In Another Time

Sketches of Utah History

D1560913

In Another Time

Sketches of Utah History

first published in

The Salt Lake Tribune

HAROLD SCHINDLER

Utah State University Press
Logan, Utah
1998

Utah State University Press
Logan, Utah 84322-7800

Typography by WolfPack
Cover design by Barbara Yale-Read

Cover painting: *Search for the Pass* by Howard Terpning
© 1988 The Greenwich Workshop, Inc., Shelton, CT

Library of Congress Cataloging-in-Publication Data

Schindler, Harold, 1929-
In another time : sketches of Utah history / Harold Schindler.
p. cm.
Includes bibliographical references (p.) and index.

ISBN 0-87421-247-2
ISBN 0-87421-242-1 (pbk.)
1. Utah–History–Anecdotes. I. Title.
F826.6 .S35 1998
979.2–ddc21
98-9028
CIP

Contents

Illustrations

Preface

In 1994 with the approach of the Utah Statehood Centennial (January 4, 1996), *Salt Lake Tribune* editor James E. Shelledy asked a number of staff members for feature story ideas, in anticipation of the celebration. His experience as editor and publisher of the *Moscow-Pullman Daily News* and executive editor of the *Lewiston Morning Tribune* in Washington and Idaho had brought him in contact with several centennial observances, and he well knew the importance of planning in such matters. Something more than a year earlier, he had been struck with the notion that I should write a history series to give readers a better sense of what made Utah tick. I was skeptical. Fortunately, Shelledy was not.

And so, from that notion was born the series of articles called "In Another Time." It was published three Sundays a month from 1993 through 1997, when I retired from the *Tribune*. The columns varied widely in content and ranged from the sublime (how ninety pairs of English sparrows were imported in 1877 to brighten the Great Salt Lake Valley and feed on the hordes of grasshoppers infesting Utah crops) to the mundane (the color and composition of Utah's early sales tax tokens). Still other articles considered such offbeat topics as the impact of the 1849 California gold rush on the impoverished settlers of Great Salt Lake City and Utah's unusual methods of executing condemned murderers! Of the hundred or so stories that "In Another Time" comprised, forty of the best and most representative are presented here. You will read of John Baptiste, the ghoul who was branded, manacled, and banished for life to an island in the Great Salt Lake in 1859 after he was caught robbing graves, and of Wilford Woodruff, a Mormon apostle who made history as a member of the pioneer company that crossed the plains to found Great Salt Lake City and in the process became the first fly fisherman to test the trout streams west of the Mississippi River.

The sketches from "In Another Time" are framed by the "Centennial Collection Series," a dozen columns published monthly during 1995 as a prelude to the Utah Statehood Centennial, which depict Utah from its prehistoric period to 1996. Through them I attempted to show readers of the *Tribune* the fibre and sinew of Utah's progenitors. Who *were* these people who built over the soil and sage of the Great Salt Lake Valley the robust and resourceful crossroads of the West— host to the world in 2002? When Shelledy proposed this series in 1994 (creating perhaps the first newspaper "history beat" writer in America), the ground rules were a virtual *carte blanche*: "Write what you want, at whatever length is necessary. But tell the story." In the business of journalism, where brevity is the essence, that is an astonishing free pass.

The series was to tell of the people and the deeds, good or bad, that formed the backbone of Utah Territory, to describe the progenitors of today's movers and shakers. With an abiding interest in western history and playing under Shelledy's rules, I was willing to give it a try. Having written *Orrin Porter Rockwell: Man of God, Son of Thunder*, the biography of a Mormon stalwart; and co-edited a new edition of *West from Fort*

Bridger: The Pioneering of Immigrant Trails across Utah, 1846–1850, I felt reasonably prepared. But to the despair of copy readers and page editors, I did knowingly take unconscionable advantage of the elastic limit on space and produced some of the longest feature stories to appear in the *Tribune* in this century. Shelledy kept his promise and made the room. But, of course, there was always his last word on the subject to be considered: "Do this centennial series right," he said, "and you won't have to do it the next time around."

PART I

The members of the Domínguez-Escalante party were among the earliest whites to see Utah. Illustration by Dennis Green, the *Salt Lake Tribune*.

1

The First Utahns

People of the Desert Culture First Inhabited the Great Basin
11,000 B.P. to A.D. 1776

Even prehistory has to start somewhere. In Utah, it's likely that could be 11,000 B.P. (before the present). That, at least, is a verifiable date, according to evidence unearthed by archaeologist Jesse D. Jennings in his storied excavation of Danger Cave east of Wendover in the 1950s. Perhaps, just perhaps, the earliest inhabitants of that portion of the Great Basin we now know as Utah were people of the Desert culture.

The prevailing theory among scientists for years has been that early man migrated to the North American continent across the Bering Strait land bridge between Siberia and Alaska in about 20,000 B.P. During the ensuing centuries, these small bands of nomads—hunters of bison and other big game—made their way south to warmer climes, reaching the caves around Great Salt Lake along the way.

Jennings's dig showed the Danger site antedated all but a few of the excavated campsites in North America and was perhaps as old as Clovis man (named for the Clovis, New Mexico, site discovered in the late 1920s). What the archaeologist had unearthed was a "full and intimate glimpse into an entire lifeway geared to an ecosystem we could visualize and understand." The thirteen-feet-deep layers of trash in the floor of the cave surrendered the story of early man, and data gleaned from other cave sites—Jukebox, Hogup, Raven, Cowboy, and Sudden Shelter—all played a role in reconstructing an image of early Holocene life.

Jennings later learned the same adaptation to desert environment revealed by the cave excavations was found in the ethnological record of historic Numic-speaking tribes (Shoshoni, Ute, and Paiute) of the West. His findings at Danger Cave suggested to the archaeologist the existence of a long-lived and widespread Desert culture in the Great Basin and that Danger Cave had been home until recently (say, 250 years ago) to the Shoshoni-speaking Gosiutes. The desert way of life persisted, and as historian Dale L. Morgan explained, "The lives of all these peoples were shaped by the peculiar nature of the country they occupied."

When the Spanish introduced horses to the New World, it was but a matter of time before the animals migrated north via the Utes and Comanches to the Shoshonis. While horses revolutionized the lives of all these tribes, Morgan pointed out the animal was of little service to the Paiute and Shoshoni bands in western and southern Utah, whose lives continued to follow more closely the Desert culture pattern.

There were no horses at all in the West—or anywhere else in America for that matter—when the Spanish conquistador Hernando Cortés landed on the coast of Veracruz in 1519, bringing with him ten stallions and six mares. As the

A recreated scene of early man hunting waterfowl six thousand years ago in a marsh near Hogup Cave (upper right) on the southwestern flank of the Hogup Mountains in the Great Salt Lake Desert. Utah State Natural History Museum diorama.

Spaniards moved inland against the Aztecs in Mexico and on into the American Southwest, they brought more and more horses for use as mounts and pack animals. Then, in 1680, came the revolt of the Pueblos of New Mexico against their white masters. Thousands of horses, now without owners, ran loose, to be taken by any Indian with the opportunity and the will. Within fifty years of the revolt, as a result of intertribal trading and theft, the Shoshonis and Comanches had horses.

Canadian explorer and map-maker David Thompson spent the winter of 1787–88 in the tent of an old Piegan warrior named Saukamappee, who told him of the band's first glimpse of a horse in 1730 after a raid in the south on the Snakes (Shoshonis). Thompson, then a Hudson's Bay Company apprentice and clerk living among the Piegans, made notes in his journal of the old warrior's story:

"After all the war ceremonies were over," Saukamappee said, "we pitched away in large camps with the women and children on the frontier of the Snake Indian country, hunting the bison and red deer, which were numerous, and we were anxious to see a horse, of which we had heard so much.

"At last, as the leaves were falling, we heard that one was killed by an arrow shot into his belly, but the Snake Indian that rode him got away.

"Numbers of us went to see him, and we all admired him; he put us in mind of a stag that had lost his horns, and we did not know what name to give him. But as he was a slave to man, like the dog, which carried our things, he was named the Big Dog."

While the lifestyle of the Plains Indians now underwent a radical change, with the horse enabling them to become nomadic hunters on a scale undreamed of before, the situation was quite different in the Great Basin. "Lacking buffalo, this desert region could not support a horse culture, and the best uses to which these Indians could have put horses would have been to eat them. The Indians

Utah Indians in Utah Valley. After an etching by John Hafen; LDS Church Archives.

here necessarily were hunters of small game and gatherers of seeds and roots," Morgan writes. The historian is quick to point out, however, that the Desert culture represented a necessary adjustment to the conditions of environment. "Theirs was a technology no less specialized than the techniques of living worked out by the Plains tribes. The desert country except in special situations would not allow large concentrations of population."

When the first white men entered Utah is still, and always will be, a matter for conjecture. Myths and tale-tellers will forever cloud the slate upon which history is recorded. But insofar as the record is recoverable, it is the Spanish to whom the honor of being first is bestowed . . . until some other evidence is discovered.

As the Spanish moved ever north along the Pacific Coast, they had by the 1770s established a half-dozen missions in California. The next logical step was to connect these with Santa Fe, the first capital of the new Mexico. To that end, two Franciscan fathers, Atanasio Domínguez and Silvestre Vélez de Escalante, formed an expedition to trace a route to Monterey. The two friars had agreed to leave on their journey July 4, 1776, a date otherwise well remembered in American history, but unforeseen developments, including Escalante falling ill, postponed departure from Santa Fe until July 29.

They were accompanied by Don Bernardo Miera y Pacheco, a retired artillery officer and militia captain who was to be the expedition car-

tographer; Andrés Muñiz, the interpreter, and his brother, Antonio Lucrecio Muñiz; Don Pedro Cisneros, the alcalde (mayor) of Zuni; Don Joaquin Lain; Lorenzo Olivares; Juan de Aguilar; and Simon Lucero. Later, the party would include runaway servants Felipe and Juan Domingo; Atanasio, a Sabuagana Yuta (Ute) Indian; and Silvestre and Joaquin, Laguna Yutas from Utah Lake. The three Yutas acted as guides.

Escalante believed the way to Monterey most likely would be north and west of the Hopis, through the lands of the Yuta to the north. During August, the expedition made its way through present Colorado—reaching the area of Dolores and Montrose and crossing the Colorado River west of Rifle—to the vicinity of Rangely and then into Utah near Jensen, where the explorers crossed the Green River.

By September 23, 1776, the priests and their party reached a Laguna village at Utah Lake. In succeeding days, they visited other villages in the vicinity of Spanish Fork and as far north as American Fork, where the Lagunas listened to the messages translated by Andrés Muñiz and expressed a willingness to become Christians. The friars discovered a fishing culture in the region, bearded Indians who seined the lake and whose men wore bones as nose ornaments. They also heard of a salt lake to the north.

With winter coming on, the priests were in a quandary: whether to push on to Monterey, which Miera insisted was less than a week's journey away, or to return to Santa Fe and plan an expedition the following year to the Lagunas. The friars decided to cast lots and put the decision "in the hands of God." And so they did on October 11 just north of present Cedar City. The choice fell to Santa Fe, and the expedition turned south, leaving what is now Utah at a point east of present St. George. After a grueling journey through Arizona following the base of the Hurricane Cliffs eastward, passing south of Pipe Springs and Fredonia, across the Kaibab Plateau, and down into House Rock Valley, they reached Lee's Ferry. They reentered Utah briefly near Wahweap Lodge, eventually located the old Ute Ford (later named Crossing of the Fathers in their honor), and waded across the Colorado, heading south to Oraibi and on into Zuni, New Mexico, in late November. The padres finally arrived at Santa Fe on January 2, 1777.

For all their peregrinations, had the priests turned north another forty miles that September at the main Laguna village at present Provo, the annals would have read quite differently: *Great Salt Lake discovered by the Spanish priests Dominguez and Escalante in 1776.* But that would have to await the next whites through Utah, legions of often unrecorded fur trappers and traders, some from Canada and not a few from New Mexico–Taos trappers, mostly.

So it stood until the turn of the 19th century.

A Ute Indian family. Photo by C. R. Savage; LDS Church Archives.

2

Mountain Men

Opening the Gate to Western Expansion
1803–1840

President Thomas Jefferson's curiosity about what lay beyond the Missouri River prompted him in 1803 to quietly order an expedition to explore the land west–land held by France. Twenty years had passed since the Revolutionary War, and the infant United States was feeling growing pains. Jefferson's plan to send Captain Meriwether Lewis and Lieutenant William Clark clandestinely into a powerful, but friendly, foreign nation's territory could have been embarrassing. Then an odd coincidence occurred. While negotiating with France for the purchase of the port of New Orleans, the American envoy was told his nation could have the seaport–if it took all of Louisiana with it, for $15 million! Napoleon was stretched to the limit supporting two armies, one in San Domingo in the Caribbean and another policing Louisiana Territory. The French treasury was feeling the pinch and in need of replenishment; the sale would benefit both countries.

Jefferson was roundly criticized at home for agreeing–even at the bargain price–yet when the purchase treaty was signed in March 1804, America doubled in size at the stroke of a pen. Louisiana added 800,000 square miles to the nation. France was ceding land north up to the British possessions, south to New Orleans, and west to the Rockies and the Continental Divide. However, territory west of the Divide–including

what was to be Utah–still belonged to Spain. Nevertheless, the acquisition of Louisiana transformed what would have been a reconnaissance of foreign territory into an official and quite proper survey of U.S. land.

Lewis and Clark's mission was to follow the Missouri River to its headwaters and then forge west in search of a passage to the Pacific Ocean. The Corps of Discovery departed May 14, 1804, and returned to St. Louis September 23, 1806, having journeyed 7,690 miles. The trove of information the group collected made possible the first detailed map of the Northwest, setting the stage for continued exploration and western expansion. However, the expedition left another, less fortunate, legacy as well. When, on the homeward journey, Lewis became embroiled in a scrape with Piegan braves and one was killed, the tribe, part of the Blackfoot confederation, became implacably hostile to white explorers, trappers, and traders and remained so for decades, at the cost of many lives.

On the last leg of the return trip, one of the party, John Colter, was granted permission to leave the corps to join a pair of trappers headed into Teton country. This hardy independent spent another four years in the mountains, and in 1807–8, traveling alone, he roamed the Wind River Valley of west central Wyoming, crossed the Continental Divide, descended the Pacific slope, and recrossed the Snake River to the Teton range. Colter thus became the first white to see and report the marvels of Yellowstone. And in 1808, he was involved in one of the most talked-about incidents in mountain man annals.

Colter and another trapper were working the upper Missouri when they were jumped by Blackfeet. In minutes, Colter was taken prisoner and his partner killed, riddled with arrows. Colter was stripped to the skin and challenged to run—for his life. The mountaineer began sprinting. He was allowed a minute head start, then the warriors, whooping and yelling, bounded after him. Colter ran, ran, ran. His bare feet cut and bleeding, his body torn, his flesh scratched and scraped as he crashed through the underbrush, John Colter somehow kept going.

After three miles he had outdistanced all but one of the braves, and as Colter would later tell it, he turned on the Indian and in a ferocious struggle managed to kill the Blackfoot with his own spear. A week later, naked and more dead than alive, Colter stumbled into a trapper's fort 150 miles away. His ordeal has been told and retold as one of the most astonishing escapes in frontier history.

Trappers in search of beaver, fox, and other peltry now were becoming increasingly familiar with the land beyond the hundredth meridian. The era of the fur brigades was dawning. Until the Treaty of Ghent ended the War of 1812 between Great Britain and the United States, though, the risk of venturing into the beckoning new territory for commercial purposes was too great. So long as the British conspired with the tribes of the upper Mississippi and the Missouri, fur parties kept their distance. With the war over, St. Louis companies looked seriously to the West. The Hudson's Bay Company sent men deeper south, and American traders turned their attention to Santa Fe and Taos as well.

In St. Louis, William Henry Ashley and Andrew Henry spoke of mounting an expedition to the Rockies, and Ashley hit upon a brilliantly simple idea to recruit men for his new company: he would use newspapers. His now celebrated want ad first appeared February 13, 1822, in the *Missouri Gazette and Public Advertiser*, seeking one hundred "enterprising young men" to ascend the Missouri to its source, "there to be employed for

Peter Skene Ogden,. Hudson's Bay Company brigade leader. Utah State Historical Society.

one, two or three years." The annual pay would be $200 a man.

The advertisement attracted free spirits and stalwarts such as Jedediah S. Smith, Thomas "Broken Hand" Fitzpatrick, the brothers Sublette (William and Milton), Jim Bridger, James Clyman, Hugh Glass, Moses "Black" Harris, and Jim Beckwourth. These and other "Ashley men," along with Taos trappers the likes of Etienne Provost and *engagés* in the employ of Peter Skene Ogden and the Hudson's Bay Fur Company, would in the decade to come roam the country west of the Rockies and trap the waters of Utah, Wyoming, Idaho, and Colorado. Their names would be indelibly linked with trails, rivers, streams, and landmarks long after their deeds had faded from memory. Though they may not be as easily brought to mind as those mentioned in the lyrics of the popular melody "Route 66," most western travelers will recognize the names attached to Fort Bridger, Colter's Bay, and the cities of Ogden, Logan, and Provo, as well as Beckwourth Pass, Weber Canyon, Weber River,

Etienne Provost, fur trapper. Utah State Historical Society.

Sublette County, Henry's Fork, and Clyman Bay of the Great Salt Lake.

The discovery of the Great Salt Lake has generally been attributed to Jim Bridger, but his partner Louis Vasquez made claim, in an October 1858 interview in the *New York Times* and the *San Francisco Bulletin*, that he and several other trappers had first seen the lake in 1822. Vasquez confused his dates and could not have been in the region until the winter of 1825–26. He was known to have been in St. Louis the season previous to when Ashley's party first reached the Great Salt Lake Valley.

Etienne Provost, however, was trapping the Utah Lake outlet (Jordan River) in October 1824 when a Shoshoni war party attacked and killed eight in his company of ten men. Provost's camp placed him in sight of the Great Salt Lake several months before Bridger reached the valley with Ashley's outfit. Years later, mountain man William Marshall Anderson added his voice when he wrote the *National Intelligencer* insisting that to

Provost belonged the credit for having first seen and made known the existence and whereabouts of the inland sea. And in July 1897, J. C. Hughey of Bellevue, Iowa, wrote to the *Salt Lake Tribune* claiming John H. Weber, a onetime Danish sea captain, had been in the mountains in 1822 as a fur trapper and had in later years often told Hughey he had discovered the lake in 1823. And, Hughey wrote, the captain also discovered Weber Canyon and Weber River, both of which bear his name. Weber described the lake as "a great boon to them, as salt was plentiful around the border of the lake, and for some time before they had used gunpowder on their meat, which was principally buffalo."

In 1824, a trapping party, including Thomas Fitzpatrick and James Clyman, led by Jedediah Smith along the Continental Divide pushed through a swale in the Wind River country and crossed to the western slope. This remarkably gentle twenty-mile saddle in the central Rockies was the South Pass; it would open the Oregon Trail to the fur trade as never before and serve as a gateway for wagon traffic west to the Pacific.

With Americans now in the mountains, it was only a matter of time before a confrontation would occur, and that time was May 23, 1825, when a brigade of Hudson's Bay Company trappers under Peter Skene Ogden bumped into Canadians and Spaniards from Taos led by Etienne Provost. They had come up from New Mexico and were supplied from St. Louis by way of the Santa Fe Trail. As Dale L. Morgan remarked, "trappers were swarming from everywhere." Indeed, before nightfall, still another band, this composed of two dozen or more Americans, "rode up brazenly with 12 or 15 of Ogden's Iroquois." They made camp within a hundred yards of the British outfit, hoisted an American flag, and shouted to Ogden's men that as they were in U.S. Territory, "whether indebted or engaged," all were now free.

Next morning, Johnson Gardner strode from the American side to Ogden's tent and announced that Britain had ceded its rights to this country, and as Hudson's Bay had no license to trade or trap, Ogden would be wise to leave. Ogden replied they would depart only if ordered by the British government, not before. "Then remain at your own peril," Gardner snapped. In the harangue that followed, twenty-one of Ogden's trappers deserted to the Americans—taking with them their furs—and Ogden retreated with Gardner's taunts ringing in his ears: "You shall shortly see us in the Columbia, and this Fall at the Flat Heads and Kootenais, as we are determined you shall no longer remain in our territory!" The locale of this showdown is generally considered to be Mountain Green, in Weber Canyon southeast of the city of Ogden. Peter Skene Ogden had reached the spot by crossing the divide now traversed by the Trapper's Loop highway from the mountain valley that has been known from the time of the fur brigade as Ogden's Hole.

By the 1830s, these intrepid trappers and traders had ventured throughout the West's mountains and valleys, leaving their blaze on Indian and game trails as they searched for pelts. Hugh Glass survived his legendary encounter with a wounded grizzly, which chewed and mauled him so severely his companions left him for dead—only to have Glass crawl from the grave and eventually reach a Sioux village, where he was nursed back to health.

As the decade ended, beaver was largely trapped out and the beaver hat market in Europe ruined by the introduction of the tall silk topper. The last fur rendezvous was held in 1840. The era of the mountain men and the fur trapper was on the wane. Utah trading posts such as Fort Davy Crockett and Fort Robidoux were about to become relics of a bygone day.

South Pass now represented the gateway to western expansion. It was time for the covered wagons and the settlement of the far frontier.

3

The Ways West

California-Oregon Dream Lures Scores to Utah and Beyond
1841–1846

South Pass over the Continental Divide is not truly a mountain pass in the romantic sense; it is neither craggy nor treacherous as might be imagined. On the contrary, this gateway in the Wind River country of the Rockies is a gentle twenty-mile saddle easily traversed in season on horseback or by wagon. Because it is no real obstacle to wagons, the pass became integral to the move west that was shaping "in the States" in the 1840s. After the fur-trapping brigades launched their forays across the Rockies, the siren call of California was played with increasing intensity across the pages of Missouri and New York newspapers reporting the adventures of mountaineers and explorers.

California was extolled as a sunny paradise, where land was for the taking and summer was forever. It was a dream to capture a nation's imagination. When fur companies brought supplies by wagon to trappers at their annual rendezvous, it demonstrated dramatically that wheels could make it across the rugged slopes. Soon the promise of Oregon and a fresh start in new country drew scores of prospective overland travelers to the Western Emigration Society, organized by Missourians to help emigrants prepare for the journey west. Still, there was no clear perception of a wagon route beyond the Rockies. The prevailing mindset was to head for Oregon by way of South

Pass and Fort Hall, the Hudson's Bay Company trading post, and from there west the best way possible, the mountaineers reckoned.

Wagon teams clustering at the Kansas River in May 1841 formed an unsure, insecure group with no discernible leader. One blustering individual, John Bartleson, insisted on being elected captain and threatened to pull out of the enterprise if ignored. Though it was obvious that "Captain" Bartleson knew little more about plains travel than the next man, the emigrants obliged him. Hearing that the famous mountaineer Thomas "Broken Hand" Fitzpatrick was guiding a small contingent of Catholic missionaries to Flathead country in present Montana, the emigrants wisely waited to join them.

When on May 18 the company set out, it was with fifteen wagons and four solid-wheel Red River carts. Counting the Catholics, there were sixty-six men, at least five women, and a few children. With the trail-wise Fitzpatrick pointing the way, they made it to Soda Springs in present Idaho by August. There in the mountain fastness, difficult choices were made. The Catholic missionaries, Jesuit priest Pierre-Jean De Smet among them, continued north to the Flatheads. Bartleson with three others rode to Fort Hall seeking trail information, and thirty-two of the travelers in nine wagons chose to press on for California, moving

John Bidwell, California pioneer and Bidwell-Bartleson party chronicler. Utah State Historical Society.

into the Great Salt Lake. Bidwell confided dourly in his journal, "This is the fruit of having no pilot—we pass through cash valley, where we intended to stop and did not know it."

Bartleson and the three who rode to Fort Hall caught up at the campsite now called Connor Springs. The end of August found the party plodding westward just north of the lake, taking wagons where none had been before. Past Locomotive Springs and through Park Valley they struggled. They had no fresh water; their animals had no grass. On September 6, 1841, Bidwell wrote, "We travelled about 10 miles a day in a southwest direction and camped on a small brook. Today we killed some rabbits and an antelope. Game being scarce here we were compelled to kill oxen."

A week brought them to yet another milestone in western annals, as Dale L. Morgan described it: "the first immigrant arrival at Pilot Peak." It was costly. Four years later, John C. Frémont's pack expedition reached this critical watering hole after a venturesome crossing of the Salt Desert, and in 1846 emigrant companies would stumble here out of the desert as though to salvation itself.

Now a refreshed Bidwell-Bartleson party moved on to the Pequop Range in present Nevada, where, after surviving five months of tortuous trail-breaking travel, the remaining wagons were forsaken, their hulks grim guideposts to future emigrants. It was early November before the hardy pioneers actually reached California. Their achievement stirred the nation's pulse, and before five more years had passed, the move west was on in earnest. The Bidwell-Bartleson route proved too arduous and lengthy, so succeeding emigrant parties would take the Oregon Trail from Soda Springs to Fort Hall, then turn southwest to City of Rocks and follow the California Trail west.

Frémont's 1843 exploring expedition took him to the Great Salt Lake in the fall. He and a small party including Kit Carson paddled an India rubber boat to an offshore island west of the mouth of the Weber River, where Frémont took topographical readings while Carson amused himself by cutting a cross "under a shelving rock" on the island summit. (When Captain Howard Stansbury surveyed the lake in 1849, he rejected Frémont's choice of Disappointment Island as a

slowly until Bartleson could overtake them. The rest of the group chose Oregon.

In the California company was John Bidwell, whose daily journal left a record of the experience. History would recognize him by dubbing the nine wagons the Bidwell-Bartleson party. They planned to seek out Cache Valley and there await Bartleson. The company jolted south in the general vicinity of the Bear River, and would by mid-August reach the site of today's Cornish, Cache County, thus becoming the first emigrant wagon party to travel northern Utah.

During the next few weeks, they wandered desperately, reaching the site of present Smithfield before turning west to what is now Fielding, making a northern loop to cross the Malad River, then veering south again to the future location of Corinne. Here scouts brought word the party was within ten miles of where the Bear River emptied

An inner view of the Fort Hall trading post. Drawing by Osborne Cross, 1849; Utah State Historical Society.

name, and instead called it Fremont, in tribute to its discoverer.)

Frémont made his way to Sutter's Fort and returned to the States early in 1844. He reached Independence, Missouri, in late July to a hero's welcome. His official *Report of the Exploring Expedition to the Rocky Mountains in the Year 1842, and to Oregon and North California in the Years 1843–'44* was a literary hit as well, and it played a significant role in persuading the Mormons to settle the Great Salt Lake Valley in 1847. But the ever-restless Frémont, now a brevet captain, embarked on his third expedition, which would include the desert west of the Great Salt Lake. This time he camped on the site of Salt Lake City in October 1845, taking observations for latitude and longitude and visiting the largest island in the lake. There he found grass and water and numbers of antelope. "In memory of the grateful supply of food they furnished I gave their name to [Antelope] island."

It was this exploration–its course skirting south of the lake across the Salt Desert to Pilot Peak and on to Sutter's Fort–that spurred Lansford W. Hastings into promoting his theoretical "short-cut" wagon road to California. How Hastings seized on Frémont's achievement to substantiate his own untested speculations and then persuaded emigrant wagon parties to use the route is a compelling drama and tragedy of overland trail history.

Backtracking Frémont through Nevada and Utah, Hastings, with James Hudspeth and a few others, reached the Fort Bridger trading post by the first week in June 1846. In his party was mountaineer James Clyman, an Ashley man who had circumnavigated the Great Salt Lake two decades earlier in a buffalo-skin boat. Hastings had hoped to leave word of his cutoff at the trading post but learned that Jim Bridger had been absent for several weeks. Hastings insisted on waiting, and Clyman was for moving on. They went their separate ways.

Historians Roderic Korns and Dale L. Morgan, writing in *West from Fort Bridger*, said Hastings chanced upon Wales B. Bonney, a lone traveler from Oregon heading east in the vicinity of South Pass, and used this "providential" circumstance to write an open letter to California-bound travelers. Though no copy of Hastings's letter survives, diarists have provided clues as to the burden of its message. Hastings invited them to concentrate their numbers and strength and to take his new route, which he promised would materially shorten the distance. (In truth, the "cutoff" was almost one hundred miles longer.)

THE PIONEERS.

An immigrant wagon train on the Plains, as depicted in *Harper's Weekly*. Utah State Historical Society.

While most of the emigrants elected to take the sure way, Hastings's pitch worked with several parties, among them Edwin Bryant and William H. Russell's mule-pack outfit, the George Harlan-Samuel C. Young wagon company, George and Jacob Donner's party, and James Frazier Reed's wagon company. In all, some seventy-five wagons risked the Hastings Cutoff in 1846. Other overland travelers stayed with the Fort Hall trail to California, which bypassed all of Utah except the extreme northwestern corner.

The Bryant-Russell mule party moved faster than wagons and entered Utah through Thomas Canyon west of today's Evanston, Wyoming. They followed Crane Creek across what is now Deseret Livestock Company land and descended Trail Creek Canyon and Lost Creek to the Weber River near present Croydon, Morgan County. After a futile effort to penetrate Weber Canyon, they backtracked to present Henefer and rode up Main Canyon to Dixie Creek and the floor of East Canyon and then back along an Indian trail to the Weber River about two miles below present Morgan.

The men camped while their guide, James Hudspeth, once more scouted Weber Canyon and reported that he had encountered a train of some forty wagons, with Hastings as guide, at the mouth of Echo Canyon. The pack party broke into the Great Salt Lake Valley above Ogden, turned south, and on July 31 forded the Jordan River where 2700 South in Salt Lake City is today. From that point, they headed their mules due west past the site of Grantsville and across the Salt Desert to the Pilot Peak oasis soon to be known as Donner Spring. Pushing on through present Nevada, the party picked its way across Secret Pass at the north end of the Ruby Mountains, then to Sutter's Fort by August 31, making them the first overland immigrants to California that year.

Remains of a Donner party wagon. LDS Church Archives.

Back on the trail, the wagon companies were not faring well. The Harlan-Young party and Hastings had managed to overcome the tangled underbrush, trees, and boulders choking Weber Canyon, but not without great difficulty. Once in the valley, they found a ford on the Jordan near today's North Temple street and crossed over at that point. Before venturing on to the Salt Desert, the company rested at Twenty Wells, so named for its many springs. It is now known as Grantsville. There James Frazier Reed and two others from the struggling Donner wagon train came up and persuaded Hastings to return long enough to show them a better route from the mountains than Weber Canyon.

He rode with them as far as Big Mountain summit in Emigration Canyon and offered his advice regarding a wagon road; then Hastings turned back to rejoin Harlan-Young and the others. After much labor, the Donner-Reed company hacked its way from Big Mountain Pass to Little Mountain and down Emigration Canyon to the valley. It took them a dozen precious days.

From the mouth of Emigration, they crossed the Jordan slightly south of 2700 South to reach Tooele Valley about August 24. Here one of the company, a lone traveler named Luke Halloran, who had joined them at Fort Bridger, died of tuberculosis. In his last days, he had been cared for by Tamsen Donner, and it was to her he left his property, $1,500. Halloran, a Master Mason, was buried near John Hargrave, who succumbed to typhoid pneumonia two weeks earlier at the Harlan-Young camp. Hargrave thus became the first overland emigrant laid to rest in Utah soil and Halloran the first Mason buried in Utah. Neither gravesite has been located.

More hardship was in store for the wagon parties. The Salt Desert extracted a cruel toll. What the emigrants expected to be a forty-mile drive without grass and water was twice that distance. Some families lost oxen, wagons, and personal belongings in the unforgiving and brutal terrain. Finally at then Pilot Spring, the emigrants were in truly critical straits. Farther west they would be thwarted at Secret Pass, which they found impassable by wagon. Forcing an eighty-mile detour around the southern tip of the Ruby Mountains to intercept the California Trail, this prolonged drive made the Hastings Cutoff no

A Donner party monument in California. LDS Church Archives.

shortcut. Indeed, it was considerably longer than the Fort Hall road it was to supersede.

The Harlan-Young company was the last wagon train to safely cross the Sierra Nevada ahead of the Donner-Reed party. The Donners' tragic tale of being trapped late in the season in the high mountains during the ferocious winter of 1846–47, with its spectre of starvation and cannibalism, is one of the darkest chapters in the annals of overland travel.

Yet the trail they carved by toil and tears in the wilderness to the Great Salt Lake Valley would become a wagon highway. For in April 1847, even as the Donner survivors were being rescued, members of the Church of Jesus Christ of Latter-day Saints prepared to set out from Winter Quarters in Nebraska to seek their promised valley in the Rockies.

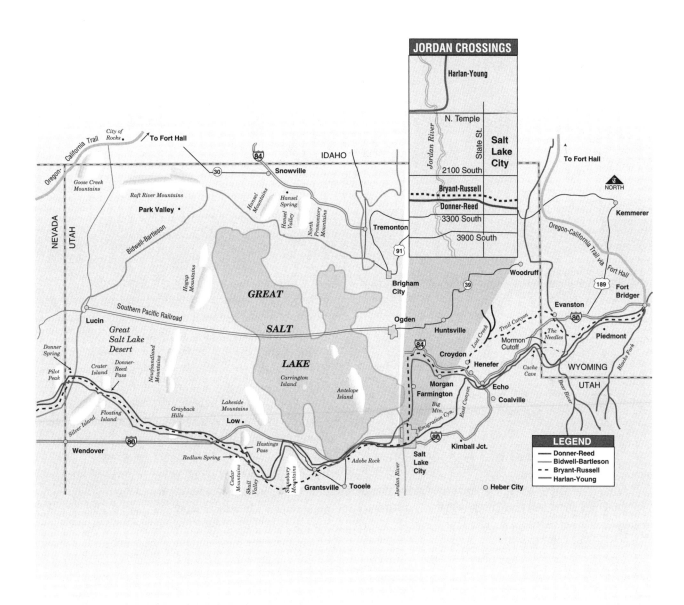

Emigrant trails across Utah. Map by Mark Knudsen and Dennis Green, the *Salt Lake Tribune*.

4

Ho! for the Great Salt Lake

Mormons Give Up Livelihoods in a Rush for the Promised Land
1846–1847

By the middle of May [1846], it was estimated that 16,000 Mormons had crossed the Mississippi and taken up their line of march with their personal property, their wives and little ones, westward across the continent to Oregon or California; leaving behind them in Nauvoo a small remnant of a thousand souls, being those who were unable to sell their property, or, who having no property to sell, were unable to get away.
—Gov. Thomas Ford in *History of Illinois*

The Church of Jesus Christ of Latter-day Saints, reacting to threats from Illinois citizens if it did not leave their state, began an exodus from Hancock County in February 1846—its ultimate destination neither Oregon nor California but the Great Salt Lake Valley.

Orson Pratt, a member of the church's Council of Twelve Apostles, had in November 1845 sent a message to Mormons throughout the eastern and middle states, urging them to join the hegira as early in the spring as "grass would grow or water run." Exhorted Pratt, "We do not want one saint to be left in the United States after that time. Let every branch in the east, west, north and south be determined to flee out of 'Babylon,' either by land or sea, as soon as then." Those who could acquire teams during the winter were advised to go by land, but those who preferred to leave by boat were not dissuaded.

Illinois Mormons were surrendering their homes and property for pennies on the dollar after clashing with "old settlers" over church doctrine and political power and suffering the assassination of their two leading elders, the founding prophet Joseph Smith Jr. and his brother Hyrum, at the hands of a mob at Carthage Jail in June 1844. The threat of civil war between the Mormons and their enemies gradually eased but never quite vanished. Being forcibly expelled from Nauvoo, a city church members literally had lifted from swamplands, marked a bitter end to years of squabbling with their non-Mormon neighbors. With state militia eager to torch homes and oust them with musket and bayonet, there was little choice but to go.

As early as January 1845, church leaders were mulling the idea of sending a company to California to seek a suitable place of refuge for the church. (The *Nauvoo Neighbor* on January 29 printed a story reporting that Captain John C. Frémont had reached the Great Salt Lake in the fall of 1843 on his third western expedition.) In late August, the council agreed on the California expedition. But a week later they resolved, instead, to send fifteen hundred pioneers to Great Salt Lake Valley and began collecting information on immigration. What happened in that week to change plans so drastically has never really been resolved by historians. Prevailing opinion is that

Carthage Jail, Hancock County, Illinois, scene of the assassination of Joseph and Hyrum Smith. LDS Church Archives.

The Mormon exodus from Nauvoo. LDS Church Archives.

The Nauvoo Temple sat on the city's high ground. LDS Church Archives.

Mormon leaders distrusted Illinois Governor Thomas Ford, who strongly recommended the move. But the more likely explanation is Brigham Young's unwavering insistence on settling in a location no one else coveted: Great Salt Lake Valley met the requirement in all respects.

By the third week in December, Franklin D. Richards was reading aloud to council members Frémont's *Report of the Exploring Expedition to the Rocky Mountains in the Year 1842, and to Oregon and North California in the Years 1843–'44,* which gave an account of his travels to California and described in some detail the country around Great Salt Lake. A few days later, Parley P. Pratt was doing the same with Lansford W. Hastings's recently published *Emigrants' Guide, to Oregon and California.*

As part of his plan to plead the LDS Church's case, Young and his counselors had writ-ten President James K. Polk and every governor in the United States except those in Missouri and Illinois, seeking sanctuary for the Mormons or support of the church's "Great Western Measure," which sought to colonize Oregon or some location remote from the United States. Those who answered declined assistance; some urged the Mormons to move to Oregon, California, Nebraska, or Texas.

To borrow a phrase, the die was cast. February and March 1846 saw Mormons pour-ing across the Mississippi to the snow-crusted Iowa shore by the hundreds and by the thou-sands. They were preparing, not for a blind, wan-dering trek across the frontier, but for what would be a carefully planned and organized jour-ney to a specific locale west of the Rockies, where they would settle and worship as they pleased, these first citizens-to-be of the Territory of Utah.

Samuel Brannan, restored to favor after being disfellowshipped, took 238 men, women, and children of the LDS Church aboard the chartered vessel *Brooklyn* to sail from New York to Yerba Buena (San Francisco) by way of Cape Horn and the Sandwich Islands (today's Hawaii). *Brooklyn* cleared the harbor on its southward voyage February 4, 1846.

Meanwhile, the first families began crossing the frozen Mississippi on that same frigid February day, with temperatures barely above zero. They began gathering for a camp at Sugar Creek in Iowa territory, about nine miles from Nauvoo. Nine babies were born that first freezing night at Sugar Creek, some in tents, others in wagons, in rain, sleet, and snow. Five hundred wagons formed the vanguard of the caravan rolling from that encampment ever south and west, reaching Council Bluffs in mid-June. But before Council Bluffs came camps at Richardson Point, Chariton River, Locust River, Garden Grove, and Mount Pisgah. It was at Chariton River that order and discipline were restored to the mass evacuation; the camp's affairs were set in order and families organized into "hundreds" and "fifties" with captains over each. The whole was named Camp of Israel, with Brigham Young unanimously elected its president.

The camp settled in at Council Bluffs, while Young and his council planned the next move. But on June 26 at Mount Pisgah occurred an incident of great importance. U.S. Army Captain James Allen rode into that camp with *A Circular to the Mormons* explaining that Allen had been instructed by Colonel Stephen W. Kearny, commander of the Army of the West, to recruit five hundred volunteers from among the Mormon membership for service in the war against Mexico, declared the month before. Contrary to later remarks by Brigham Young that the federal government unfairly demanded volunteers during a desperate time for the Mormons, the recruiting call, in fact, had come in response to urgent pleas by church elder Jesse C. Little—acting on Young's orders—for President Polk's "assistance in moving the Saints to California" as part of Kearny's army.

The volunteer battalion of Mormons was raised and marched out under Allen's command to Fort Leavenworth, Kansas, where it was outfitted for what was to become, by some estimations, the longest infantry march in U.S. military his-

tory—twelve hundred miles along the Santa Fe Trail and beyond to San Diego. Before leaving the Camp of Israel, however, battalion members were instructed to tarry once they reached California until the mountain passes were free of snow before attempting to rejoin the main body of pioneers somewhere in the Great Salt Lake Valley "in one or two years." And so the bone and sinew of the Mormon camp—five hundred of its best men—marched off to Fort Leavenworth. The Camp of Israel retrenched, settled in for the winter, and made plans for the pioneer advance party to strike out for the Great Basin.

In anticipation of a spring departure by a pioneer party, the main body of Mormons moved to the west bank of the Missouri River and began laying out a secure "Winter Quarters" camp of log cabins enclosed by a stockade. Upward of 1,000 houses were built on 820 lots within 41 blocks. Winter Quarters eventually became Florence, Nebraska, and today is within Omaha's city limits.

Spring of 1847 found the pioneer company gathering at the Elkhorn River, a tributary of the Platte, ready for the trek west. Coincidentally, Parley P. Pratt and John Taylor, two apostles who had been on a Mormon Church mission to England, returned and joined the company in early April. Taylor had brought with him "scientific instruments" ordered by Brigham Young for use by the pioneers. On the evening of April 13, they unpacked "two sextants, one circle of reflection, two artificial horizons, two barometers, several thermometers, telescopes and so forth." The pioneers also were furnished with maps of the route to Oregon and maps of Frémont's route to California via the Great Salt Lake in 1843 and of his return in 1844 by way of southern California, the Mojave River, Las Vegas, the Rio Virgin, the Sevier River, Utah Lake, Spanish Fork Canyon, the Uintah River, and so on to Pueblo, Colorado, and the east—further evidence of the knowledgeable planning and scope of the Mormon migration.

On the afternoon of April 16, the Pioneer Camp numbered 143 men, 3 women, and 2 children (down one man from the "twelve times twelve" originally called for, because Ellis Eames took sick on the 18th and returned to Winter Quarters). The women were Harriet Page Wheeler Young, wife of Brigham's brother, Lorenzo D. Young; Clarissa Decker Young,

Mormons driven from Nauvoo. Illustration by C. B. Hancock; LDS Church Archives.

The Nauvoo Temple in ruins. Illustration by Frederick Piercy; LDS Church Archives.

Pioneer odometer. LDS Church Archives.

Brigham's wife; and Ellen Sanders Kimball, wife of Heber C. Kimball. The children, Isaac Perry Decker and Lorenzo Sobieski Young, were those of Harriet Young. These and the men of the company would be the first citizens of Great Salt Lake City of the Great Basin of North America. There were 73 wagons in the camp, 93 horses, 52 mules, 66 oxen, 19 cows, 17 dogs, and a clutch of chickens. The travel organization of the pioneer company was completed with the naming of two captains of hundreds, Stephen Markham and A. P. Rockwood; captains of fifties, Tarlton Lewis, John Pack, and Shadrach Roundy; and captains of tens, Wilford Woodruff, Ezra T. Benson, Phineas H. Young, Luke Johnson, Stephen H. Goddard, Charles Shumway, James Case, Seth Taft, Howard Egan, Appleton Milo Harmon, John S. Higbee, Norton Jacob, John Brown, and Joseph Mathews. The company also included three slaves, Hark Lay, Green Flake, and Oscar Crosby, Utah's first black citizens.

On April 19 the camp moved out under the supervision of the various captains, covering twenty miles the first day on a line of march along the north side of the Platte. The south bank had by now become the Oregon Trail from Independence, Missouri, to the Willamette Valley. By 1847 it was a national wagon road as far west as Great Salt Lake because the Harlan-Young and Donner-Reed companies had pushed it through the year before. The trail went all the way to California by the Fort Hall route. The Mormon pioneers followed the north bank to Fort Laramie, at which time they crossed to the south side. They made it through Pawnee lands with minor abrasions.

In buffalo country the company hunters knocked down a meat supply, and in mid-May the pioneers noted the addition of an "odometer" to their wagon train. William Clayton, who was keeping a journal of the trek, had been frustrated in attempts to accurately estimate the distance traveled each day. He appealed to scientist-mathematician Orson Pratt to help him out. Pratt designed a device that would attach to a wagon wheel and would turn 360 revolutions in a mile, each mile then being ticked off on a small secondary gear. With Pratt's design, Appleton Milo Harmon, a skillful carpenter, fashioned a model from wood, and it was mounted on one of Heber C. Kimball's wagons that had the proper circumference wheel. From that day forth the pioneer trek was more accurately measured for the benefit of Mormon companies that followed. While not

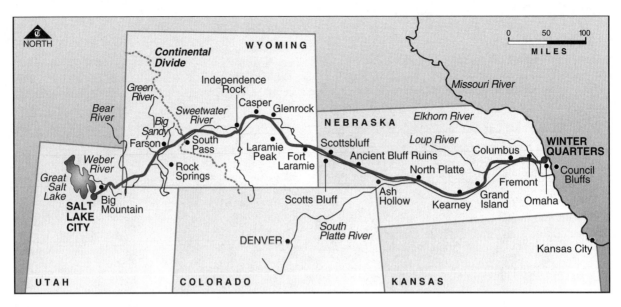

The Mormon trek from Winter Quarters to Salt Lake City. Map by Rhonda Hailes Maylett, the *Salt Lake Tribune*.

unique, the Clayton-Pratt-Harmon odometer can be considered among the earliest uses of the device in overland travel.

Halting for two days at Fort Laramie to refit the wagon train, making needed blacksmith repairs and such, the pioneers learned that a Mississippi detachment of church members plus a sick detachment released from the Mormon Battalion were en route from Pueblo, in today's Colorado, to join the main company and accompany it to the Great Salt Lake Valley. Young also received information that some two thousand wagons of immigrants were on the road west for Oregon and California and advance companies were but two days from Fort Laramie. That was enough to hurry the Mormon camp back on the trail.

Mid-June brought them to the upper Platte River crossing, where an advance work party of Mormons had prepared a ferry to take the pioneers over. Once across they would follow the Sweetwater River to South Pass, the saddle of land that separates the waters of the Pacific from the Atlantic, the passage over the Rocky Mountains to the western slope, 275 miles (by odometer) from Fort Laramie.

The pioneers now came in frequent contact with Oregon immigrants and occasional eastbound parties of trappers and mountaineers. At Pacific Springs west of the pass, they encountered noted mountain man Moses "Black" Harris, who

gave them issues of the *Oregon Spectator*, the first newspaper published on the Pacific Coast, and a number of copies of the *California Star* published by Samuel Brannan, the Mormon elder who had taken the sailing ship *Brooklyn* to Yerba Buena the year before. Also at Pacific Springs was Thomas L. "Peg Leg" Smith, who operated a trading post on Bear River near Soda Springs, in present Idaho. Two days later, near present Farson, Wyoming, they met Jim Bridger, who suggested it was imprudent to bring a large population into the Great Basin until they were sure grain could be grown; the mountain man's pessimism was such that he offered $1,000 for the first ear of corn raised in the valley "or the Utah Outlet," which the Mormons would name the Jordan River.

At Green River on June 30, Samuel Brannan himself, direct from San Francisco, rode into the Camp of Israel. He gave the pioneers an account of the *Brooklyn* voyage and told of the Donner party disaster in which so many immigrants had succumbed in the Sierra Nevada to the elements and starvation. Brannan also attempted without success to persuade Young to lead the Mormons to California, rather than the Great Salt Lake Valley. About this time an advance company of the so-called Pueblo detachment (the sick and disabled) of the Mormon Battalion, caught up with the Camp of Israel.

Five days later, the pioneers had reached Fort Bridger, at which point they left the Oregon Trail and followed Lansford W. Hastings's cutoff, which would lead them into Great Salt Lake Valley. They followed a route "dimly seen as only a few wagons [Harlan-Young and Donner-Reed] passed over it last season," wrote Orson Pratt in his journal.

Then, on July 10, the Mormons met the red-haired mountain man Miles Goodyear guiding a small party making its way from the Bay of San Francisco to the States. Goodyear intended to meet the Oregon immigration and do some trading. He held a "considerable conversation" with the leading elders and downplayed the Salt Lake Valley as a place for the church. He told them of his "farm" in the "Bear River" Valley (today's Fort Buenaventura in Ogden) and pointed out a trail to take them to the head of Red Fork (Echo Canyon). They parted with this "first white settler in Utah" for the moment, but the Mormons would have further dealings with the mountaineer once in the valley.

From Echo Canyon the wagon train followed the earlier Donner party trail to Main Canyon, East Canyon, and Big Mountain, then down a difficult descent to Little Mountain and into Emigration Canyon. From the summit of Big Mountain itself, Orson Pratt and John Brown "had a view of the valley for the first time." On the early morning of July 22, Mormon journals report, an advance party comprising Pratt, Brown, George A. Smith, Erastus Snow, Orrin Porter Rockwell, Joseph Mathews, John Pack, J. C. Little, and another man, whose name was not recorded, entered the valley. That ninth man was Hark Lay, one of the black slaves. The main group reached the floor of the Great Salt Lake Valley later that day, while Brigham Young, who had contracted a type of "mountain fever,"

Samuel Brannan. LDS Church Archives.

remained behind with several wagons until he felt well enough to proceed.

On the morning of July 24, with Young bundled in Wilford Woodruff's easier-riding carriage, the last contingent moved to join the Camp of Israel. "President Young," Woodruff noted in his journal "expressed his full satisfaction in the appearance of the valley." That, in essence, was Brigham Young's seal of approval, his agreement that "this is the place."

5

Great Salt Lake Valley, "The Place"

First Few Years in "Deseret" Test Pioneers' Mettle
1847–1850

When the main party of Mormon pioneers entered the Great Salt Lake Valley on July 22, 1847, two days ahead of their fever-stricken leader Brigham Young, they set about plowing, planting potatoes, and grazing their cattle and horses. Young, suffering from "mountain fever," had lagged behind with several other wagons until he felt up to making the final drive from Emigration Canyon to the present site of the Salt Lake City and County Building in what would become "Great Salt Lake City of the Great Basin of North America." And now it is, as it has always been, the 24th of July—the day Brigham Young reached the valley—that is celebrated as founder's day. More than one wag has wondered aloud what would have become of those potatoes, if Young had not agreed that this was the place.

Most of the members of the Church of Jesus Christ of Latter-day Saints were delighted to finally reach their new mountain home, while others had doubts. Of the three pioneer women who made the journey, Harriet Young, the eldest, said: "Weak and weary as I am, I would rather go a thousand miles farther than remain in such a forsaken place as this!" Ellen Kimball echoed her sentiments, while Harriet's daughter, Clarissa D. Young, wife of Brigham, seemed satisfied. "My poor mother was almost brokenhearted; terribly

disappointed because there were no trees. I don't remember a tree that could be called a tree."

Now the pioneers moved quickly; the first field was plowed and five acres turned. Potatoes were cut and planted and ditches dug for irrigation. "We gave the ground quite a soaking," wrote Orson Pratt in his journal for July 24. (Early LDS records locate the plowed ground as bordered by 200 and 300 South between Main Street and 200 East.) It has been popularly accepted that this marked the birth of modern irrigation, and that may be true, although there were earlier examples of irrigation in the Southwest and it is just as likely that Miles Goodyear at his trading post in Ogden's Hole had irrigated first in Utah. Goodyear was not alone at Fort Buenaventura; he had a partner, an English mountaineer named Wells who tended the fort while the younger man was off horse trading. Dale L. Morgan described Wells as Utah's first agriculturist, a man with a green thumb who tended a goodly corn patch and vegetable garden as well as a herd of horses, some cattle, and a large flock of goats and sheep with Goodyear that summer. Where and how Goodyear acquired sheep remains a puzzle, but it is likely he trailed some up after one of his trips to Santa Fe.

Using engineering instruments brought from England, Pratt and Henry G. Sherwood began to survey the city plat during the first week of

Council Bluffs ferry on the Mormon Trail. Illustration by Frederick Piercy; LDS Church Archives.

Loup Fork ferry on the Mormon Trail. Illustration by Frederick Piercy; LDS Church Archives.

Cache Cave (Redden's Cave) near the head of Echo Canyon on the Mormon Trail. Photo by Harold Schindler.

Elk Horn River ferry on the Mormon Trail. Illustration by Frederick Piercy; LDS Church Archives.

First glimpse of the Great Salt Lake Valley. Painting by H. L. A. Culmer; LDS Church Archives.

The "This Is the Place" monument overlooks Salt Lake City, crossroads of the West, founded by Brigham Young and his followers in 1847. Photo by Harold Schindler.

Wild bulls stampeded through the camp of the Mormon Battalion during its march to California. Illustration by C. B. Hancock; LDS Church Archives.

August. It was sufficiently accurate that the heart of Great Salt Lake City "has all its lines today as Pratt laid them out in 1847," said J. Cecil Alter, first director of the Utah State Historical Society. Of primary concern in that initial survey was selection of a site for the proposed Mormon Temple. Alter studied Wilford Woodruff's diary entry and noted the following account: "We walked from the north [pioneer] camp," writes Woodruff, "to about the center between the two creeks [this would have brought them approximately to the site of the Kearns Building, or in the street in front of it, or possibly as far east as the *Tribune* building, Alter says], where President Young waved his hand and said: 'Here is the forty acres for the temple; the city can be laid out perfectly square, north and south, east and west.'" However, when it came to actually laying out the design on the plat, four central city blocks seemed entirely too much ground, and the temple square was reduced to a quarter that size, a regular city block in relation to which all streets were to be named and numbered.

By the second week in August, the pioneers were well into building the adobe walls of the fort that would house the men remaining in the valley while Young and a return party went back for the rest of the Mormon camps at Council Bluffs and Winter Quarters. The company of Mississippi Saints and the Mormon Battalion sick detachment they had joined at Pueblo followed the pioneers into the valley on July 29. Mormon Battalion men were assigned ox teams and wagons as vanguard of the return company. Young and his apostles on horseback followed with thirty-six wagons two weeks later. They would rendezvous at Winter Quarters and lead the rest of the Mormons to the valley in late summer of 1848.

Those who stayed behind in Great Salt Lake City were left with little but their own devices to face the coming winter. Fortunately, it was mild. These first citizens of Great Salt Lake City proved their mettle time and again in the months and years to come. The wagon parties that had trailed the pioneers from Winter Quarters began streaming into the valley in late September 1847. In the next months, ten companies totaling 1,690 immigrants emerged from Emigration Canyon, overrunning the valley with 2,213 oxen, 887 cows, 124 horses, 358 sheep, 35 hogs, and 716 chickens. The encampment now was a city on wheels, the wheels of 566 wagons, all dutifully recorded by Camp of Israel historian Thomas Bullock.

One can only wonder how Miles Goodyear, Jim Bridger, and Peg Leg Smith regarded this tumultuous disruption of their solitude. For Goodyear, the answer was to move. Captain James Brown returned from California in November with a saddlebag crammed with Spanish doubloons—back pay for members of the sick detachment of the Mormon Battalion. Brown was authorized by a LDS Church high council to buy Goodyear's property if a fair price could be agreed upon. For $1,950, Fort Buenaventura and its improvements were sold to Brown, and Goodyear pulled out for California.

The influx of Mormons was almost disastrous. The meager gardens planted in such haste in late July—potatoes, buckwheat, and turnips, with some corn in tassel—lasted only "until the first company [of immigrants] came in and turned their cattle loose; they devoured crops that would have been ready to harvest in a few days," anguished John Steele. Brigham Young returned in the autumn of 1848, leading even more church members. Three large divisions of wagon companies arrived in the valley in September and October, increasing the population to some five thousand.

Young was in Great Salt Lake Valley to stay; he would never again journey east. The church leader now turned his efforts to building a mountain empire. During the winter, the valley Mormons managed to put up nearly twelve miles of fence, enclosing more than five thousand acres. Fall wheat was sown on two thousand acres, and plowing was continuous so long as the weather permitted. The haunting fear was that the crop would fail as many of the mountaineers had direly predicted.

March and April 1848 passed, and by May the grain promised a strong healthy growth, but the appearance of so much wheat attracted swarms of large black crickets; they descended on the fields, clumsily hopping a scant foot at a time, but with an appetite defying description. And they came, it seemed, by the millions, ravaging the wheat, turning yellow fields to ugly brown patches of ruin. Then followed what church members to this day describe as "the miracle." From the islands in the Great Salt Lake came the California gulls to

swoop down on these "black Philistines of the mountains," the Mormon cricket (*anabrus simplex hald*), which Thomas L. Kane described as "wingless, dumpy, black swollen-headed, with bulging eyes in cases like goggles, mounted upon legs of steel wire and clock spring, and with a general appearance that justified the Mormons in comparing them to a cross of the spider and the buffalo."

A cannibal by nature, the Mormon cricket has a voracious appetite, moving it to devour everything edible until nothing remains. It will feast comfortably on its own kind as easily as a shawl or sheet used to protect plants or vegetables. And they swarmed in clouds of "thousands of tons." Then God sent the gulls—so said the Mormon pioneers. Flocks of birds came gliding in to feast on the crickets. They killed and ate until they were filled, then vomited and ate again. It was a loathsome time. Every morning for three weeks, the gulls sailed in and attacked the insects. Pile after pile of dead crickets littered the fields. The pioneers gathered the filthy mess in baskets, sun dried them, roasted them, and made them into a silage that lasted for months. Most of the crops were saved; in fact, the harvests of 1848 were generally excellent.

While life was hard for the settlers in Great Salt Lake Valley, some improvement was in the offing. In California, gold had been discovered at Sutter's sawmill on the American River, and as word spread east the United States was about to experience its first full-blown gold rush. For adventurers in the States, there were but two ways to reach the diggings: by ship—around Cape Horn to San Francisco or across the isthmus of Panama by pack train and then by ship again to San Francisco—or overland on the Oregon-California Trail. The overland route would take many gold seekers, with a mind to trade, through the City of the Saints. California's gold bonanza thus brought its own peculiar prosperity to the Mormons.

Meanwhile the political scene was changing almost as rapidly. The Treaty of Guadalupe Hidalgo on February 2, 1848, ended the war with Mexico; the southern boundary of Texas was set at the Rio Grande. Upper California and New Mexico were ceded to the United States for a payment of $15 million. Brigham Young and his followers, who had fled what they considered religious persecution in Illinois to settle in Mexican

First South in Great Salt Lake City looked like this to Captain Howard Stansbury during his 1850 visit. Utah State Historical Society.

territory, found themselves once again within American boundaries. Never one to waste time, Young issued a call for a convention to "all citizens of that part of Upper California lying east of the Sierra Nevada." The convention met in Great Salt Lake City on March 8, 9, and 10, 1849, and it was agreed to petition Congress for a territorial form of government. Meanwhile the convention adopted a constitution for a Provisional State of Deseret, pending action by Congress.

An election was conducted on March 12, and to no one's surprise, since candidates were unopposed, Brigham Young was named governor; Willard Richards, secretary; Newell K. Whitney, treasurer; Heber C. Kimball, chief justice; John Taylor and N. K. Whitney, associate justices; Daniel H. Wells, attorney general; Horace S. Eldredge, marshal; Albert Carrington, assessor and tax collector; Joseph L. Heywood, surveyor of highways; and bishops of several Mormon wards were named magistrates. A military unit, the Nauvoo Legion, was organized with Daniel H. Wells as major general and Jedediah M. Grant and Horace S. Eldredge brigadiers.

When the petition to Congress was sent east in May, it was twenty-two feet long and bore 2,270 signatures. It sought a territory to be named Deseret to include all of the country between Oregon and Mexico and between the Rockies and the Sierra Nevada, plus a strip of the California seacoast. In July, the provisional government drafted another memorial, this one seeking outright statehood in preference to territorial status. It

was this petition rather than the earlier memorial that ultimately was presented to Congress. But there were forces at work to thwart their efforts.

General John Wilson arrived in the city in August on his way to California. He claimed to be acting as an emissary of President Zachary Taylor to deal for Mormon cooperation in blocking proslavery factions. Young was asked to join with California (newly won in the war with Mexico) in forming a single large state. President Taylor believed, Wilson said, if such a huge land mass could be admitted to the Union leaving the question of slavery to its residents, it would offset the recent acquisition of Texas (a slave state) and thus ease the terrible possibility of a proslavery-antislavery fight. Wilson agreed to Brigham Young's condition that California and Utah would be separated after two years and each would be an independent state. In return, Young would see that the Mormons dropped all petitions, memorials, and applications to Congress and concentrate solely on early admission of the State of Deseret.

In the end it was California that balked at tying itself to the Mormons and opted to pursue its own interests. Later, when Taylor was confronted in Washington with allegations of his "confidential deal," he denied all. The fiasco was a crushing setback to Mormon plans, and Young never forgave the chief executive. Taylor had entrenched himself in the Mormons' Hall of Infamy alongside notables such as President Martin Van Buren, who had agreed their cause was just, but could do nothing for them; Missouri Governor Lilburn W. Boggs,

Lilburn W. Boggs, Missouri governor responsible for the 1838 Mormon war. Utah State Historical Society.

who told his citizens to exterminate them; and Illinois Governor Thomas Ford, who had promised the Carthage Greys would protect Joseph Smith. In a speech a year after Taylor's death in office, Young said, "I know Zachary Taylor; he is dead and damned." Lest he be misunderstood, the church leader later explained, "I love the government and the Constitution of the United States, but I do not love the damned rascals who administer the government."

Such was the situation when word came of the California rebuff. When next Congress considered the Mormon petitions, it proclaimed the name "Deseret" to be repulsive, and instead approved the Territory of "Utah" on September 9, 1850. Celebration in Great Salt Lake City was enthusiastic; the territory had completed its first important step to becoming part and parcel of the United States of America. But the joy was in large measure premature, as Brigham Young was soon to discover. Utah politically was about to come face to face with the real world.

Sketches

A FORT FOR DAVY CROCKETT

WHEN IT COMES TO TRADING POSTS IN THE WEST, most history-minded folks can easily recall Fort Bridger, Fort Hall, and Fort Buenaventura (Miles Goodyear's place near Ogden), even Fort Uintah, southeast of Roosevelt. But Fort Davy Crockett? That's pushing it, some might say: Davy Crockett didn't make it to Utah; he was killed in the Alamo fight in 1836.

Even so, a trading post was named for the legendary folk hero by his admirers—and it was located on the Green River, ten miles or so above the Gates of Lodore in the valley of Brown's Hole. As romantic as it sounds, the trading post had a short life, in the twilight of the fur trade. It was built in 1837 and abandoned in 1840. It was destroyed and put to the torch, probably by Utes who in 1845 burned Fort Uintah near the confluence of the Green, Duchesne, and White Rivers.

As trading posts go, Fort Davy Crockett, across the river from Hoy Draw in present northwestern Colorado, was not much pumpkins. A small, inferior establishment at best, it was at worst a squalid insect-infested place, and the few diarists who saw it had little good to say of it. A German traveler, Frederick A. Wislizenus, complained he couldn't get an hour's rest there because of the mosquitoes. Wislizenus stayed over in 1839 and described it as "the worst thing of the kind that we have seen on our journey. It is a long one-story building . . . of wood and clay, with three connecting wings and no enclosure. The whole establishment appeared somewhat poverty stricken." It was bad enough despite the sublime natural setting, Wislizenus added, that the trappers called it Fort de Misere (Fort Misery). T. J. Farnham also dropped by that year and described it as "a hollow square of one-story log cabins with roofs and floors of mud."

Brown's Hole—a valley some fifty miles long stretching from the eastern border of Utah's Daggett County through western Moffat County in today's Colorado—took its name from one Baptiste Brown, a Hudson's Bay man who quit in 1827 and with his native wife drifted down river to settle in the beautiful basin. (John Wesley Powell euphemistically renamed the locale Brown's Park.)

It came to pass in 1837–38 that mountaineers William Craig, Prewitt Sinclair, and Philip F. Thompson pooled their resources to build a trading post in Brown's Hole; it was a marvelous setting and a favorite wintering place of Indians and whites. Trapping and trading aside, whatever other skills the partnership enjoyed, cabin construction was not among them. They hoped to capitalize on the winter season at Brown's Hole, where as many as fifteen thousand Indians could be found at one time. Still, the enterprise was shaky at best. By 1839 the men of the mountains could sense their time had come. In these autumn years of the fur trade, just before the founding of Fort Bridger, Brown's Hole had become a watering hole and gathering place of choice for free trappers. Precisely why the partners chose to name the post after Davy Crockett has never been absolutely clear, but it probably was Thompson's idea, since he, like the frontiersman, also was a Tennessean.

By the first of October 1839, thousands of trappers and Indians fresh from the rendezvous at Horse Creek (Wyoming) thronged to winter at Brown's Hole. Here were Kit Carson, Joe Walker, Jim Baker, and old Jack Robertson. Joe Meek and his brother-in-law, Robert "Doc" Newell, also arrived with their wives, a pair of Nez Perce sisters. Most of the mountaineers at Fort Davy

James Baker, mountain man. Utah State Historical Society.

Joseph R. Walker, mountain man. Utah State Historical Society.

Crockett that season had lost their livelihood since the disbanding of the American Fur Company and were much concerned about the future. Already a number—William Craig among them—were considering a move north to Oregon territory.

Such was the setting for an incident which split the ranks of mountaineers and led to the scattering of Brown's Hole inhabitants. The coming of winter had seen some horse stealing among the whites and while this was considered common warfare among Indians, trappers considered their horses safe among other trappers. When a white man stole from another white man, it was a matter for comment, and even Doc Newell, sparing of word and judgments, was so shocked as to remark, "Such thing has never been known till late."

An eyewitness to subsequent events, E. Willard Smith, picks up the story in his journal: On the evening of November 1, 1839, a party of Sioux who had tracked a band of Snake Indians

discovered Brown's Hole and its secret. The war party located the horse herd and made off with 150 head. So confident had the trappers and the Snakes become about their wintering place they allowed their mounts to run loose and unguarded in the valley. It was secure from hostiles—or so they thought.

The raid caused considerable commotion at the fort, and the victims were determined to recapture their property. But the next morning the idea was abandoned as impractical and ill-timed. Instead, a dozen men under Philip Thompson set out for Fort Hall, the Hudson's Bay supply post two hundred or so miles to the northwest. Thompson's party stole a number of horses at Fort Hall, even though they had always been treated well there. On the return ride the trappers stopped at a small camp of friendly Snakes—and ran off forty horses from them—an unthinkable breach of mountain ethics. When Thompson's bunch rode into Fort Davy Crockett, they found themselves roundly cursed as thieves by the better element among mountaineers.

Thompson and his renegades took the horses and headed south, following the ice-covered Green to the White River. Not far behind, the remaining mountain men set out to retake the stolen herd before tribes sought vengeance on all trappers, friendly or not. It brought about the demise of Fort Davy Crockett and broke up the Thompson-Sinclair-Craig partnership. Sinclair wasn't at Brown's Hole at the time, and Craig joined the "posse" chasing his partner.

In this group were Kit Carson, Joe Meek, Doc Newell, and twenty-five others—all under the leadership of Joseph R. Walker. They tracked the renegades to the vicinity of Fort Uintah and encircled them, cutting off retreat. While Walker's men didn't relish the notion of spilling the blood of their comrades, they were determined. Thompson, however, recognized his dilemma and surrendered the horses to Walker, who returned them to the tribes at Brown's Hole, thus avoiding an Indian war. So ended the great horse raid of 1839.

Fort Davy Crockett was abandoned as the trappers scattered to the winds—the curtain was falling on the fur trade era. The later record is silent about the trading post except for the rare remark from passing travelers. Over the next century traces of the log fort vanished and eluded historians attempting to locate the site from vague descriptions and John C. Frémont's flawed star sightings. Possible locations ranged from ten miles into Utah to a dozen miles east into Colorado. Then, in 1975, Glade Ross, a ranger at the Lodore Station of Dinosaur National Monument, decided to again check the area near Sterling Spring. On a steep cutbank near the river he found some large river cobbles which couldn't have come there naturally. In the bank itself, two feet below the surface he spotted a definite line of charcoal. A team of archaeologists from Denver examined the site and found trader's beads, musket balls, melted lead, a percussion cap, gun flints, a musket hammer, a brass gun forestock, presumably from a Hawken rifle, and some five-hole buttons. The remains of a log wall 140 feet long were uncovered.

Fort Davy Crockett had been found; its location is now on the National Register of Historic Sites and is protected by the National Wildlife Service.

FRÉMONT AND CARSON LEAVE A MARK ON A GREAT SALT LAKE ISLAND

ONE HUNDRED AND FIFTY-FOUR YEARS AGO, Lieutenant John C. Frémont of the U.S. Corps of Topographical Engineers, with four members of his survey expedition, paddled an inflatable rubber boat from the mouth of the Weber River due west to a small island in the Great Salt Lake. Hungry and short of provisions, Frémont hoped to find game while surveying the lake from the island summit. This was the second of the explorer's military expeditions—the first in 1842 had taken him to South Pass and the Wind River Mountains along the Continental Divide. John C. was becoming famous, and ambitious.

With Frémont on this September morning in 1843 were Christopher "Kit" Carson, an intrepid hunter and guide who already enjoyed a position of respect among men of the mountains, and Charles Preuss, a gifted, literate map maker who kept careful diaries written in his native German but whose outward demeanor rarely mirrored his waspish personal thoughts. Two employees, French Canadian engagés Baptiste Bernier and Basil Lajeunesse, had served with Frémont before and comprised what the lieutenant regarded as his "small family." Before setting out for the island, eight of the party of seventeen were sent north to Fort Hall, a Hudson's Bay Company trading post in present Idaho, for supplies; and four others were assigned to remain ashore to guard the baggage and horses while the survey party did its work.

The decision to land on the smaller island was Frémont's choice because of the food shortage. After a meal of yampah root, seasoned by "a small fat duck," the expedition was tiring of boiled birds and becoming restless. The men warmed themselves at the campfire on the night of September 8 and wondered what the new day would hold in store. "We fancied that we should

Christopher "Kit" Carson, 1863. Utah State Historical Society.

John C. Frémont, explorer and topographer. Utah State Historical Society.

find every one of the large islands a tangled wilderness of trees and shrubbery, teeming with game of every description that the neighboring region afforded, and which the foot of a white man or Indian had never violated," Frémont wrote in his logbook. Preuss, as usual, was not so enamored of the adventure. He was more interested in how his food tasted. "So close to the Salt Lake and we have to get along without salt!" he complained to his diary.

But Frémont's plans for an early start were soon dashed. In unpacking the India rubber (*gutta-percha*) boat, they discovered that instead of being strongly sewn like one used a year earlier in exploring the canyons of the Upper Platte River, this boat's air cylinders had been pasted together, and poorly at that, by a manufacturer rushed for time. He had been told to cram two months' work into a week, and this was the result. At sunrise the rubber raft was inflated, with men alternating on the bellows. When two of the lengthy cylinders leaked and threatened to sink the boat, one man was constantly at the bellows while the others rowed for all their worth.

Frémont noticed immediately the radical change between the mouth of the Weber and the beginning of the lake at the marsh line. "The lake water was saturated with common salt," he said. Midway to their intended landing point, the wind grew stronger and the air cylinders started to collapse. Again the bellows were pumped feverishly. At last, the boat made it to the island beach. It was about noon on September 9.

Carson, who was no stranger to danger and hard times as a mountaineer, recalled in his autobiography, "We found nothing of any great importance. There were no [fresh water] springs and the island was perfectly barren." Preuss was even less charitable in his diary. "We ferried with our miserable rubber boat to the island, which Frémont christened Disappointment Island because he expected game there but did not find it." Having thus unburdened himself, he turned to exploration. "We found plenty of salt and have boiled down some of it. I believe that three, or certainly four pounds of water make one pound of salt. I have never seen anything like it.

We found the salt fifteen feet deep near the island."

While Frémont and Preuss set up their instruments to begin the survey, Carson took the opportunity to stroll around the island. On the eight-hundred-foot summit he rested near a schist rock formation and left his mark. Perhaps it was Bernier or Lajeunesse who stood with him, but in later years, this famous plainsman recalled, "We ascended the mountain, and under a shelving rock cut a large cross, which is there to this day." When Captain Howard Stansbury took his survey party to the island seven years later, he noticed the cross but had no clue as to its origin. He passed it off with just a single sentence in his famous report on the Great Salt Lake.

The Mormons, who had settled the Great Salt Lake Valley in 1847, were aware that Frémont had named the land mass Disappointment Island, but because of its shape, the Saints renamed it Castle Island. To Stansbury, however, fell the official responsibility of placing it on a U.S. map. He chose to recognize the adventurous explorer who first set foot upon its shore. He set it down as Frémont Island, and so it remains today.

When Frémont's party departed on the morning of September 10, the lieutenant was dismayed to discover he had left the lens cap to his "spy glass" on the summit and ruefully observed it would probably remain there undisturbed by Indians, to furnish "matter of speculation" for some future traveler. The lens cap was found in the 1860s by Jacob Miller, a Mormon using the island as a sheep range.

For Frémont, clambering aboard Preuss's "miserable rubber boat" and returning safely to the mouth of the Weber was easier said than done. Carson's recollection was understated: "We had not gone more than a league, when a storm came up," he said. "The boat was leaking wind." Frémont urged them to "pull for their lives," Carson remembered, because "if we did not reach shore before the storm, we would surely all perish." Pulling at the oars with all their might, they barely made it. "Within an hour, the waters had risen eight or ten feet," Carson said. Scrambling through the brushy wetlands, Frémont ordered his men to carry the baggage the quarter mile to firm ground, while Preuss and Lajeunesse set off on foot to the main camp and the horses, some nine miles distant.

The expedition continued its mission, and in October 1845 visited other islands in the Great Salt Lake, among them the largest, which supplied the party with fresh meat. Frémont named it Antelope Island.

GONE FISHIN'

IZAAK WALTON'S DELIGHTFUL 1653 TOME, *THE Compleat Angler*, dealt with fishing as a pastime. And so it should be. But in the early years of western expansion, beginning in the 1840s, those hardy pioneers fished not for the pure pleasure but for survival. Journals of the period mention anglers only infrequently and then not in great detail. Mostly the emigrants were concerned with pushing onward, and during the gold rush, for instance, nothing short of calamity could delay them.

So when the occasional Waltonian account bobs to the surface in western history, it demands attention. The first fly fisherman in America probably experimented with the English artificial lure in the late 1700s and escaped the historian's notice. Fortunately, western annals leave a stronger clue and point directly to a Utahn—no less a figure than Wilford Woodruff, fourth president of the Church of Jesus Christ of Latter-day Saints and a totally committed angler.

Woodruff made the trek west as a member of the LDS Council of Twelve Apostles and traveled in the vanguard of pioneer Mormons to reach and settle the Great Salt Lake Valley in July 1847. He also was one of the most diligent and important diarists among the Mormons, keeping note of everything he did for more than a half-century. And when he fulfilled an LDS Church mission to

England in 1841, he brought back a fly rod and an assortment of artificial flies.

Because of his fondness for angling, he became a sort of clearing house for matters piscatorial. Woodruff always remembered to inquire of trappers and traders on the prairie where the best fishing was. And when someone had some luck, they passed the word to Woodruff.

As a measure of his commitment, his diaries are sprinkled with revealing comments on the subject. On May 28, 1847, for instance, he made note of a clear stream not more than three miles long, which rose from a large pure spring near Scotts Bluff in present Nebraska. Beaver dams and lodges dotted the course, and, Woodruff remarked, "At one place it raised the water about two feet which was lined with fish, a share of which was speckled trout, so the brethren informed me. This is the first stream I have met with containing trout since I left the New England States. Therefore I name it Trout Creek."

When the pioneers reached Independence Rock on the overland trail, Woodruff was the first Mormon to climb it, a distinction he dutifully recorded in his journal. But Woodruff's true claim to fame for sportsmen came when the wagon train reached Fort Bridger in early July. He may not have been the first to cast an artificial fly on waters west of the Mississippi, for there are earlier accounts of bass caught on flies in the South. But Wilford Woodruff surely was the first fly fisherman west of the Continental Divide.

Bridger's trading post of crude log houses on Blacks Fork of the Green River was a place emigrants could stay a day or so to rest and feed their livestock, repair wagons, and generally gird for the final push to the Great Salt Lake Valley or points west. And here Woodruff made his mark. In his own words, and colorful spelling:

> As soon as I got my breakfast, I rigged up my trout rod that I had brought with me from Liverpool, fixed my reel, line & artificial fly & went to one of the brooks close by Camp to try my luck catching trout.
>
> The men at the fort said there were but very few trout in the streams. And a good many of the brethren were already at the creeks with their Rods & lines trying their skill baiting with fresh meat and grasshoppers, but no one seemed to ketch anything.

> I went & flung my fly onto the [water]. And it being the first time I ever tried the Artificial fly in America, or ever saw it tried, I watched as it floated upon the water with as much intens interest As Franklin did his kite when he tried to draw lightning from the skies. And as Franklin received great Joy when he saw electricity or lightning descend on his kite string in like manner was I highly gratified when I saw the nimble trout dart [at] my fly, hook himself & run away with the line, but I soon worried him out & drew him to shore. I fished two or three hours including morning & evening & I cought twelve in all. And abought one half of them would weigh about ¾ of a pound each while all the rest of the camp did not ketch during the day 3 lbs of trout in all, which was proof positive to me that the Artificial fly is far the best thing now known to fish [for] trout with.

Wilford Woodruff went on to fish the Bear River (not with an artificial fly, however) on horseback in the middle of the stream, casting baited hooks into eddies. Like anglers of today, he discovered that fish are fickle: "Some of the time I would fish half an hour & could not start a fish. Then I would find an eddy with 3 or 4 trout in it & they would jump at the hooks as though there was a bushel of trout in the hole. And in one instance I caught two at a time."

As he wound his way to the valley of the Great Salt Lake he would periodically assemble his English bamboo rod for flies and become the first to test those streams that crossed his trail. On July 17, "I fished with a fly and caught several trout." On the twenty-first of that month he cast his line on the Weber near the mouth of the canyon "and caught eight." And later in 1849, after the Mormons settled the valley, he wrote a friend that trout abounded in Zion, that a Brother Whipple irrigated his fields with Mill Creek Canyon stream and having shut the water off, strolled through the field and picked up "any quantity he wished of very fine trout."

Emigrant wagon trains and packers heading for California the year before the Mormon exodus west also left accounts, albeit sketchy, of their adventures with Walton's pride. Edwin Bryant, part of a nine-man pack train heading for California in 1846—just ahead of the Donner-Reed party—also noticed that Blacks Fork near Fort Bridger "abounds in spotted mountain trout." By the time the party reached the mouth of Weber

Canyon near today's town of Uintah, on July 26, 1846, Bryant, a former newspaper editor, had lapsed into prose as purple as the sunset.

Wrote he, "Returning to camp Hyrum O. Miller, who had employed his leisure in angling, exhibited a piscatory spectacle worthy [of] the admiration of the most epicurean icthyophagist, he had taken with his hook about a dozen salmon trout, from eight to eighteen inches in length; and the longest weighing four or five pounds. A delicacy such as this, and so abundant, we determined to enjoy, and from the results of Miller's sport we feasted this evening upon a viand which epicures would give much to obtain."

And again the following day, "Fishing apparatus was in great demand this morning; and most of the party . . . were enjoying the Waltonian sport, in angling for the delicious salmon-trout with which the stream abounds. Our bait is the large insect resembling the cricket, heretofore described, myriads of which are creeping and hopping among the grass and other vegetation of the valley. Every angler was more or less successful."

Two other diarists, both writing in 1848, left evidence of an angler's experience. One Addison Pratt showed promise, and according to his journal entry for September 17, in the neighborhood of Clear Creek, south of present Naf in Cassia County, Idaho, after catching some "beautiful trout," the "brethren complimented me highly for my skill as a fisherman and remarked jocularly that I could catch a mess of trout if I could only find rainwater in a cow track." Henry W. Bigler, one of the participants in the gold discovery at Sutter's Mill in January of 1848, also was returning to his family in Great Salt Lake Valley when from his camp on the Malad River that September, he recorded, "Here the boys ketchd fish all most as fast as they threw their hooks in. . . . We found an abundance of chubs . . . in Malad Creek."

Those were the days.

WHAT'S IN A NAME? SAMUEL HENSLEY—NOT HANSEL—DISCOVERS A CUTOFF

SETTING THE RECORD STRAIGHT—THAT'S WHAT this is all about—doing what needs to be done to restore Samuel J. Hensley's rightful place in history. And that means changing a few names on Utah maps. It isn't easy, but it can be done, and in this case it should be done.

First, a little background on Sam Hensley: A native of Kentucky, he was born in 1816, and in his teens took up what was known as "the mountain life." He became a trapper and hunter in the wilder regions of Missouri. It was in this enterprise that he made the acquaintance of many of the most famous mountaineers of his day—the Sublette brothers, Jim Bridger, Joseph R. Walker, Peter Lassen, and others—as they roamed, trapped, explored, and hunted the boundless region from the Rockies to the Pacific, from the British possessions on the north to Mexico on the south.

By 1843, he had joined the Joseph C. Chiles (rhymes with "miles") party and made his way to California. Hensley found work with John A. Sutter at his fort in the Sacramento Valley, and when the Bear Flag Revolt broke out three years later, Hensley joined the insurgents as a captain in John C. Frémont's California Battalion. In the controversy over Frémont's role in siding with Commodore Robert F. Stockton and his falling out with General Stephen W. Kearny, Frémont was ordered to Washington and arrested. Hensley accompanied Stockton to the States and testified at Frémont's court martial, which ran from November 1847 to January 1848. After the conclusion of the trial, Hensley, with a handful of men, probably discharged soldiers, took up the return journey to California—and that is where his role in Utah history begins.

As Hensley and his pack party headed west that spring on the Overland Trail, Mormon settlers had made it through their first winter in Great Salt Lake Valley and were bending to the

Outer view of the Fort Hall trading post. Drawing by Osborne Cross. Utah State Historical Society.

task of building their city in the mountains. The Hastings Cutoff through the Great Salt Lake Desert had for the most part been shunned since the Donner-Reed debacle of 1846. And word of the gold discovery at Sutter's Mill in late January 1848 would not explode in the East for months yet. What Hensley would accomplish on his westward journey was to find a shortcut to California, one that avoided the dangerous Hastings route and still saved 150 miles or so along the accepted trail north of the Great Salt Lake.

The first contemporary mention of his presence in Mormon country appears in a letter from LDS Church authorities in Great Salt Lake City updating Brigham Young, who then was making his way from Winter Quarters in Nebraska to the valley with the main body of Latter-day Saints. Buried in the August 9 letter was this: "Ten of the U.S. Troops under Capt. Hensley lately arrived in our valley on their way to California; they tried the Hastings route, but the desert was so miry from heavy rains that they have returned and gone on by way of Fort Hall." Fort Hall was the Hudson's Bay Company trading post near present Pocatello.

Hensley's dilemma was more graphically described by Richard Martin May, who encountered the Californian at Goose Creek just west of City of Rocks. May had first met Hensley at Independence Rock in today's Wyoming, and now Hensley and his packers had overtaken May's wagon train. The words are precisely as May wrote them:

He [Hensley] intinded to pass to Fort Bridger & Thence South of Salt lake intending to follow [Hastings] Trail. He passed on without difficulty untill he Reached the South western portion of the Lake and Traveled Several Miles upon an incrustation of Salt and unfortunately for the Major and his Train (10 in number) There fell a heavy rain which so weakened the incrustation that they were verry near perishing in the mire. They were under the necessity of Cutting Loose the packs to Save the animals. In this way they lost their provision or nearly So with part of their clothing They were 48 hours without food or water and hard at work most of the time to Save the Property They then retraced their Steps to the Mormon City and there replenished their Larder.

Once they were again fit to travel, Hensley and his party headed north toward Fort Hall, following wagon tracks made the previous March by Mormon dissidents Hazen Kimball and James Pollock, who had chosen California over the Great Salt Lake Valley. Hensley did not follow the tracks all the way to Fort Hall, though; rather he veered west after crossing the Malad River, thus pioneering a new route—the Salt Lake Cutoff to the California Trail. The cutoff joined that trail at City of Rocks about seven miles north of today's Utah-Idaho border.

Hensley, indeed, is credited with discovering the "nigher" route. In late August, he rode into a camp of discharged Mormon Battalion members far down the Humboldt Valley. They were on their way home—to families in Great Salt Lake City. Henry W. Bigler, one of the discoverers of gold at Sutter's Mill, wrote in his diary that "Capt. S. Hinsley [and] a packing company of 10 men" provided the battalion with a "way bill," a description of a new route to the valley. He told the battalion boys they could go not "by Ft Hall and save a bout 8 or 10 days travel." It would also shorten the distance by "a bout 150 or 200 m.," Bigler said.

While the distance was less, the traditional Fort Hall road was easier. Yet when the gold rush was in full fury the following year, emigrants grasped every opportunity to "get there first," and the Salt Lake Cutoff became a valuable link for the twenty-five thousand or so gold seekers who took the trail in 1849 and 1850.

Trail historians Dale L. Morgan and J. Roderic Korns noted that the meager obituary of the man who made the effective discovery of the Salt Lake Cutoff route for overland travel does not mention the achievement and that Utah has repaid its debt to Samuel J. Hensley shabbily by corrupting his name upon its map. They agreed "a poor memorial is better than none, and the 'Hansel' Mountains, Peak, Spring, and Valley have pre-

served down through the generations, after a fashion, the memory of Samuel J. Hensley. But our maps should now be corrected." Morgan proposed in 1951 that the Utah State Historical Society "request an official ruling from the U.S. Board on Geographical Names by which this change in name or spelling, shall be approved and thereafter used on the map of Utah." As of this writing, however, the name Hansel persists.

And how did Samuel J. Hensley fare after he reached Sacramento? Well, he joined the gold rush and worked the Feather River placers. He made enough money to open a trading post at Sutter's Fort with a couple of partners. In the early 1850s he went back east to organize a steamboat venture, which ultimately expanded to include the "entire steam navigation interests of the rivers of California and the Pacific Coast." He married, settled in San Jose, and raised a family. The rigors of his earlier years took a toll on his health and he fell ill. Samuel J. Hensley died at Warm Springs, Alameda County, California, on January 7, 1866, leaving a widow and a son and daughter. He was forty-nine.

A WAR OF EXTERMINATION

EIGHTEEN MONTHS AFTER THE MORMON PIONEERS first entered the Great Salt Lake Valley, they launched a war of extermination on predators, intending to save their crops and livestock but winding up feuding among themselves.

The situation arose during a mid-December meeting in 1848 of the General Council of the Church of Jesus Christ of Latter-day Saints. The council's fifty members were responsible for establishing early law and organizing a municipal government until the settlement stabilized and formally took hold. After grappling with a number of problems, including a common herd ground for cattle and horses as protection from predators and raiding Indians, someone suggested a campaign to eliminate the more troublesome and destructive animals.

John D. Lee was all for rubbing out the "wasters and destroyers" and spelled out the

specifics in his journal. Here is Lee at his colorful best, the flavor of his remarks as well as his inventive spelling are as he wrote them 146 years ago:

> [Taken into consideration were] . . . the wolves, wildcats, catamounts [in most cases catamounts are mountain lions, but Mormon settlers apparently grouped bobcats and lynxes in this category], Pole cats, minks, Bear, Panthers [mountain lions], Eagles, Hawks, owls, crow or Ravens & magpies, which are verry numerous & not only troublesome but destructive. $1000s of dollars worth of grain and stock have already been destroyed by those Wasters, & to check their career it was thought best to have a Hunt.

> Acordingly Pres. B. Young nominated J. D. Lee & John Pack captains to carry on a war of extermination against the above named wasters & destroyers.

A few days later the captains met at Lee's home to hash out rules for the shoot. It was Christmas Eve 1848 when they signed articles of agreement for the war of extermination against those "Ravens, Hawks, owls, Wolves, Foxes, &c. now alive in the valley of the Great Salt Lak [sic] & in the regions roundabout." To make it interesting and to encourage competition, the captains felt there should be an incentive, a reward, at the close of the hunt. It was serious business as far as they were concerned; the two were by nature strong-willed men. At this point, Lee's journal entries refer to it as the Hunt, with a capital H. Again, Lee carefully outlines the "Rules":

1stly. The two cos. are to partic[i]pate in a Social Dinner with their Ladies to be given at the House of Capt. John Pack's on a Day hereafter named & to be paid for by the Co. that produces the least No. of game.

2ndly. The game shall count as follows. The Right wing of each Raven Shall count one; a Hawk, owl or Magpie two. The wings of an Eagle 5. The skin of a Wolf, Fox, wild cat or Catamount ten. Pole cat or mink Five. A Bear or a Panther Fiffty.

3rdly. The Wings of the Birds & the Skins of the animals shall be produced by each Hunter at the Recorders office on the first Day of Feb., 1849, at 10 o'clock A.M. For counting & examination, at which time the day for recreation shall be appointed.

4thly. Isaac Morley & Reynolds Cahoon shall be the Judges or counters of the game and to designate the winners. And Thos. Bullock to be the clerk to Keep a Record of each man's skill & to publish a list of the Success of each in [sic] Individual.

5thly & lastly. The man who produces the most Proof of his success Shall recieve a Publick vote of thanks on the Day of the Feast. The article of agreement having [been] drawn, The foll[ow]ing Persons were chosen to participate in the Hunt . . . .

And there followed two columns of ninety-three names each, comprising the teams. How they were selected isn't discussed, but it probably was by draw, since Lee (as Brigham Young's adopted son) would not have allowed the church leader to be on Pack's team without an argument. Nevertheless, Pack drew Young and some sharp-eyed shooters the likes of Porter Rockwell,

Chauncey West, Lewis Robison, and Dimick Huntington, while Lee's team included George Bean, Judson Stoddard, Jefferson Hunt, and Thomas S. Williams.

Lee also came up with Hosea Stout, who had been, and would be, at various times a militia officer in Nauvoo, Illinois, and Utah; chief of police at Nauvoo; ex-officio chief of the "old police" during the exodus from Nauvoo; and territorial attorney general. In a nutshell, Stout was a smart, tough Mormon lawyer. He, too, kept a diary, and on that same Christmas Eve, he confided to it: "Snowed to day. I learned today that John Pack and J.d. Lee had lead out to see who should kill the most crows & and other noxious vermin each to choose 100 men and the party who killed the least number, counting the first of Feb next was to pay for a dinner for both parties &c I also learned that I was chosen on Lee's side but I declined to accept the office not feeling very war like at this time."

As Christmas dawned, Lee remarked that the report of gunfire could be heard in every direction, "which is nothing uncomon about chrismas times, but insted of waisting their Powder as usual on such ocasions, hundreds of Ravens no doubt were killed on that day. The Boys being full of shoot as well [as] the Spirit of the Hunt went it steep." By the end of January, the teams having made such rapid "havock" among the "Wolves & Foxes, especially" the captains agreed to continue the killing another month, to which the general council consented. Lee and Pack met on February 1 to notify their marksmen of the change in plans. The emphasis on "Wolves," incidentally, is probably misplaced. The settlers likely were being pestered by coyotes, which they were in the habit of calling "prairie wolves."

When the month extension ended and March 1 rolled around, the Council House was almost buried in pelts and feathers. The counting began. Lee's journal again follows the action:

"Some 5000 [points] were counted on Capt. John Pack's Side & some 2000 on Capt. J. D. Lee's side. Only about one third of Capt. J. D. Lee's men counted, not having Notice in time; but the greater part of Capt. John Pack's game was brought in on that day. The poles close[d] about Dark, leaving Capt. J. D. Lee above 3000 in the rear." And that did not sit well with John D. Lee. He was not comfortable being a loser. He took the matter to higher authority.

Fort Utah on the Provo River, 1850. LDS Church Archives.

Two days after the count, Lee brought the subject to the attention of the general council, at the time occupied with sending militia to Fort Utah (Provo) to punish an Indian band for stealing settlers' cattle. The council allowed laggard hunters additional time to bring their game to be tallied. Lee's luck was about to take a decided shift:

> At 10 morning the skins of the Wolves, Foxes, mi[n]ks &c. & the wings of Raven, Magpies, Hawks, owls & Eagles were roling in to the clerk's office in every direction to be counted, each Hunter eager to gain the contest. At 4 P.M. poles closed, giving J. D. Lee a majority of two thousand five hundred & 43 skelps. The entir No. brought on both sides was estimated between Fourteen & Fifteen Thousand. Thos. Williams on Capt. J. D. Lee's Side, won the vote of thanks by a majority of about 300 skolps. He brought in about 2100 skelps. Capt. J. Pack was rather wo[r]sted & sadly disapointed when he found that one 100 men [team] beat two Tribes of Indians & the white Tribe of the valley. . . .

Lee made the mistake of rubbing it in too deeply with Pack. The late Juanita Brooks, Lee's biographer, thought that Lee might have been hinting that Pack used Indians in the region to help him run up the score. But that was never proven or openly discussed. In any case no one got the dinner. Pack sulked and cried foul, complaining that March 1 was the official day of counting, while Lee insisted the council's four-day extension nullified the deadline. Since the ladies of the settlement were to have been guests at the social dinner, it is fair to assume they lost the most in the three-month hunt. The journals are silent in regard to their reaction.

But it was not yet over for Lee and Pack. Their personal differences growing out of the "war of extermination" dragged on. Because of the nagging problem with the Indian tribes of the region (who were fighting each other as well as the white settlers), the old Nauvoo Legion was resurrected to protect the town. Hosea Stout explained, "One circumstance took place today which I never saw before–John Pack & John D. Lee were each put into nomination for Majors by regular authority & both most contemptestuously hissed down. When any person is thus duly nominated I never before knew the people to reject it But on this occasion it appears that they are both a perfect stink in every body's nose. The reasons of which is not needful to relate."

It would have been easier to go Dutch on the dinners.

Spanish Doubloons and Mormon Gold

WITH TEN THOUSAND OR SO MORMONS POPULATing the Great Salt Lake Valley and neighboring settlements by summer of 1849 and with more on the road, the need for some sort of hard cash in the economy was acute. The barter system had worked for a while, but as more members of the Church of Jesus Christ of Latter-day Saints heeded the call to gather in their new mountain home, the principle of "What have you?" and "What do you need?" began to wear thin.

According to historian J. Cecil Alter, Brigham Young, while sojourning in Winter Quarters that first winter, remembered how the boys in the valley were wearing out their pockets reaching for money they did not have and brought with him on his return in September 1848 about $84 in small change. But in a burgeoning population that was chicken feed and disappeared in the crowd as if it had never been.

An effort was made in December 1848 to circulate paper money, using handwritten scrip signed by Brigham Young and Heber C. Kimball, with Thomas Bullock, clerk, as a counter signee. The scrip was issued in one dollar and five dollar denominations backed by gold dust, which was prevalent in the valley but awkward and inexact in common use. (A pinch of dust varied from thumb to thumb.) After several other attempts, including the reissue of Kirtland Safety Society anti-banking notes from the Mormon Church's failed venture in organizing an Ohio bank, Brigham gave up on paper currency. What was needed was coin.

The first solid money showed up in Great Salt Lake Valley in December 1847 after Young had left for Winter Quarters to prepare the rest of the Saints for the journey to Utah the following spring. Captain James Brown had ridden into the valley from San Francisco, his saddlebags heavy with Spanish doubloons—back pay owed the Pueblo Detachment of the Mormon Battalion. The precise sum is a matter of debate; church records have it ranging from $5,000 to

$10,000. But whatever the amount, the doubloons, probably coins of eight-escudo denomination (twenty dollars in U.S. value), had been paid by the U.S. Army paymaster to Brown, who held powers of attorney from the Pueblo veterans. Depending on the sum involved, Brown would have had from 250 to 500 of the Spanish coins in his pouches.

These gold escudos (worth today on the numismatic market about $500 each in good condition) were readily accepted by Americans. With approval of the Mormon High Council in Brigham's absence, Brown spent $2,000 to buy Fort Buenaventura from Miles Goodyear; the balance is said to have gone to battalion members.

Still, the reluctance of travelers to accept Mormon scrip or Kirtland Bank notes as legitimate money continued to be a problem. As Alter explained it, "To those who knew the sound of his voice, Brigham Young's signature made the new money legal tender by common consent." But with transients, who from 1849 became an important segment of the population, at least in summer, it was a different matter entirely. They were moving onward and would carry the money into a land that knew not Joseph Smith's successor, consequently emigrants not only paid out good money for what they bought but demanded money they could use in California and Oregon in exchange for wagons, livestock, groceries, clothing, tools, and implements they sold in the valley. And, Alter pointed out, that not only threatened depletion of the meager supply of U.S. money but of the gold dust deposits held in security as backing for the paper money issued. It was imperative that a coin be struck that in itself was intrinsically worth the amount claimed on its face, which would be acceptable and usable by Mormon residents, Mormons abroad, and non-Mormons in Great Salt Lake City and elsewhere.

With the discovery of gold at Sutter's Mill early in 1848, gold dust was finding its way into

William Clayton. LDS
Church Archives.

the Mormon economy in increasing amounts. There are numerous cases of Mormons paying their church tithing in gold dust (at fifteen dollars an ounce). This "church treasure," as Alter described it, was to be melted and rolled into strips from which coins could be stamped.

The extent to which Mormon authorities had concerned themselves over the situation is evident in a letter from Brigham Young to Thomas "Peg Leg" Smith, who ran a trading post in the Bear River Valley:

[I] understand that you have a desire to dispose of your establishment, cattle, stock, &c. now in the Bear River Valley. I send herewith Mr. Lewis Robison, a friend of mine, who is fully authorized to treat with and make suitable arrangements for pay, transfer of property, &c. Whatever arrangements he may make in regard to the pay, you may consider me responsible for the amount.

The coined money, I have now not on hand, but we are preparing to put the gold dust into coin without an alloy, which if you are disposed to take, you can have . . . but if you choose the American-coined money we can probably get it by the time you want it. If not, it will probably save me some little trouble.

All that remained in the planning process was for Young to order the design of such coins and create the dies to stamp them with. Part of that task took place November 25, 1848, when Brigham Young, with John Taylor and John M. Kay, sketched out the coin designs and decided upon inscriptions for them. Alfred B. Lambson forged the dies, the punches, tools, and collars; Robert L. Campbell engraved the first stamps for the coins; a drop hammer was forged by Martin H. Peck; and John Kay engraved the dies and minted the coins. William Clayton and Thomas Bullock acted as accountant and weigher, respectively. Originally, the plan was to mint two-, five-, ten-, and twenty-dollar gold pieces, and while this ultimately was done, the ten-dollar coin was the first struck; with twenty-five minted the first day.

The first design called for an obverse with the motto "Holiness to the Lord" and an emblem of the LDS priesthood—a three-pointed Phrygian crown over an All-Seeing Eye of Jehovah. On the reverse, the two-, five-, and twenty-dollar coins were inscribed "G.S.L.C.P.G." (Great Salt Lake City Pure Gold) over two clasped hands symbolizing friendship, then with the value and the year. The ten-dollar coin bore the words "Pure Gold" on its reverse, rather than the initialed phrase. This was altered in later coins so the obverse inscription would read "Deseret Assay Office, Pure Gold," then the year 1860 and at the base "5 D." On the reverse side was a crouched lion, surrounded by "Holiness to the Lord" written in Deseret Alphabet characters.

The coins were .899 fine, with a bit of native silver, but no other alloy, for strength. Most of the coins bore the date 1849, but a great many were issued in 1850 and later. With hard cash a reality, Daniel H. Wells and Thomas Bullock spent September 10, 1849, destroying the Mormon paper currency. "They tore up and burned between $3,000 and $4,000," according to church records.

When the coins were first circulated in St. Louis by Salt Lake merchants, who used them to pay for merchandise, the twenty-dollar coins were accepted at eighteen dollars because of the touch of silver alloy. In the valley, however, the coins went for face value. But over the long account, the Mormon minters had the last laugh, because the numismatic value of these golden treasures is manyfold what the Saints asked for them. A twenty-dollar 1849 Mormon gold piece, for example, is valued at between $25,000 and $50,000, according to Alvin Rust's *Mormon and Utah Coin and Currency*.

The day of the Mormon coiners came to an effective close when the new San Francisco Mint went into operation in 1854, producing U.S. gold and silver hard money by the bagsful daily. The last Mormon gold was minted in 1860.

UTAH STRIKES IT RICH IN 1849

IT WAS TOUGH TIMES EARLY IN 1849 IN GREAT SALT LAKE CITY. Mercantile goods were scarce and what was available was not cheap, having to be freighted from the East. For the early citizens of the provisional State of Deseret, as they called their mountain settlement, money was in short supply, crickets and grasshoppers had done considerable damage, crops were meager and nothing to rave about, and their Indian neighbors were becoming testy. All things considered, morale was a mite low and the community, such as it was, was in need of some encouragement.

At a Sunday meeting in April one of the speakers was Heber C. Kimball, a member of the First Presidency of the Church of Jesus Christ of Latter-day Saints who was, next to Brigham Young, the most powerful man in the valley. No one ever dozed when Kimball spoke; he was well known for

saying things to capture an audience's attention, for he minced no words in speaking his mind. New York newspaper publisher Horace Greeley would say of Kimball that in conversation with a Gentile, the apostle had announced, "I do pray for my enemies! I pray they may all go to hell."

Kimball in 1849 had not yet reached full stride as a pulpit pounder, but he had a knack for making a point. Some said he was coarse and listened to him tight lipped, but on this Sabbath he was moved to inspire those around him, to lift their spirits. They were down, they were hungry, and they barely had clothes on their back. Matter of fact, almost every man in the congregation was clad in animal skins of one sort or another. Kimball stood and, after a few opening words, came to the point: "Never mind, in less than a year there will be plenty of clothes and everything that

Daguerreotype of Heber C. Kimball. LDS Church Archives.

Charles C. Rich. Photo by Savage & Ottinger; LDS Church Archives.

we shall want will be sold here at less than St. Louis prices."

Charles C. Rich, a fellow apostle sitting nearby, was astonished at the remark. "I don't believe a word of it," Rich said, in what may have been crowd consensus. George A. Smith, also an apostle, looked up and said, "Brother Kimball, you have burst your boiler this time sure." Kimball was somewhat startled himself. As he sat down, he muttered he was "afraid he had missed it some."

In the East, a virus was taking hold—gold fever. Stories of fantastic riches springing from the discovery at Sutter's Mill in California spread with astonishing speed. Extravagant claims of fortunes made overnight appeared in newspapers, along with accounts of gold lumps of "16 and 26 pounds" being exhumed from the rivers. Within a few months the rush was on. In May an emigrant from St. Joseph, Missouri, who signed his name *E Pluribus One of `Em*, wrote the *New York Tribune* that nine hundred wagons were on the trail west, averaging three men to a wagon, which would make nearly three thousand gold seekers, allowing for the considerable number going with pack mules.

In early June, A. W. Babbitt with a small party carrying the U.S. mail to Great Salt Lake City reported he "counted," as he passed on the north bank of the Platte, six thousand wagons heading west on the Oregon-California road near Fort Laramie. Another correspondent writing to St. Louis newspapers reckoned there must be a scarcity of firearms in the States because the emigrants "are covered with them." Every man had a rifle and revolver or two. One man had three Bowie knives in his belt.

By the time the "rushers" reached the plains west of Fort Laramie, they were starting to shed some of their gear and provisions. The grass was showing the heavy demand of horses, mules, and oxen; and firewood was fast vanishing. "Thousands of pounds of the finest flour and bacon were offered for sale at $1 per hundred, and no takers. It was left by the road," the St. Louis correspondent noted. At Fort Laramie flannel shirts were selling for a dime, wagons for five dollars to twenty-five dollars. One party bought a "cord" (a pile eight feet long, four feet high, and four feet wide) of clothing at such rates.

Once over South Pass, the "fever" reached epidemic proportions. Eastern newspapers estimated that by the third week in June there were twenty thousand people and sixty thousand animals in a headlong dash to be first to California! Now they began lightening their loads in earnest. At the outset the gold seekers overstocked on everything. They brought sawmill parts, blacksmith shops, gold-digging equipment, grindstones, chain, and a thousand sundry items. The overland trail was littered with valuable plunder as the travelers jettisoned these encumbrances one by one. But the emigrant's loss was the Mormon's gain. While much was abandoned on the plains, more reached Great Salt Lake City.

The first forty-niners arrived at the City of the Saints in mid-June. Brigham Young had anticipated the increased trail traffic and sent a party of missionaries to the Green River to trade and operate a ferry. On a twenty-mile stretch west of present Casper, Wyoming, they reported finding at least $50,000 in iron, trunks, clothing, and other discarded belongings, strewn among the several hundred rotting ox carcasses adding their stench to the sweltering summer prairie. When the first gold seekers strode from Emigration Canyon that June morning Heber C. Kimball's extravagant prediction began coming true—in spades. The Mormons were about to reap a most welcome and completely unexpected harvest.

Every mule in the valley suddenly increased tenfold in value. A light Yankee wagon could be traded for three or four heavy Murphy models with a yoke of oxen to boot. The argonauts were consumed with a desire for speed. Common domestic muslin, which sold for five to ten cents a yard in St. Louis, was offered by the bolt at the same price to Mormons in trade for green vegetables. The finest in spades and shovels went for fifty cents each as the forty-niners trimmed their baggage. Full chests of joiner's tools priced at $150 in the East traded for $25. Smaller merchants, hoping to deal in the gold fields, switched from wagons to pack horses in Great Salt Lake City and found it expedient to leave whatever could not be rolled easily into a bundle or tied safely onto a pack animal.

In one respect merchants were fortunate in finding Mormons to share their losses; others had no consumers to absorb the supplies. Between South Pass and Fort Hall, roads were choked by hundreds of entirely helpless wagons; many of their teams drowned in crossing streams or starved for want of grass. Men, maddened because they could not get by or go ahead at trail passes blocked by broken-down wagons and teams, fought and killed each other.

Benjamin Johnson was in his field when he saw a company of argonauts roll from Emigration Canyon. "Almost their first inquiry was for pack saddles and fresh animals in place of their jaded ones," Johnson recalled. "I traded them a jack and a jenny and began the making of pack saddles, rigging them with rawhide. And oh! what a change! I could now get flour, bacon, sugar rice, soap, tea powder, lead, tobacco, the finest clothing, with wagons and harness in exchange for pack outfits, which I could supply in quantity."

Historian Brigham D. Madsen in his *Gold Rush Sojourners in Great Salt Lake City* tells of sharp bargains by Mormons who were reluctant to part with their strong and healthy animals but would finally give in to overly generous offers. For instance, Chapman Duncan started bargaining with one yoke of oxen and by autumn had two yoke of oxen, two colts, two mules, and one horse. George Morris found that after some haggling, he would take two large footsore oxen, a third ox, and ten dollars in trade for his smaller team of two oxen. Then he turned his newly acquired livestock to run loose in marshy grass for a few days, salving their sore feet. Thus refreshed, the animals attracted other travelers who offered two yoke of oxen, $15, and a $110 wagon for Morris's three oxen. By the end of the tourist season, Morris owned five yoke of oxen, a wagon, four cows, plus clothing, boots, shoes, bread, and groceries enough to make his family more comfortable "than we had ever been before."

Zadok Judd parlayed two horses and a proper reluctance into trades which brought him three yoke of cattle, a good wagon, a cook stove, a dozen shirts, a silver watch, some tools, and a half-barrel of pork. One gold seeker went to Benjamin Johnson's home late on a Saturday night, according to historian Madsen, and wanted to buy pack saddles, insisting he could not wait until Monday for his party was leaving at sunup. Johnson labored the night through until time for church to make up the order. The emigrant gave Johnson three sets of harness and a new wagon "with more camp outfit, clothing and goods in it than a fair price to pay four-fold for my work. When they got what they wanted, the gold-seekers cared for nothing they had to leave."

As for Brigham Young, he considered such transactions to be a "mutual blessing." But the record is silent on whether Heber C. Kimball was tempted to crow, "I told you so."

SUPPLY AND DEMAND IN THE OLD WEST

IN THE DAY-TO-DAY WORLD OF THE 1990s, consumers on a tight budget have learned to "shop around," to find out where they can get the best buy for their hard-earned cash. And while goods were much less expensive in the early settlements of the West—a dollar could buy a lot more—there were fewer dollars to be had. In early Utah especially, goods had to be packed or freighted from the East and that drove the cost up. The settlers in the Great Salt Lake Valley knew right away they were going to have a tough winter; the crops planted in the summer of 1847 likely would get them through, but they also knew clothes and other essentials would be in short supply until the emigration brought fresh supplies in 1848.

The first "storekeeper," if you could call him that, to open trade in the valley was a Hudson's Bay Fur Company man, Captain Richard Grant, who ordinarily held forth at his Fort Hall trading post. But on November 19, 1848, Grant rode into the Salt Lake settlement at the head of a pack train laden with skins, groceries, and other goods. He pulled in on the south side of the old fort and opened for business as long as the merchandise lasted. His goods were on the pricey side because of the transportation problem, but all in all, leaders of the Mormon community were pleased that he didn't exploit the situation and gouge the buyers.

As it was, Grant sold sugar and coffee at a dollar a pint (an amount less than a pound), his twenty-five cents a yard calico went for fifty and seventy-five cents a yard, and other articles were priced proportionately. Why did Grant not sell higher? pondered *Deseret News* editor Albert Carrington in a newspaper article written years later. "Perhaps he had some conscience, and it is probable he thought the then poverty of the settlers would not admit of any dearer rate and it must be confessed the [prices mentioned] were pretty high figures."

Captain Grant's pack horse storefront was short-lived in any case. And in early 1849 the first regular stock of goods for Utah markets was brought in by the partners Livingston & Kinkead, who hauled $20,000 in St. Louis merchandise into the valley and began dealing from an adobe house in the vicinity of South Temple and Main. The following year Holladay & Warner became the city's

Fort Hall. Photo by W. H. Jackson; Utah State Historical Society.

second mercantile firm, operating from a small schoolhouse on Brigham Young's block east of today's Eagle Gate. Then came John and Enoch Reese who opened shop on Main Street, and J. M. Horner was the fourth Utah merchant.

With these outfits in business and dealing with the Mormon population and Gentile transient traffic, things seemed to be moving right along, but some of the city's leaders were not entirely delighted. Livingston & Kinkead seemed to be "fa'r and squar," while other stores appeared to be operating on the sharp side. And Carrington, the public watchdog in his position as newspaper editor, wasn't happy. It was bad enough the U.S. mail was months late from the States and he wasn't receiving his exchange newspapers and correspondence, but when he felt he was being gouged by the shopkeeper, well, that cut it. He picked up his pen and swung it like a sword.

In a September 28, 1854, *News* editorial he pointed out that Livingston & Kinkead had established the prevailing prices by virtue of being first; the figures were based on cost, interest, and

expenses. Nothing wrong with that, opined Carrington. The merchants offered sugar and coffee for forty cents a pound and good calico for twenty-five cents a yard. True, they brought little iron and steel—a few nails, mill irons, and heavy irons—which because of their weight did not bring a proportionate return for the dollar. (You could carry more coffee, sugar, calico, and sundries if you passed on the iron and steel.) "To their credit be it known that they never raised their regular price on an article even when they had all there was in the market, never kept incorrect accounts, nor even failed to deal as fairly with a child or a person ignorant of value and price, as with the most knowing and influential, and it is . . . just [and proper] that this conduct be remembered and the people stand by those who have been tested and found to deal fairly."

Fair or not, the prices across the board were still a bit steep in the editor's estimation, and he muttered editorially that it was time for consumers (he called them buyers) to make their presence felt. Wagon train after wagon train of staple goods had

Great Salt Lake City, first capital of the Territory of Utah, in 1850. Utah State Historical Society

begun reaching Great Salt Lake City, with rumors of many more on the road. And because money was always scarce in the settlement, the merchants, who had bills to pay too, were showing signs of concern. Competition was just around the next bend and they could sense it.

Carrington pointed out that some folks who had a little cash were not ready to "squeeze themselves out of shape when a new store opened in order to buy a yard of ribbon or a flumdiddle for a new wife. . . . [Webster is as much at sea on flumdiddle as the rest of us.] And to the credit of the [Mormon ladies], we have seen but little teasing or crowding on their part to purchase Gentile wore fog, commonly called belgerine, gauze, coarse delaines, nor the foolish expenditure of hard earnings for silks, satins, and artificials, to the neglect of more useful appropriate goods."

So what happened when the merchandise trains brought in the goods? The firm of J. M. Horner & Co. was induced to take the lead and drop the price of sugar to three pounds for a dollar, which prompted Livingston & Kinkead to cut their sugar price to thirty cents a pound and calico

to eighteen cents a yard and generally to slash prices of their "large and splendid stock" by 25 percent across the board, with a guarantee that they would not be raised later. "Competition," exulted Carrington, "did it."

And that emboldened the journalist to take the case a step further. "Can a Mormon, with cash and good credit, buy as cheap as a Gentile in the markets of Babylon? He can [or he doesn't belong there]. Can he freight his goods as cheap? He can or he has no skill in freighting. Can he rent or build rooms, and hire clerks, etc., as reasonable? If not, it is his own fault. Then why can he not sell as good an article as low as the transient trader?" The answer, editor Carrington said, was obvious. If a Mormon could not do these things, it is because he has been duped or is selfish and greedy. He had one last bit of advice for all concerned: "Sooner or later merchandizing here [in Utah] will have to come to the fair living level, and whoever pursues an even honorable tenor in that channel, will receive the support of the people."

Buyers are learning the wires, he said. Don't deal with shops where they ask fifty cents a pound for candles, $2.50 a bunch for cotton yarn, and will only give you $10 a ton for your hay and pay you in goods at their high prices, only to resell your hay for $15 cash. "Hay," Carrington wrote, "is worth $15 and will soon be worth $20. Can you not wait a little? Keep out of HIGH PRICED STORES until you are compelled to go into them, which if you are wise, will never happen." That is 1850s advice that is just as sound 148 years later.

HAVE YOU SEEN THE ELEPHANT?

THERE ARE ALL SORTS OF CATCH PHRASES IN history, some born of the moment, such as Don't shoot until you see the white of their eyes! Others are creations of frustration: Pike's Peak or Bust! And still others mark the poignancy of tragedy: Remember the Alamo! The chronicles are full of such phrases, and in rare cases their origins are so cryptic as to defy solution. For instance, not a GI in World War II can explain the root beginnings of that mysterious declaration discovered in every theater of combat from Atlantic to Pacific: Kilroy was here!

However, there is catch phrase that should intrigue western history students, and it, too, has escaped satisfactory explanation for the better part of a century and a half: Seeing the elephant! Anyone familiar with the California gold rush of 1849 has come across that puzzling statement at one time or another. Gold seekers were off to "see the elephant." Successful fortune hunters said they had "seen the elephant," or "tracked the elephant." Unsuccessful forty-niners, down on their luck and flat busted, complained of having "seen the elephant" and wanted no more of it.

For all of its turns of phrase, rare is the journal which explains the whys and wherefores of this fabled critter. Most of the theories are as lame as the excuses for not finding gold in El Dorado. Whatever else, the phrase came to signify some bizarre wild adventure or improbable escapade. But two explanations seem to claim the most respect for reasonable logic.

The first was laid out for 1856 readers of the *Deseret News,* who found this account–under the headline "Origin 'Seeing the Elephant'"–in their November 19 edition (since the article was overwritten by half, what follows is a pruned and pared synopsis): Some years before 1856 (probably antedating the 1848 gold discovery at Sutter's Mill), a pageant was in rehearsal at one of the Philadelphia theatres in which it was necessary to enroll an elephant. Alas, no elephant was to be had, and the property man, stage managers, and director had fits worrying about it.

However, the article went on, Yankee ingenuity prevailed, as it always has, and a pachyderm was made to order from wood, skins, paint, and varnish. So far, so good, but they failed to find a means of making the contraption travel. But wait! The property man had an inspiration. He would hire two agile young knockabouts, two true and genuine "b'hoys" who could carry off the role without complaint. And so, the young men were installed as legs.

Ned C––, the article explained, was in charge of the forelegs, and his cohort brought up the hindermost. The role was a tedious one, as the elephant was obliged to be on stage about an hour and young Ned was rather too fond on the bottle to remain so long without "wetting his whistle." So he set about calculating a way of providing himself with a wee drop. Because the eyes of the elephant were two port bottles with the necks turned in, Ned recognized an opportunity. He would fill the two bottles with the good stuff, and once accomplished, he willingly undertook to play the forelegs again.

Saturday night came on–the theatre was packed with denizens of the Quaker city. The music was played in the sweetest strains, the curtain rose, and the pageant began. Ned and the "hindlegs" marched out upon the stage. The elephant was greeted by round upon round of applause. The decorations and trappings were gorgeous. Again and again the "elephant" and the prince seated upon his back were loudly cheered.

As the play proceeded, the pachyderm was marched round and round the stage. The forelegs got dry, withdrew one of the corks and treated the hindlegs; then he drank to the health of the audience with a bumper of genuine Elephant Eye whisky, a brand, by the way, till then unknown. On went the play and on went Ned, toasting the music, the lights, and the cheers. The grand finale signal was given, and forelegs staggered to the front of the stage. The conductor tugged the elephant's ears to the right—forelegs wobbled to the left and, with the footlights obstructing his view, stepped smack into the orchestra pit! Forelegs crashed onto the conductor's fiddle, and, of course, the elephant overturned, sending the prince and hindlegs into the middle of the orchestral pandemonium.

Onstage, the managers stood horror-struck: the prince and hindlegs lay confounded, box seat patrons were in convulsions, the actors choked with laughter, and poor Ned, casting one look—a strange blend of drunkenness, grief, and laughter at his predicament—fled hastily from the theater, with the conductor in close pursuit waving the wreckage of his fiddle and performing various cuts and thrusts in the air. The curtain fell on the shambles. No more play, no more forelegs. Pit, boxes, and gallery rushed from the theater shrieking between every breath: "Have you seen the elephant?"

That, it is said, is how the phrase came to be associated with the bizarre and improbable. In the years 1849 and 1850 it was not unusual to hear the phrases "the elephant's tracks" or "the elephant's tail" uttered by those who turned back, insisting that view was sufficient to satisfy their penchant for adventure. Many a wagon was decorated with the query Have you saw the elephant?

There remains, however, another explanation. This one preferred by most authorities, or so it seems: At a time when circus parades first featured elephants, a farmer, hearing of such an event, loaded his wagon with vegetables for market in town. He had never seen an elephant and very much wished to. On his way he encountered the circus parade led by the aforementioned beast. The farmer was thrilled, but his horses terrified. Bolting, they overturned the wagon and ruined the vegetable harvest. "But I don't give a hang," he said, "for I have seen the elephant!"

The same can be said for the gold rush of 1849: Was it worth the trials, tribulations, and hardship? Was it enough just to have seen the elephant?

FIREARMS: A DANGEROUS NECESSITY IN THE OLD WEST

THERE IS A TENDENCY ON THE WESTERN SLOPE OF the Continental Divide to lose perspective occasionally and confuse the myth of the West with reality. That can be dangerous, especially now that Americans are becoming ever more conscious of guns and recall a time in frontier history a half-dozen generations gone by when carrying a pistol in public was as commonplace as wearing a hat. The image of the square-jawed man-of-few-words with a six-shooter on his hip come to tame a town is the stuff of daydreams and childhood fantasies.

More likely is the picture of an overland traveler in a weathered and worn prairie schooner pulled along by a double yoke of trail-weary oxen.

Inside the wagon, one would probably find within easy reach a handgun, which might or might not function each time it was called upon. And there would be a musket, a muzzle loader that required a lead ball be rammed in place down the barrel atop a measured amount of black powder. A percussion cap would complete the firing chain. All very primitive by today's standards and not always dependable by any standard. But always dangerous.

Western myth holds that pioneers, settlers, mountaineers, and all other manner of frontier citizens knew their way around guns. It was part and parcel of their everyday lives. True, in most

Daguerreotype of Brigham Young, 1850. Utah State Historical Society.

In 1847, during the Mormon hegira from Winter Quarters, Nebraska, Brigham Young took special pains to instruct the advance party of pioneers to travel in groups of ten, "as we were in Indian country and for every man to carry his gun loaded." But, he stressed, percussion caplocks were to rest on a piece of buckskin with "caps ready to slip on in an instant in case of attack, or if it is a flintlock it should have cotton in the pan and a powder flask handy to prime quick." The reason for this caution, he said, was to prevent accidents.

On an evening in June, however, as the advance company moved into camp on the Sweetwater River, nineteen-year-old John Holman, musket in hand, was herding several of Brigham Young's horses. He jabbed one in the flank with the muzzle of his rifle, the hammer caught on his clothing, and the gun discharged into the best horse in camp. The shot tore into the animal's abdomen. It died a few hours later. Thomas Bullock, camp historian, ruefully noted it was the third horse accidently killed on the trail. There is no record of Young's reaction to the death of his favorite mount.

A gold seeker, Joseph Waring Berrien, headed for California was camped on the Big Blue River in Kansas on a cold and disagreeable Sunday in April 1849 when he heard the report of a gun in a wagon "about eight paces distant." He heard someone cry, "Sacre! Oh, mon Dieu!" and saw a body fall "with a heavy squelch to the ground," from the back of the wagon. "It proved to be a young Frenchman, Nicholas Boismenue by name. . . . He had crawled into the back part of his wagon and finding his gun there had attempted to draw it towards him with the muzzle pointing directly at his breast; something coming in contact with the lock raised the hasp which coming down on the cap exploded the gun, the contents of which he received in his breast ranging downwards towards his hip and causing his death almost instantly," Berrien wrote in his diary.

Frederick Gardiner was with a group of Mormon missionaries headed east in May 1857 when one of the party, a fellow from Big Cottonwood in the Great Salt Lake Valley, pulled a rifle muzzle-first from a wagon. It discharged and the heavy lead ball took away half his head. "We buried him on the Little Sandy," Gardiner said.

respects. With firearms so accessible the danger, ironically, was less that hot tempers would provoke an endless round of gunfights than that careless disrespect of such weapons would produce disastrous consequences. Annals of the West are rife with examples.

Early emigrants on the overland trail constantly abused or ignored the most basic precautions. Medorem Crawford, guiding a wagon train to Oregon in July 1842, sadly recorded the death of a man named Bailey near Independence Rock, "shot while walking through camp by accidental discharge of a gun from a wagon. He lived an hour." Wrote Crawford, "My feelings on this occasion can hardly be described. A young man in the vigor of youth and health taken from our company, wrapped in a buffalo robe & buried in this dismal prairie. What sad tidings for his parents & friends, who like my own are far from here." Three days later, he noted in his journal, "Mr. Bennett's daughter slightly wounded by an accidental discharge of a gun."

Similar incidents abound. When a group was sent from Salt Lake City in October 1853 to settle near Fort Bridger, it reported one of its members, Silas Pratt, suffered a wound in the hand when a pistol accidentally fired. And when Mormon guerrilla leader Lot Smith regrouped his company after burning a government supply train at Simpson's Hollow in present Wyoming, he suffered the only casualties of the raid. Smith was reloading his weapons and had placed a pistol atop a large clump of sagebrush. In picking it up the trigger caught on a sage branch and the gun fired. "The ball passed through Orson P. Arnold's thigh, breaking the bone in a fearful manner, struck Philo Dibble in the side of the head, and went through Samuel Bateman's hat just missing his head." Young Arnold, suffering greatly, was sent home and recovered.

A HANDBOOK FOR AMERICA'S PIONEERS

FAMILIES PLANNING A CROSS-COUNTRY TRIP TODAY find it a simple matter to get from the local automobile club a map and checklist to make the experience as comfortable and pleasant as possible, but in the days of the prairie schooner circumstances were different—a lot different. For someone then to ignore or overlook a bit of trail advice might cost dearly, perhaps even a life. In today's world it is still possible to find books trumpeting "Enjoy that trip on $5 a day!" or "Travel made easier: 200 tips to better motoring." But in great-grandpa's time, authoritative advice was scarce as wheels on a snake.

For the most part, overland pioneers such as the Bidwell-Bartleson party of 1841, the Harlan-Young company of 1846, the Donner-Reeds in that same year, even the Mormon pioneers of 1847, paid close attention to experience when it was offered. And they sought out, where possible, guides familiar with the country.

It's easy to see, then, why Captain R. B. Marcy proved to be a godsend for overland pilgrims. Marcy was one of the ablest officers in the old frontier army, and he was as handy with a pen as pistol. During his gloried career, he commanded a number of expeditions in the West; his mission to discover and chart "what was over the next hill." And more than once his derring-do almost did him in.

In 1859 he wrote *The Prairie Traveler; The Classic Handbook for America's Pioneers*. It proved to be just what the unskilled wagonmaster needed to take himself and family across the western plains. And it came from someone who knew of what he spoke; during his career Marcy led no fewer than five military explorations. In 1849 he escorted the largest California-bound emigrant train along the southern route from Fort Smith, Arkansas, through dangerous Indian country to beyond Santa Fe, New Mexico; and in 1853 he explored the headwaters of the Red River and the dread Llano Estacado, the Staked Plains of the Texas panhandle.

His *Prairie Traveler* was, hands down, the best "how-to" of its day and remained so for years. With his handbook, even the most bumbling city dweller had a chance. Marcy told emigrants why mules can only cross rivers if they don't get water in their ears. And which tree bark and leaves could be smoked if tobacco ran out. He also offered opinions on the best—and worst—treatments for rattlesnake bites. He drew from many years of frontier life for material and he was skillful with words.

Swimming mules? Oh, it seems if they get water in their ears they usually drown. It has something to do with disorientation and their sense of balance. "Whenever a mule in the water drops his ears, it's a sure sign that he has water in them and should be led out as soon as possible." He recommended easing mules into deep water slowly without crowding to ensure safe crossing.

As for his writing qualifications, Marcy had hoped "someone more competent than myself" would take on the book job. Ever modest, he did not understand how sharply that restriction would narrow the field of authors. Of his contemporaries among mountaineers, Marcy would say, "Our frontiersmen, although brave in council and action, and possessing an intelligence that quickens in the face of danger, are apt to feel shy of the pen. They shun the atmosphere of the student's closet; their sphere is in the free and open wilderness." To them the field of literature remained a *terra incognita*.

Thus having set himself to the task, Marcy became a fount of knowledge ranging from proper trail selection to picking the best and most practical equipment for the journey and where it could be obtained: "There are stores at Powderhorn and Indianola, Iowa, where the traveler can obtain most of the articles needed. . . . Supplies of all descriptions necessary for the overland journey may be procured at Fort Smith, or at Van Buren on the opposite side of the Arkansas." Organization was essential. Without it, he warned, it would be impossible for a party of any magnitude to travel together for any great length of time. Discords and dissensions would arise sooner or later. Select a captain, he suggested, and once picked, "he should be sustained in all his decisions unless he commit some manifest outrage." Only then should he be deposed and another more competent leader selected.

The best wagons for overland travel came from Concord, New Hampshire, he said. Used in carrying passengers and the mails on some routes across the plains, they are considered superior to any others, he added. And they were sturdy, made of close-grained oak, and well seasoned. Marcy didn't mention cost, but newspapers of the day in St. Louis and Independence advertised them at $150.

He cautioned that wagons with six mules should never on a long journey be loaded with over two thousand pounds, unless grain was the cargo, in which case another thousand pounds was permissable, provided it was fed out daily to the team. For emigrants interested in optional "under-the-hood" specifications, Marcy opined that for a trip of less than one thousand miles, mules were the preferred power supply, but if the march extended to fifteen hundred or two thousand miles or was over rough, sandy, or muddy roads, young oxen would endure better than mules. And they were more economical: a team of six mules cost $600, while an eight-ox team on the frontier ran

about $200. Oxen were much less liable to be stampeded or driven off by Indians. Besides, in a pinch, if food ran short, they could be used as beef—a bit tough, but better than mule meat.

Under the heading "Stores and Provisions," he had these suggestions: Bacon should be packed in strong sacks of a hundred pounds to each or, in very hot climates, put in boxes and surrounded with bran, which in great measure prevented fat from melting away. Flour should be packed in stout double canvas sacks well sewed, a hundred pounds to each sack. Butter could be preserved by boiling it thoroughly, and the scum skimmed off as it rises to the top until it was quite clear like oil. It then should be placed in canisters and soldered up. This mode of preserving butter had been adopted in the hot climate of southern Texas and was found to keep it sweet for a great length of time, its flavor but little impaired in the process, he said. Sugar could be well secured in India rubber or *gutta-percha* sacks or so placed in the wagon as not to risk getting wet.

Marcy was big on desiccated vegetables— "They have been extensively used in the Crimean War and by our own army in Utah"—prepared by cutting fresh vegetables into thin slices and subjecting them to a very powerful press, which removed the juice and left a solid cake. After having been dried, a small piece about half the size of a man's hand, when boiled, swelled to fill a vegetable dish, sufficient for four men. A single ration weighed but an ounce, and a cubic yard contained sixteen thousand rations. "I regard these compressed vegetables as the best preparation for prairie traveling that has yet been discovered," Marcy noted.

Marcy also handed out his caveats: "It is true that if persons choose to pass through Salt Lake City, and the Mormons happen to be in an amiable mood, supplies may sometimes be procured from them; but those who have visited them know how little reliance is to be placed upon their hospitality or spirit of accommodation." (Keep in mind that Marcy was a prominent member of the Utah Expedition, which Mormons considered to be an invading mob in 1857–58, so he had his biases as well.)

For the medicine chest, he advised: "A little blue mass, quinine, opium, and some cathartic medicine, put up in doses for adults, will suffice." As for weapons, he preferred the revolver, to be worn in the belt, ready for instant use, if necessary. "There is a great diversity regarding the kind of rifle most efficient and adapted to Indian warfare. A majority prefer the breech-loading arm; others the old-fashioned muzzle-loader. Border hunters and mountaineers insist on the Hawken rifle." However, "I look upon the Colt new patent rifle as a most excellent for border service, giving six shots in more rapid succession than any other rifle I know of. If I were alone upon the prairies and expected an attack from Indians, I am not acquainted with any arm I would as soon have in my hands as this."

He placed a stampede of horses and mules high on the list of most dread disasters on the plains. Many animals are irretrievably lost, he said, and the journey thus defeated. Indians were the principal cause of such calamities. "They [Indians] approach as near the herds as possible without being seen, and suddenly, with their horses at full speed, rush in among them, making the most hideous and unearthly screams and noises to terrify them, and drive them off before the astonished owners are able to rally and secure them."

Marcy also related a number of snake bite cases, with most remedies involving slicing open the wound and sucking out the venom. His personal preference: "Of all the remedies known to me, I should decidedly prefer ardent spirits. It is considered a sovereign antidote among our Western frontier settlers, and I would make use of it with great confidence." Intoxicants stop the action of the venom, he said. "It must be taken until the patient becomes very much intoxicated, and this requires a large quantity, as the action of the poison seems to counteract its effects."

(So much for the notion that whiskey should be poured on the wound, not into the victim.)

And for campfires when wood was unavailable, Marcy was on the side of the French *bois de vache*, otherwise known as the wood of the prairie, or as the mountain men called it, "buffler chips." Since it burns evenly and hot, "This dried dung of the bison burns well when perfectly dry, answers a good purpose for cooking, and some even prefer it to wood."

Marcy had much more to say for the benefit of prairie travelers, but his wide open spaces don't apply to the limits on print here. And so Marcy, with his trove of knowledge and decades of plains experience, must be left to history.

PART II

THE UNITED STATES EXPEDITION TO UTAH.

The Utah Expedition marched from Fort Leavenworth, Kansas, to suppress a Mormon "rebellion." Engraving from T. B. H. Stenhouse, *The Rocky Mountain Saints* (1873).

6

Pulling toward Zion

Young Calls Flock to Travel to Mountain Home by Handcart
1850–1856

President Millard Fillmore's first appointees to the new Territory of Utah were, bluntly speaking, a disaster. Despite his support and sympathy for the Mormons, the nation's chief executive managed to select men remarkably unfit for important territorial positions; the situation did not improve with time. It was said Fillmore had once thought of appointing Utahns to the posts, but the pressures of patronage shouldered that possibility aside. He did, however, appoint Brigham Young as Utah's first governor. The territorial legislature gratefully named its capital city Fillmore, county of Millard, in the president's honor.

First to arrive in the territory was its new Chief Justice Lemuel G. Brandebury, a colorless man with no strong personal convictions. Then came Broughton D. Harris and his wife. He was a twenty-seven-year-old easterner who took his appointment as territorial secretary seriously, so much so he developed a wilfulness that infuriated Brigham Young. Harris brought with him $24,000 in gold earmarked as government operating funds, but he refused to heed the governor's instructions and withheld monies in a feud with Young over procedures. The legislature had completed a territorial census, but because it was not done with the proper bureaucratic paperwork in the presence of Harris (neither the forms nor Harris were avail-

able at the time), the secretary insisted on a new census, a demand Young rejected out of hand.

A third appointee, Associate Justice Perry S. Brocchus, was patronizing, pompous, and windy. Invited to speak to the citizenry on the subject of supplying a Utah marble block for the Washington Monument, Brocchus discoursed on patriotism for two hours to a restless audience. He was intoxicated by his own eloquence and, having noticed an unusually large number of women in attendance, turned to a mention of polygamy and the importance of virtue. He expressed a hope that the "sweet ladies of the congregation would become virtuous." Instead of applause, he found himself suddenly in imminent peril of an unpleasant death at the hands of an incensed throng. He later said he feared the people would "spring on me like hyenas and destroy me." Brigham Young stood to calm the tempest and in doing so unburdened himself of a few recent aggravations by scorching Brocchus. He accused Brocchus of excessive political ambition, profligate debauchery, and lechery and measured him as "one of those corrupt fellows" for sale by the handful. (Young later would remark he could have loosed the women of the congregation on Brocchus by "crooking his little finger.")

Ashen, Brocchus informed Brandebury and Harris that he intended to return to Washington as

Kanosh, chief of the Pahvant Utes. Photo by C. R. Savage; LDS Church Archives.

Uncle Sam, a Ute Indian. Photo by C. R. Savage; LDS Church Archives.

soon as possible. Good idea, they would likewise. Harris informed a fuming Brigham Young that he was taking the $24,000 back with him, leaving the governor free to argue the point with the secretary of the treasury. The trio, joined by another appointee, Indian sub-agent Henry Day, departed Utah and for a time became a cause célèbre in the national press. In the years to come, however, the incident of the "runaway officials" would be pointed to as an example of Utah's rebellious nature.

Back in the territory, Brigham Young had other problems; his efforts to suppress slave trading among the tribes had precipitated an Indian war. Walker, or Walkara, war chief of the Utes, took to raiding outlying settlements in 1853 before peace was restored. Then, late in the fall, a wagon train bound for California became involved in an incident with some Pahvant Utes near Fillmore. Several Indian men were wounded, and one, the father of their war chief, died. Some weeks later, a war party, vowing vengeance on whites, moved

toward the Sevier River—where Captain John W. Gunnison and his Pacific Railroad surveying expedition had camped. The Pahvants ambushed the government party, massacring Gunnison and seven others, among them their Mormon guide.

Persistent rumors that Brigham Young was somehow implicated in Gunnison's murder would prove groundless. Chief accuser was Judge William Wormer Drummond, appointed by President Franklin Pierce to replace Leonidas Shaver, who died in Great Salt Lake City in June 1855 of an inflammation of the inner ear (compounded by the jurist's use of opium). Shaver had succeeded Brocchus, the "runaway," as associate justice of the Territorial Supreme Court of Utah. Drummond was one of a batch of Pierce appointees, as was Lieutenant Colonel Edward Jenner Steptoe, who was ordered to Utah to arrest and punish the murderers of Captain Gunnison and also to be military governor replacing Young. But Steptoe, a career army officer, could see no

Ute Indian mother and child. Photo by C. R. Savage; LDS Church Archives.

advantage to being subjected to the whim of Washington politicians. He declined the honor and recommended Brigham Young's reappointment. It was an unexpected answer, but Steptoe's endorsement with other powerful Utahns urging Young be renamed gave Pierce reason to allow Young to stay in office.

His choices for the territorial court, however, proved a mixed bag, indeed. Pierce appointed John F. Kinney as chief justice, with Drummond and George P. Stiles as associate justices. Kinney was an Iowan with experience. Drummond—a hypocrite, liar, adulterer, gambler, bully, and horse trader—was also ruthlessly ambitious. He would figure prominently in scandals to come. Stiles was a wavering Mormon from Nauvoo.

The situation with the judiciary was especially delicate because of the Mormon Church's decision in September 1852 to publicly acknowledge its doctrine of "a plurality of wives." This thunderbolt from the pulpit was embarrassing to many of the church's missionaries, who had not been forewarned and still were denying its existence. The shock wave of excommunications for apostasy because of the proclamation was swift in coming. Mormon critics found renewed ammunition for their tirades, and the bitterness of the national press was typified by the *New York Mirror's* denouncement of Mormonism as "an immoral excrescence." The *New York Herald*, the *New York Sun,* and the *New York Tribune* joined its outrage in print. Brigham Young countered with editorials in

Great Salt Lake City, 1853. LDS Church Archives.

the church-owned *Deseret News*, the *St. Louis Luminary* in Missouri, the *Mormon* in New York, and, in San Francisco, the *Western Standard*. That there was no law against polygamy only enraged critics who called it to one of the "twin relics of barbarism," the other being slavery.

While this turmoil was festering, it was time for Brigham Young to push ahead with another "noble experiment," one he had been mulling since the Saints took root in the Great Salt Lake Valley—he spoke of immigration by handcart. Young had alluded to the plan in 1851 in a general epistle on the subject of "Gathering to Zion." He stated then, in part, "you have been expecting the time would come when you could journey across the mountains in your fine carriages, your good wagons, and have all the comforts of life that heart could wish; but your expectations are vain, and if you wait for those things you will never come . . . . Some of the Saints now in our midst, came hither with wagons or carts made of wood, without a particle of iron, hooping their wheels with hickory, or rawhide, or ropes, and had as good and safe a journey as any in the camps . . . *and can you not do the same?*"

Young now was asking for the "gathering" to begin in earnest, for converts in the East, in Europe, and elsewhere to pack up and set out for Great Salt Lake Valley—their Zion in the mountains. On October 31, 1855, he made his case for handcarts: "We are sanguine that such a train will out-travel any ox train that can be started. They should have a few good cows to furnish milk, and a few beef cattle to drive and butcher as they may need. In this way the expense, risk, loss and perplexity of teams will be obviated, and the saints will more effectually escape the scenes of distress, anguish and death which have often laid so many of our brethren and sisters in the dust." The "expense" and "perplexity of teams" may have been nullified, but even Brigham Young's confident assurances couldn't mask the fact that distress, anguish, and death were realities handcart companies would face on the trail.

Iowa was to be the terminus, the jumping-off place where immigrants would be issued handcarts. It was summer 1856. The first two companies—led by Edmund Ellsworth (266 people, 52 handcarts) and Daniel D. McArthur

(220 people, 44 handcarts)–left on June 9 and 11, respectively. A third, smaller company, led by Edward Bunker, left Iowa City on June 23. After the expected rigors of such an overland journey the Ellsworth-McArthur companies reached Great Salt Lake City on September 26; the Bunker party pulled in six days later. But the handcart experiment was far from an unqualified success. There were two other companies that fall and their thirteen-hundred-mile trek would become an ordeal hauntingly paralleling the debacle ten years earlier when the Donner-Reed wagon train was caught by winter.

James G. Willie and Edward Martin captained the remaining companies of 1856. In all, 980 immigrants were in their care. Willie's mob of Liverpool Saints was ready to leave on June 26. But their tents and handcarts were not finished; the crushing demand brought a great sacrifice in quality. The already frail structures now were fashioned of green unseasoned wood; the wheels went without metal tire bands. Compounding this problem, Martin's company had a "disproportionate number of women, children, aged and feeble emigrants," Franklin D. Richards, who passed them on the trail, would recall.

Willie's group trundled across Iowa to Winter Quarters (since renamed Florence), Nebraska, in twenty-six days. They debated whether to continue so late in the season and risk mountain storms or spend the winter in Florence. A majority of the elders in charge decided the issue: Onward to Great Salt Lake Valley! Departing August 19, Willie's company made 265 miles by September 5, but lost thirty head of cattle along the way. The immigrants, city dwellers mostly, had no interest in herding animals; they were occupied pulling handcarts. At Platte River they experienced the first severe frost. It would get worse.

By September 30, they reached Fort Laramie–still five hundred miles from their destination. Now the food supply, already meager, was rationed. Barely enough to sustain life. At Willow Creek on the Sweetwater River just east of South Pass, fierce storms caught the handcarts and swept them into drifts. Dysentery broke out in the camp, frostbite was common, and death a constant companion. Fifteen perished in the days before the Willow Creek camp, and expectations of a relief

train from Great Salt Lake buoyed spirits briefly, but the howling storms smothered hope that help would reach them in time.

Each morning the immigrants crawled from their tents, numb, exhausted, unable to properly feed themselves, faced with the realization of making miles. The camp was a disaster of disease and pain; dysentery reduced the handcarters to apparitions. As they steadily weakened, John Chislett, one of the company, was later to confide, "Life went out as smoothly as a lamp ceases to burn when the oil is gone. At first the deaths occurred slowly and irregularly, but in a few days at more frequent intervals, until we soon thought it unusual to leave a camp without burying one or more persons." Many a father pulled his cart with his little children on it until he died, Chislett said.

Captain Willie and another started out alone to find help, before all in the camp went under. He stumbled on the relief train a few miles distant, and returned with fourteen wagons. Eight wagons remained with the Willie company and six pressed on to Martin's handcarts stranded farther back. Once over South Pass and descending into Green River Valley, the weather moderated such that many of the frozen and disabled could be carried in wagons. Willie's company arrived in Great Salt Lake City on November 9–the total number of deaths seventy-seven.

Martin's company fared even worse. With a larger number of women and children and many aged and feeble, coupled with the delayed start and poorly made handcarts, they could not overcome two-foot snowdrifts and ice. Children who tried to ride in the carts only caused them to break down more readily. Martin and his company reached Green River by November 21 and by the 28th made it to the Weber River. Two days later they struggled into Great Salt Lake City.

Chislett said of Martin's company that of six hundred who started, more than one-quarter perished. One hundred and fifty deaths. "Their campground [on the North Platte] became a veritable graveyard before they left," Chislett wrote. That number plus Willie's death toll, brought the total to 227, not counting other casualties. For years, frostbite survivors without feet, toes, or fingers could be seen in the territory–many crippled for life, Chislett said. But the handcart experiment was not abandoned. A company traveled east from Utah in April 1857, two smaller parties journeyed to the valley from the States that summer, still another company trekked to Utah in 1859, and two made the westward trip in 1860—that was the last use of that method of travel.

And so it was that handcart pioneers added their strength, spirit, and indomitable will to Utah's legacy in its struggle for statehood.

THE HAND-CART EMIGRANTS IN A STORM.

Handcart pioneers suffered terrible hardships in the vicious 1856 winter storms near South Pass. Engraving from T. B. H. Stenhouse, *The Rocky Mountain Saints* (1873).

7

The Utah War

The Hold Mormons Had on Utah Is Broken
1857–1858

If any particular period could be considered critical in Utah's history, it likely would be 1857–58, when the U.S. Army marched on the Mormons and forever cracked their shell of isolationism. In the brief span of two years, Brigham Young would be deposed as governor of the territory, troops would be sent to protect his successor, and a horrific episode known as the Mountain Meadow massacre would cloak the Mormon Church in a black shroud of shame and disgrace.

The army eventually withdrew, leaving behind millions in materiel, which the Mormons bought for pennies on the dollar. On the surface it seemed an unalloyed Mormon triumph, but in truth Brigham Young lost the total domination he once enjoyed over the citizens of Utah. It was far from a fair exchange. Who gained the advantage? It depended on which side was asked.

The confrontation had been long simmering, starting in the early 1850s with the runaway officials—those federal appointees who vacated Utah after clashing with Governor Brigham Young on how things should be run in the territory. In the next few years, the situation became complicated when Jim Bridger was forced out of the trading post he built on Blacks Fork in present Wyoming. The Mormons accused him of intriguing with the Indians. Brigham Young offered to buy the property but dealt with Louis Vasquez, Bridger's partner. Young paid Vasquez $4,000 in 1855 with a promise of another $4,000 to close the deal.

At the same time, Albert Carrington, editor of the *Deseret News*, railed against William M. F. Magraw, the U.S. mail contractor, accusing Magraw of dereliction in delivering eastern mail to Utah. So vociferous were the complaints that Magraw, sullen and vindictive, finally threw up his hands and abandoned the contract to a much lower Mormon bid.

Then, of course, there was Associate Justice W. W. Drummond, in 1855 the latest federal appointee to the Supreme Court of the Territory of Utah. Drummond was related by marriage to a Mormon, and he rated them somewhat lower than horse thieves on the social ladder. If anything, the feeling was mutual. Brigham Young, in one of his more solicitous moments, referred to Drummond as "a rotten-hearted loathesome reptile."

Drummond became a stench within his jurisdiction once he introduced "Mrs. Drummond" to Mormon social circles and it was discovered that she was, in fact, Ada Carroll, a prostitute he had picked up in Washington. It also became public then that Drummond had deserted his wife and children at Oquawka, Illinois. A letter from the real Mrs. Drummond was published in the *Deseret News,* exposing his scandalous behavior with the Carroll woman and "his general perfidy." During

President James Buchanan. LDS Church Archives.

Drummond's tenure among the Saints, he was hard pressed to keep Ada interested; there just wasn't enough action in Zion to entertain a city woman. So on the days Drummond held court, she joined him on the bench and, according to several diarists, offered her counsel on handing out sentences.

Dale Morgan summarized the problem succinctly in stating, "Drummond launched a wholesale assault upon the Mormon courts as being founded in ignorance, and he discovered an ally in Judge George P. Stiles, who had at one time been a Saint in good standing but who had, as the Mormons saw it, gone lusting after strange gods." Stiles, the wavering Mormon, was excommunicated for immoral conduct—adultery.

Then Bill Hickman, who divided his time between being a desperado and a lawyer, let it be known if Drummond pulled any such shenanigans on him, he would inflict on the judge painful bodily injury. The message reached Drummond, who decided it was time to hold court in a more distant corner of Utah Territory—Carson City, for instance. From there he and his lady Ada went to San Francisco and booked ship passage to the East.

Stiles's abrasion with Utah lawyers came in February 1857 when James Ferguson and Hosea Stout, a couple of true hard cases, raised Cain in the court and intimidated Stiles into adjourning. The judge's law office was ransacked and certain papers in his office burned in a nearby outhouse, giving rise to subsequent charges that Stiles's law library and court records had been destroyed. (They had not been.) The judge appealed to Brigham Young as governor to protect him in the discharge of his office but was told that if he could not sustain and enforce the laws, the sooner he adjourned the court the better. Stiles closed shop and also packed to leave the territory.

The national election in November 1856 had seen James Buchanan defeat John C. Frémont for the presidency. Bitter reports brought east by those who departed Great Salt Lake City proved to be a last straw, writes Dale Morgan in *The Great Salt Lake*. Characterizing the Mormons as being in open rebellion, Buchanan ordered a sizable military force to Utah as an escort for new federal appointees (including a governor to replace Brigham Young) and to reestablish the supremacy of government.

This Utah Expedition was to be commanded by Brigadier General William S. Harney, but he was temporarily reassigned to Kansas and Colonel Albert Sidney Johnston named to take his place. Because of this change in orders, the expedition—consisting of the Tenth Infantry Regiment, the Fifth Infantry Regiment, the Fourth Artillery, and elements of the Second Dragoons—got off to a late and erratic start from Fort Leavenworth, Kansas. Civilian contractors Russell & Majors were hurriedly called upon to supply the expedition as well as the western army posts. The short notice resulted in mass confusion along the frontier as wagons, mules, oxen, and men were recruited and assembled for the massive campaign.

The Department of the Army dispatched Captain Stewart Van Vliet, an assistant quartermaster, to Utah to arrange for supplies. He contacted Governor Young and turned over a confidential communication from Harney explaining the expedition's mission: to escort the new appointees and to act as a *posse comitatus*. Later instructions would allow at least two and perhaps three new U.S. Army camps in Utah. Van Vliet reached Great Salt Lake City September 8 and sought out Young. In the maelstrom Buchanan had made a critical slip; he had failed to notify Brigham Young officially that he had been superceded. Young—who had once declared: "We have got a territorial government, and I am and will be the governor, and no power can hinder it until the Lord Almighty says, 'Brigham, you need not be governor any longer,' and then I am willing to yield to another"—made the most of Buchanan's blunder. He chose to regard the troops as a mob and on September 15, 1857, declared martial law in the territory. His now famous proclamation began *"Citizens of Utah*—We are invaded by a hostile force. . . ."

Two weeks later, Young learned that an entire wagon company—men, women, and all children over the age of six—had been slaughtered in southern Utah. Only seventeen youngsters had been spared! Not until September 29 did John Doyle Lee arrive in Great Salt Lake City from Cedar City with his "awful tale of blood." According to Lee, Indians had massacred a wagon train. Brigham Young grieved for the victims, but by early October details began trickling out of California. It was Indians, yes. But whites, too—Mormons, who had betrayed the emigrants. Lee later claimed to have told Young this as well.

The wagon train was principally made up of Arkansans from Carroll County who had pulled up stakes for a fresh start in California. The company would be treacherously slain at a place called Mountain Meadow on the old Spanish Trail southwest of Cedar City. Full identities of the victims have never been totally determined and probably never will be, but it is generally accepted that some of the 120 or more slain had traveled in companies led by John T. "Uncle Jack" Baker and Alexander Fancher. Seventeen youngsters under the age of six were spared and parceled out to Mormon families. They later were recovered and returned to Arkansas. It is believed by some historians that at least one additional, unidentified surviving child remained in Utah to be reared by a Mormon family.

The history of the massacre is complex and in great measure hopelessly contradictory. Books have been written and will continue to be written on this black, bloody chapter in Utah's past. But for now, the most balanced account is *The Mountain Meadows Massacre* by Juanita Brooks. New facts continue to surface with the passage of time because of dogged research on the part of historians and scholars. But in essence, the Arkansas train was composed of well-to-do families from the Carroll County area. It has been said theirs was the richest outfit to have crossed the Plains.

They left in April of 1857 and followed the Arkansas River, crossed the Santa Fe Trail, then coursed north until they reached the Platte River in mid-June, moving slowly with a trail herd of some nine hundred cattle. Two other wagon parties—the Turner-Duke outfits, primarily Missourians—also were on the trail and traveled with the Baker-Fancher companies from time to time for mutual protection against Indians; the Turner-Duke bunch also trailed a sizable cattle herd.

Nearing Great Salt Lake City in late July, they encountered groups of Mormons making preparations to fend off the U.S. Army they now knew was on the march for Utah. There were still other scattered emigrant companies on the road, at least one from Texas, and these wagon trains, too, sought pasturage in the Salt Lake Valley for their herds. But the Mormon population, girding for an expected "invasion by a hostile force," was in no mood to banter or barter with non-Mormon "Gentiles"—especially Missourians and Arkansans (whom they now held responsible for the ambush murder of their apostle Parley P. Pratt by an angry husband west of Fort Smith the previous May). The emigrants were ordered to move their livestock off Mormon pastures and warned to keep them off!

During the next few weeks, the Baker-Fancher company first drifted north, thinking to take the upper route around the Great Salt Lake, then in late August turned about for the southern corridor to California (along today's I-15). And so, in the eye of a hurricane of Mormon war planning, the Arkansas company proceeded south on a road that would take them through outlying settlements. Trouble began almost immediately beyond Provo when they were rebuffed in efforts to buy vegetables and other hard-to-get trail provisions.

Mormon apostle George A. Smith was on a circuit of those southern settlements preparing them for the approaching Utah Expedition. In his "war talk," he warned the army might try to drive the Mormons from their homes, and, he emphasized, Utahns should husband food and provisions and not trade with Gentiles. "Store your harvest for the hard times ahead," he counseled. The stubborn refusal to part with even the smallest amount of greens and garden vegetables infuriated the wagon companies, who retaliated with threats to

George A. Smith. Photo by Savage & Ottinger; LDS Church Archives.

return when the army reached Utah and help in teaching "the damned Mormons" a lesson. It was also said the travelers turned their herds into Mormon fields and trampled fences in the towns beyond Salt Creek (Nephi) and Fillmore. Later it was reported they insulted and cursed the settlers, and some claimed the emigrants dumped strychnine into a spring at Corn Creek (Kanosh) and poisoned an ox carcass, which subsequently sickened Indians who ate the meat. Though they have become fixed in Mormon lore, such claims are difficult to prove or disprove today.

The Fancher-Baker outfits camped in Mountain Meadow to rest their animals. They reportedly left in their wake a seething string of settlements, including Beaver, Paragonah, and Parowan. Isaac C. Haight, a Mormon stake president, angrily told a church meeting on September 6 that "the Gentiles will not leave us alone. They have followed us and hounded us . . . and now they are sending an army to exterminate us. So far as I am concerned I have been driven from my home for the last time."

Mountain Meadow massacre, 1857. Engraving from T. B. H. Stenhouse, *The Rocky Mountain Saints* (1873).

Years later, John D. Lee confessed that Piede (Paiute) Indians in the region had been encouraged to attack the wagon train for its plunder. The Mormons, he said, became involved out of revenge for past grievances and to lash out at the belligerent attitude of the emigrant companies as they traveled through the settlements. Indians opened fire on the wagon camp at the south end of the meadow the morning of September 7. (Like so much else about the massacre, there is good reason to believe this commonly accepted date may be wrong.) Those first shots caught the Arkansans completely off guard, killing and wounding a dozen or more before the emigrants could circle their wagons and throw up a dirt barricade.

The cattle herd pastured a mile or so north of the camp was run off the first day. Shooting was sporadic thereafter, with the emigrants returning fire and the Indians forced to snipe from a distance. By midweek the Piedes had lost patience with the siege; two of their chiefs had been seriously wounded by the sharp-shooting whites, and the Indians demanded the Mormons help finish the job. Lee, who was a "farmer to the Indians," changed tactics to deal with the situation, while Mormon authorities—Haight in Cedar City and

William H. Dame in Parowan—organized the Iron County militia to put the emigrants "out of the way," according to historian Brooks.

Accompanied by William Bateman, who carried a white flag, Lee walked to the open country near the emigrant redoubt, where white had already been hoisted (a child wearing a white dress had been lifted to view). Two men from the camp strode out to meet the Mormons. After a brief conversation the four went to the wagon camp, where Lee persuaded the emigrants to surrender their weapons "to placate the Indians." In return he would provide safe conduct out of the meadow.

Three Mormon wagons were ordered up. The youngest children were placed in one, all the guns in another, and three or so wounded emigrants in the third. The women and older children of the camp walked out and followed the first two wagons in a disorganized march. After a quarter mile, the men started out in single file, each with an armed militia "guard" at his side. Major John Higbee of the Iron militia, on horseback, was in charge. After approximately a mile, the women and children were way out ahead, and the men had reached a point east of what is now known as Massacre Hill. Here Higbee shouted, "Halt! Do

John D. Lee. Photo by James Fennemore. LDS Church Archives.

your duty." Each Mormon turned to shoot the emigrant at his side. Up the trail, the Piedes leaped from hiding places in the brush to begin killing the women and children.

Mormons who protested the killing were to fire in the air and kneel down, remaining quiet while the Indians finished off their men. It was Friday, September 11. The bloody business, by all accounts, was over quickly. The Indians stripped and plundered the corpses, but the whites made off with most of the loot, including the wagons and surviving cattle. The whites left the scene until the next morning, when they made a half-hearted effort to bury bodies, chucking them in shallow trenches and covering them with dirt and brush.

Arguments about who should accept responsibility erupted at once. A rider, James Haslam, had been dispatched earlier in the week to notify Brigham Young that the Indians planned to attack the train. He arrived in Great Salt Lake City on Thursday, September 10. Young, who had been in meetings with Captain Van Vliet, sent the exhausted Haslam on his return south the same afternoon with instructions that the Indians must be restrained. Haslam reached Cedar City on the thirteenth, two days after the massacre.

Meanwhile, the Missouri wagon companies– Turner, Duke, and others–had been detained on the trail and, after paying Mormons to lead them, were guided on a route skirting the meadow. They had been preceded by a mail train driven by two Mormons, Sidney Tanner and William Matthews, in company with three emigrant wagons. They traveled the meadow at night a week after the massacre and arrived in San Bernadino October 1. It was from these various emigrant wagon parties that newspapers in Los Angeles and San Francisco pieced together a story of the attacks that so outraged the nation.

Twenty years later, John D. Lee alone would pay the supreme penalty for his role in the massacre. After two trials, he was condemned to die by firing squad on March 23, 1877, at, of all places, Mountain Meadow. In 1859, elements of the U.S. Army from Camp Floyd visited the massacre site and erected a cairn and monument over the collected skeletal remains. "Vengeance is mine, saith the Lord, I shall repay!" was inscribed on a cross at the cairn.

Back in Great Salt Lake City, Brigham Young was telling Captain Van Vliet he would not assist the army in any way to occupy the city; and if "Squaw-killer" Harney led his expedition into Utah, Young and his followers would reduce their homes to ashes and fight a relentless guerilla war against the troops. "Five times we have been driven–no more!" was the rallying cry by George A. Smith, and echoed by church members. Van Vliet promised on his return to present the Mormon position in his report and to halt further advance of Utah Expedition supply trains on his own authority. In the Mormon view, the problem was savagely elementary: If Harney crossed South Pass, the buzzards would pick his bones.

Brigham's first action after proclaiming martial law was to order Nauvoo Legion scouting parties into the field. Colonel Robert T. Burton was to take a detachment as far east as South Pass on the Continental Divide, Colonel Lot Smith was to command a company of guerrillas to harass and delay any government advance near the Green River crossing above Fort Bridger, while Porter Rockwell and Bill Hickman and their companies would do the same.

When, in late September, the first detachments of the Tenth U.S. Infantry Regiment, commanded by Colonel Edmund Alexander, made its way over South Pass and camped at Pacific Springs, four miles below the summit, Rockwell and a half-dozen of his men took the initiative. As the soldiers slept, Rockwell's raiders—whooping and yelping, firing their guns in the air, and clanging large cowbells—came galloping among the tents like buffalo with their tails on fire. Their objective was at once psychological, to rattle the troops (which they surely did), and tactical, to run off the huge mule herd packing troop supplies. Colonel Alexander's quick reaction in sounding stable call halted the stampeding mules.

Ten days later Lot Smith compounded the Utah Expedition's woes by surprising two civilian supply trains camped for the night at Green River crossing and setting the fifty-two wagons ablaze; at noon of the next day he encountered another train near present Farson, Wyoming, and torched all but two wagons, which he allowed the teamsters to keep. In one stroke, the Mormons had dealt a body blow to the federal force. The third train alone contained enough ham, bacon, flour, beans, coffee, sugar, canned vegetables, tea, and bread for more than one hundred thousand individual meals— provisions for an army for a winter.

Within a month Albert Sidney Johnston would overtake the advance elements of the expedition and, with the new federal appointees—including Governor Alfred Cumming—in tow, pitch a winter quarters encampment he named Camp Scott near Fort Bridger. The trading post itself had been put to the torch by its Mormon occupants before abandoning it to U.S. troops. Johnston was effectively stalled in the mountains, and the worst winter in decades was whistling over the Uinta Mountains. Without adequate clothing and with virtually no rations, the soldiers began butchering oxen and mules for food.

The army bivouac turned into a frozen hell on the night of November 6, when Camp Scott became known as the Camp of Death. Temperatures plunged to minus thirty. Horses, mules, and cattle died in their tracks. Some wandered into campfires and refused to move though they were literally roasting. Death was everywhere. The governor's lady, Elizabeth Cumming, could not finish a letter because the ink froze; but, she noted, two thousand government animals perished in that storm, and her own frostbitten foot pained excruciatingly until the skin burst. Colonel

Lot Smith, Mormon guerrilla leader against the Utah Expedition. Utah State Historical Society.

Philip St. George Cooke's report compared the final miles of the march to Fort Bridger to "horrors of a disastrous retreat." "It has been a march of starvation," he wrote, "the earth has a no more lifeless, treeless, grassless desert; it contains scarcely a wolf to glut itself on the hundreds of dead and frozen animals which for 30 miles block the road."

Johnston called on Captain Randolph Marcy to lead a volunteer party from Fort Bridger to Fort Massachusetts in New Mexico for relief supplies and livestock. All the while, Mormon scout parties continued to harass the expedition, running off what few cattle remained and infiltrating the camp itself with men disguised as teamsters. Among the thousands of soldiers and camp followers, it was impossible to tell friend from foe, and the Mormon outriders were able to keep close tabs on the federal troops and the latest rumors, while the rest of the Nauvoo Legion spent the winter at home, except for a token force in Echo Canyon.

Brigadier General Albert Sidney Johnston. LDS Church Archives.

The canyon had been fortified to some extent by the Mormons, who used it primarily as an observation point in case the soldiers moved toward Great Salt Lake City.

In February, a "Dr. Osborne" arrived in Utah from San Bernardino. He was an old friend of Brigham Young, traveling incognito—Colonel Thomas L. Kane, acting as an unofficial emissary from President Buchanan to arrange a peaceful settlement between the Mormons and the U.S. government. Kane had journeyed from Washington to San Francisco, by way of the Isthmus of Panama, with letters of introduction from Buchanan; he also was armed with a letter from Brigham Young to Cumming. In March, he rode on to Fort Bridger to meet Governor Cumming and offer to serve as an intermediary. Cumming agreed to accompany Kane into Great Salt Lake City, despite Johnston's repeated warnings that the Mormons should be considered hostile.

Kane and Cumming, with a Mormon escort, traveled through Echo Canyon at night, but the wily Nauvoo Legion commander, Daniel H. Wells, arranged to have sentries conspicuously near campfires atop the canyon walls, giving the party the impression that hundreds of legionnaires, rather than a handful, were entrenched along the fifteen-mile corridor. In his approach to the city, Cumming saw multitudes of Mormons on the road with wagons and baggage. They were moving south toward Provo. Brigham Young had announced the "Move South"—abandonment of Great Salt Lake City and preparation to burn its homes. It was Young's threat to leave the city in ashes if General Harney led the army into the valley. (Young had received word that Harney had been relieved of his Kansas duties and Johnston was en route to take over command of the Utah Expedition.)

Once in the city, Cumming was greeted by Brigham Young and recognized by all as the new governor. He was given the official territorial seal of office and shown the law library that the Mormons had been accused of destroying. In the discussions that followed, Young assured Cumming that he would allow any dissidents or apostates who wanted to leave Utah that opportunity. A galling point with officers of the expedition had been the stories that hundreds of disenchanted Mormons were being held against their will in Great Salt Lake City by "the despot Brigham Young." It was in part the reason so many of the "young turks" of the Tenth Infantry spoiled for a fight with the Nauvoo Legion. They wanted to march on the city and put Young and his Twelve Apostles in chains for treason and anything else the government could think of.

In Washington, President Buchanan had been prevailed upon by Utah congressional delegate John Bernhisel to send a peace commission to Utah to investigate the facts. Bernhisel's persistence and warnings from respected senators such as General Sam Houston, who cautioned Congress that "if the Mormons fight, [the Utah Expedition] will get miserably whipped," had been effective. So it was that Lazarus W. Powell, former governor of Kentucky, and Major Ben McCulloch of Texas were appointed peace commissioners by Buchanan, who entrusted them with a "Proclamation of Pardon" dated April 6, 1858, ironically the twenty-eighth anniversary of the founding of the Mormon Church. The document offered amnesty to all "who would submit to the authority of the federal government."

Colonel Thomas L. Kane. LDS Church
Archives.

The peace commissioners arrived at Camp
Scott within days of the return of Captain Marcy
from his relief expedition to New Mexico. The
captain returned with hundreds of horses for the
cavalry and mules for the wagons. Shortly after
the commissioners journeyed to the city to meet
with Governor Cumming and Brigham Young in
the Council House, Porter Rockwell arrived from
Echo Canyon with a message that Johnston (now
a brigadier general by virtue of a brevet promotion
during the winter) planned to march his troops to
the valley on June 14. The news was disquieting,
but was resolved by Governor Cumming in a dispatch to Johnston urging discretion.

The presidential pardon was accepted after
some discussion. Johnston announced he would
move his troops through the city on or about June
26 and encamp "beyond the Jordan on the day of
arrival in the valley," which accommodated
Brigham Young's insistence that the army move
some distance from his city. Governor Cumming
wrote a proclamation declaring "peace is restored
to our territory," and Young counseled his church
members to return to their abandoned homes.
The U.S. troops ultimately marched forty miles
south to establish Camp Floyd—named for
Secretary of War John B. Floyd—and the Utah
War was history.

8

Territory in Transition

Army Arrives to Stay, Governors and Pony Express Come and Go
1858–1869

By 1860 Utah Territory had absorbed the first shock waves created by the Utah Expedition. The shell of Mormon isolationism had cracked wide open, and the total control once enjoyed by Brigham Young now was trammeled by "Gentiles." Having marched south to Utah Valley in 1858, the expedition, commanded by Brigadier General Albert Sidney Johnston, established Camp Floyd west of Utah Lake and some forty miles from Great Salt Lake City. During the next few years it would become the largest military post in America.

The omnipresent Brigham Young now retreated from public view, preferring to limit his appearances to Sunday church meetings. Most, if not all, of the officers who originally marched with the Utah Expedition chose not to leave on extended furlough without first paying their respects to the famous church leader. Perhaps the most outstanding exception was General Johnston himself. Neither he nor Young would condescend to visit the other. The two principals of the Utah War were destined never to meet face to face. In 1861 Camp Floyd, now renamed Fort Crittenden, was ordered deactivated, its troops dispersed to other garrisons, and its military stores and equipment (valued at $4 million) sold at auction for little more than two cents on the dollar.

W. H. Russell of Russell, Majors and Waddell, the contractors who freighted goods to the army,

conceived the notion of a Pony Express, a line of gallopers that stretched 1,966 miles from the Missouri River to Sacramento, California. It has been said that Russell used the express to prove mail could be carried year-round, so he could win an overland mail contract on the central route through Great Salt Lake City. Russell was convinced mail could be carried in winter months because in 1857–58 he witnessed General Johnston's military dispatch riders make the round trip during the worst of winter between Camp Scott and Fort Leavenworth in Kansas. The use of pony relays was a tested system six centuries old conceived by Genghis Khan to communicate with his Mongol hordes as they swept the steppes of Asia in 1206.

With St. Joseph, Missouri, as the eastern terminus and Sacramento the western, Russell calculated it would take riders ten days to complete the run each way. The line was made up of five divisions under the general superintendency of B. F. Ficklin. The division superintendent in Great Salt Lake City was Howard Egan. An investment of $100,000 bought 500 horses ("200 head of grey mares—four to seven years old—with black hoofs") and a string of 190 stations about ten miles apart. Each rider was required to cover three stations as his day's work. Incidentally, the anecdote that Russell had advertised for "riders, young, wiry, preferably orphans" to carry the express sprang

In June 1858, troops of the Utah Expedition marched through a deserted Great Salt Lake City to camp forty miles to the south. Engraving from T. B. H. Stenhouse, *The Rocky Mountain Saints* (1873).

from the fertile imagination of a professional writer in 1935. No such ads ever appeared.

The first rider set out westward from St. Joseph on April 3 at 7:15 P.M.; while his counterpart set out from San Francisco to Sacramento at 4 P.M. (Pacific time). Egan himself rode the final stretch of the first western delivery from Rush Valley in Tooele County to Great Salt Lake City, some seventy-five miles, on the night of April 7, over muddy roads in a heavy rainstorm. It took him five hours and fifteen minutes and apparently was Egan's first and only stint as an express rider; he preferred his duties as division superintendent.

By mid-July 1860 two things were clear: the Pony Express was operating with clock-like regularity, and it was not profitable, nor would it ever be, given the high cost of postage (five dollars per half-ounce). When the Overland Telegraph Line was completed through Great Salt Lake City on October 24, 1861, the fate of the Pony Express was sealed: the service was officially terminated, riders dismissed, and stations dismantled.

While it was in operation, though, the Pony Express was a sensation. News of the surrender at Fort Sumter in April 1861 had reached Utah in seven days. A Pony Express Club was formed in Great Salt Lake City and headed by Brigham Young, who with a few others and the *Deseret News* paid for a duplicate copy of the California Press service. From it the *News* would get out an *Extra* edition. When an express galloped into the city, the *News* compositors had no rest until the *Extra* was set and printed, usually a six- or seven-hour foray. The club needed at least one hundred members at twenty cents each week to make it worthwhile, so Young directed "no more *News Extras*" until five hundred subscribers (at four cents each) ponied up. They did, and the club lasted as long as the express itself.

With these events, as well as the shuttering of Camp Floyd/Fort Crittenden and Governor Alfred Cumming's decision not to seek reappointment but to return to Georgia, the territory creaked and groaned with change. President Lincoln's choice

Alfred Cumming. LDS Church Archives.

for governor-designate, John W. Dawson, did not help the situation. Dawson, a forty-one-year-old Indiana newspaper editor, stepped from the stagecoach in Great Salt Lake City on December 7 and immediately thrashed about in the quicksand of Mormon politics with a long-winded message to the legislature in which he urged collection of a war tax to support the Union and thus vindicate the Utah community of "disloyalty."

Utahns in general had no abiding interest in helping the North one way or another in its collision with the South. The territory had sent no volunteers to the Civil War, and in a Fourth of July speech that year, Apostle John Taylor had emphasized: "We know no north, no south, no east, no west; we abide strictly and positively by the Constitution, and cannot by the intrigues or sophism of either party, be cajoled into any other attitude." Brigham Young was even more adamant. "I will see them in hell first before I raise an army to fight their war." His attitude toward Dawson was cold as ice.

The governor, still preening in his new role as chief executive, injected himself into Mormon society by attending a ball for the legislature. Evidently he found the company pleasant. But two days later he was humiliated by Albina Williams, widow of Thomas S. Williams, murdered in 1860 by Indians in the Mojave Desert. She drove Dawson from her house with the business end of a fireplace shovel because, the young widow said, he made a lewd and vulgar proposition. Brigham

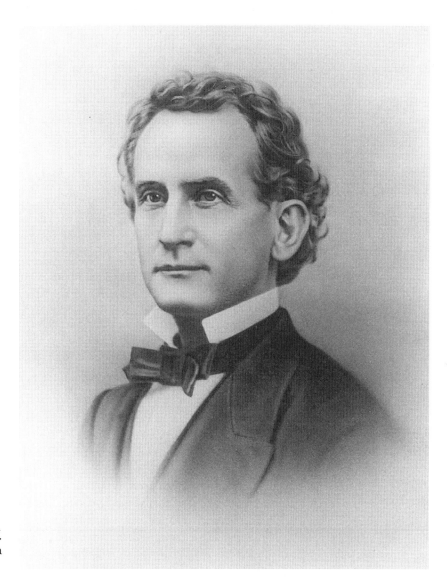

Humiliated, Governor John W. Dawson survived a beating. Utah State Historical Society.

Young was told "Gov. Dawson has threatened to shoot [T. B. H.] Stenhouse if he published anything about [Dawson's] wishes to sleep with Tom Williams' wife [or] his offer to [pay] $3,000 for her not to tell." Wilford Woodruff jotted in his journal, "Dawson cannot hold up his head in the streets and look people in the face." On December 31, just three weeks after he arrived in the city, Dawson hightailed it on the mail stage "a disgraced, debauched libertine."

But the worst was yet to befall the former newspaperman. At Eph Hank's stage station in Mountain Dell east of the city, Dawson prepared to board the stagecoach. Unfortunately for the chief executive, the driver, Wood Reynolds, chanced to be related to the outraged widow. When Dawson approached, Reynolds knocked

him down. The governor struggled back to the station, the grim-faced stage driver on his heels. Reynolds left Dawson unconscious, beaten within an inch of his life. Next morning the battered victim and other passengers departed on the eastbound coach. Reynolds returned to the city. From Bear River station near the present Utah-Wyoming border, Dawson wrote a letter to the *Deseret News* with his version of the attack and naming "the ruffians involved."

Meanwhile, an affidavit from the widow Williams, describing Dawson's "insulting behavior" in detail, was finding its way to Washington, where it would cause a minor sensation in the U.S. Senate. That body rejected Dawson's presidential appointment. And the *People's Press* in Bluffton, Indiana, also hinted darkly at Dawson's

Morrisite massacre, 1862. Engraving from T. B. H. Stenhouse, *The Rocky Mountain Saints* (1873).

past, lashing out editorially at its fellow Hoosier: "He is a poor, despised and hated ruffian, without a solitary friend of any influence on earth, outside of his own printing office. This is not the first time that [a] community has been sickened and disgusted with the infamy and crime of John Dawson."

As for the rogues named by Dawson as responsible for his rough exit from the territory, their futures were even more bleak:

—Reynolds was fined twenty-five dollars for the assault. He was killed by Indians who attacked his stage in 1863;

—Jason Luce was fined fifty dollars for his part and prior record. He was executed by firing squad in 1864 as a convicted murderer;

—Lot Huntington was killed in a gunfight with Orrin Porter Rockwell in 1862; and

—Moroni Clawson was shot and killed shortly thereafter by police who swore he attempted to escape.

Even in death Clawson could not avoid scandal. Relatives who claimed his body at the Salt Lake City Cemetery discovered his coffin had been plundered by a grave robber. Police arrested John Baptiste for that and a hundred similar crimes. Baptiste was branded, his ears cropped,

and he was banished to Fremont Island in the Great Salt Lake.

The territorial court became involved in 1862 with one Joseph Morris, a disenchanted Mormon convert from Wales, who acquired a small following after declaring himself to be the "Seventh Angel" spoken of in the Revelation of St. John. Morris joined the LDS Church in 1849. He was burned severely in an accidental fire in England, an experience, it was said, that unsettled his mind. Emigrating to Utah in 1853, he lived for a time in San Pete and Utah Counties but finally settled in Weber, where he cultivated believers to his claim as a prophet. Brigham Young gave Morris short shrift in his struggle for religious authority. T. B. H. Stenhouse said Young made "a brief and unbecoming reply to Morris's several letters claiming to be the reincarnated Moses."

Over a period of years, Morris's followers (most of them Scandinavians) organized a church of their own and located at Kingston Fort near the mouth of Weber Canyon. When dissidents complained of being held at Kingston against their will, Associate Justice J. F. Kinney issued writs of *habeas corpus* commanding the parties unlawfully detained be brought before the court. The order

Colonel Patrick E. Connor led a winter attack against Shoshoni Indians camped at the Bear River. Utah State Historical Society.

was served but rejected. A second writ, along with arrest warrants for Morris and others, was put in the hands of Deputy Marshal Robert T. Burton, who approached Kingston with a posse of several hundred militiamen and volunteers on June 12, 1862. He gave Morris just thirty minutes to surrender himself and release the dissidents.

When the ultimatum went unheeded, the posse fired a cannon into the fort area. The missile killed two women and severely wounded a third. Gunfire then erupted, inflicting casualties on both sides. After a siege lasting three days, Burton forced a surrender and entered the fort. What followed has been hotly debated. Burton swore the Morrisites rushed him and the two dozen or so posse members with him. Morris's followers on the scene claimed Burton began firing without cause. Whatever the truth, Morris was shot to death, and his counselor John Banks wounded (he died that night under questionable circumstances). Two other women also were killed.

The Morrisite adventure had cost the lives of two deputies and four women, plus Morris and Banks. Ninety-four Morrisites were arrested on charges ranging from resisting an officer to murder. The following March, some sixty appeared in court (the rest having left the territory). Those charged with armed resistance were fined $100 each; seven were sentenced to prison on the murder indictments. Three days later, Utah Governor Stephen S. Harding, the man appointed by President Lincoln to replace the battered Lothario John W. Dawson, astonished and angered the populace by granting the Morrisite defendants "a full and perfect pardon" for the offenses of which they stood convicted.

In one fell swoop, Harding "forever exonerated, discharged, and absolved [each] from the punishment imposed on them" and also forgave them the "fine, costs and charges." The governor gave no reason for his action. He was acting in the belief that he was correcting a bad situation provoked by an overzealous posse acting against bewildered farmers. But an earlier effort on his part to stifle Mormon influence in the Utah judicial system had been met by a resolution demanding his resignation. So it appears Harding also seized the opportunity to ruffle Brigham Young's feathers. It was satisfaction short lived, however, since President Lincoln, seeking to assuage the people of Utah, removed Harding from office in May 1863, appointing James Duane Doty in his place. Utah was using up governors at a steady clip.

Yet it was during Harding's tenure in office that it fell to him to greet the arrival of the Third Regiment of California Volunteers and their crusty commanding officer, Colonel Patrick Edward Connor. Connor had marched his seven companies from San Francisco to build Fort Ruby in Nevada Territory while he caught the stage to Great Salt Lake City for a quiet, unannounced "look around" in mufti as he sought a location to base his regiment. The feisty Irishman, who had volunteered himself and his command to fight in the Civil War, had been assigned instead to guard the overland mail route against Indian depredations. Connor also understood his orders to mean he was to "keep an eye on the Mormons."

He returned to Fort Ruby and cut marching orders. On October 17, 1862, they tramped into what remained of Fort Crittenden (old Camp Floyd). Three days later they started off on the final leg to Great Salt Lake City. "With loaded rifles, fixed bayonets and shotted cannon," Connor marched his men to the city's east bench and pitched tents. From its elevated location, the artillery had a clear view of the city and a "perfect and unobstructed range of Brigham's residence . . . with their muzzles turned in that direction, the Prophet felt awfully annoyed," chuckled Stenhouse. Connor himself felt the location was admirably suited for his mission. It is "a point which commands the city, and where one thousand troops would be more efficient than three thousand on the other side of the Jordan," he wrote his superior. After planting the flag and cre-

ating Camp Douglas (in honor of Senator Stephen A. Douglas), Connor set about his mission of protecting the overland mail. Reflecting on the new military post, Stenhouse said, "certainly no place could have been chosen more offensive to Brigham."

Connor's repeated entreaties to the War Department for an assignment on the fighting front fell on deaf ears. So he turned his attention to watching the Mormons and Indians. For three months his troops had grunted on work details at the post. They leveled parade ground, built barracks, quarried sandstone, and in general did the work of laborers. There were occasional patrols toward the Bear River ferry in northern Utah, where miners and emigrants complained of losing stock to marauding bands.

Major Edward McGarry caught four Indians stealing stock in the vicinity of the river crossing. After demands for the stolen animals were ignored, McGarry ordered the four prisoners summarily executed: "fifty-one shots were fired before life in all of them became extinct . . . [proving] the executioners were not good marksmen, or that the unfortunate beings who thus suffered were very tenacious of life," remarked an item in the *Deseret News*. Indian bands in the region were now truly stirred up, and forays against settlers increased.

Connor, receiving a report of two mail riders downed in a Shoshoni ambush near Portneuf, considered that reason enough to mount an attack. Then, when U.S. Marshal Isaac L. Gibbs asked for troops to help arrest certain chieftains believed responsible for other depredations, Connor saw it as an official matter. He planned a thrust against entrenched Shoshoni a dozen miles north of Franklin and on the outskirts of present Preston, Idaho. For a guide, Connor sought and acquired the services of Orrin Porter Rockwell. Marshal Gibbs asked Connor about arrest warrants for the renegade chiefs. "We won't be needing them," was the reply, "we do not anticipate taking any prisoners."

Both the cavalry and infantry figured in the campaign, which began with the march from Camp Douglas on January 22, 1863, in the most severe winter weather the troops had ever faced.

The infantry moved by day, the cavalry at night to disguise the size of the operation as the troops moved into position. They rendezvoused on bluffs overlooking the Indian redoubt along a deep ravine on the other side of the river to the west.

The minutiae of the battle from the Indian and army perspectives are detailed in *Orrin Porter Rockwell: Man of God, Son of Thunder* and Brigham Madsen's *The Shoshoni Frontier and the Bear River Massacre*. In essence, Connor's troops won the day—at a cost of fourteen dead, forty-nine wounded, and seventy-nine troopers with frozen feet (many of whom would eventually be crippled). Once the soldiers broke through into the ravine after four hours of intense combat, much of it hand to hand, the blood letting that followed had no equal among massacres in the history of the West—not Mountain Meadow, not Sand Creek, and not even the Little Bighorn. One Indian who fled up the slope of a small nearby hill was shot fourteen times in the back before he could reach the summit.

There *were* no prisoners that day. Indian dead according to army reports numbered 224; but an unidentified eyewitness from Franklin counted 386 Indian bodies, as well as many wounded. Ninety of the slain were women and children. The bands that had terrorized Cache Valley had been dealt a staggering blow.

Connor and his men returned to Camp Douglas on the night of February 2, 1863. The following month Connor was notified by telegraph that his Bear River victory had won for him a promotion to brigadier general. In their celebration that night, troops of the Third Regiment fired an eleven-gun artillery salute in tribute to their commanding officer. No one thought to notify Brigham Young. Before the roar of the last howitzer had faded to echo, Young was out of bed, dressed, and surrounded by grim-faced bodyguards ready to protect their prophet. The "false alarm" did nothing to improve relations between the embarrassed Mormons and the U.S. Army. Camp Douglas became Fort Douglas, and Brigadier General Patrick E. Connor continued his career in various posts and campaigns along the Bozeman Trail until the 1870s. Brigham Young and the citizens of Utah, meanwhile, greeted the completion of the first transcontinental railroad in May 1869 as they closed another decade in the struggle toward statehood.

Sketches

Browsing through Early Newspapers

A HUNDRED YEARS AGO OR MORE, FOLKS LOOKED to newspapers for what precious word there was about the world around them, and for a variety of reasons journalism had a different flavor to it. In many ways those old-timers were much more interesting, with their own style of writing, which was a great deal like reading someone's mail. Nineteenth-century newspaper stories could be aggravating, though. Reporters and editors never seemed to worry about using first names and completely identifying those they were writing about. "Mr. Jones" was all anyone needed, it seemed, and that was all many readers got.

Browsing through those early papers still invokes a sense of "being there." And with hindsight what it is, some of the stories bring a smile. For instance, when Colonel R. B. Mason, commandant of the Tenth Military Department, Monterey, California, wrote his official report to Washington, the *New York Tribune* in December 1848 published his impressions of the gold rush. Colonel Mason put his own interpretation on why members of the Mormon Battalion were leaving the gold fields for Great Salt Lake City and the families they hadn't seen for almost two years. No one could pass up the easy pickings the Sutter's Mill discovery had made possible, Mason decided, so this is how he explained the exodus:

> Gold is believed to exist on the eastern slope of the Sierra Nevada; and . . . at the mines I was informed by an intelligent Mormon that it had been found near the Great Salt Lake by some of his fraternity.
> Nearly all the Mormons are leaving California to go to the Salt Lake, and this they surely would not do unless they were sure of finding gold in the

same abundance as they do now on the Sacramento.

The Associated Press was still some years in the future and the country's editors worked a little harder getting a variety of news to their readers. It was a common practice for journals of the day to extract interesting items from other newspapers as part of an informal exchange agreement, with due credit to the paper of origin. Occasionally such an arrangement became a tad convoluted. Consider an item originally published by the *Frontier Guardian* in Kanesville, Iowa, quoting sources in Great Salt Lake City, extracted and printed by the *St. Louis Republican*, and reprinted in the *New York Tribune* of March 27, 1849. The story reported the murders of three men of the Mormon Battalion (Daniel Browitt, Ezra H. Allen, and Henderson Cox) by Indians in the California mountains in late June 1848—nine months earlier. The word was a bit slow making the rounds, but it was news.

Ofttimes even the most innocuous item from the past can have a tantalizing touch to it. It was a policy of the *Deseret News* in those days to publish for a nominal fee (twenty-five cents) the names of emigrants and travelers passing through Great Salt Lake City and to mail a copy of the newspaper back home. It was a service to the emigrant, plus it circulated the newspaper. The listing not only reported the wayfarer's progress but also eased the anxiety of family and friends. It was not unusual for a traveler to request an additional word or two—say, "Fat and healthy"—after his name.

So it was that on August 31, 1850, the weekly contained a brief column of names including one "N. P. Limbaugh, Cape Girardeau, Mo., arr. in the city August 8 and dep[arted] Aug. 17" in

The mail department of the Salt Lake City Post Office. LDS Church Archives.

a company of Missourians headed for the gold fields of California. Ordinarily that wouldn't arrest anyone's attention. But since 1990s radio and television talk-show host Rush Limbaugh has often mentioned that his family, including his 102-year-old grandfather, Rush Hudson Limbaugh (a lawyer still active), reside in their hometown of Cape Girardeau, well, is it possible that this gold seeker could be one of Rush's ancestors? The Limbaughs can't be certain, but they don't dismiss the likelihood, since the family has lived in Cape Girardeau for as long as they can remember, and "N. P. Limbaugh," might well be related.

Those emigrant rosters contained a number of familiar names. On September 12, 1855, the *News* listed among the new arrivals Robert Redford.

And then there were the truly short stories. As this succinct squib from the *Deseret News* of September 28, 1850, testifies: "There has been no trout in the Valley this fall." That's it, no frills. One more report from the *Deseret News*, this from the issue of November 21, 1855:

In September [1855], while excavating in Parowan, Messrs. Pendleton and Barton [there's that ambivalence with first names again] found a copper medal in cemented gravel eight feet below the surface. It was in excellent preservation. About 1½ inches in diameter and has upon one side in relief, the representation of a town with flanking towers and vessels in the harbor attacked by six ships. Around the border the words: 'He took Porto Bello with six ships only.' November 22, 1739. On the reverse, also in relief, are the figures of a man, a cannon, and a ship, and around the border, 'The British glory revived by Admiral Vernon.'

It makes a reader wonder how long before Utah Territory was settled was that medal lost so that it would collect in gravel eight feet underground, and who might have dropped it. An Indian? A fur trapper? Perhaps an engagé of the Hudson Bay Company?

But the compelling aspect of those 19th century newspapers was their outspokenness. When Nevada horse thieves were caught in Utah, the *Salt Lake Herald* treated the story on September 28,

1878, as an object lesson for aspiring outlaws. Here is the *Herald's* report:

> St. George, Sept. 27. –Jerry Sloan and W.P. Tuttle, horse thieves, with a band of stolen horses from Nevada, were followed to near this place by James Pierson, a deputy sheriff from Pioche, and posse. They were caught and the sheriff started for Pioche yesterday afternoon, and upon reaching Damron valley, twelve miles from here, four masked men took the prisoners from the sheriff and shot them dead. Sheriff Pierson sent back word, and the coroner has gone to examine the bodies.

Unfortunately, there is no way of determining whether the *Herald's* approach to crime and punishment had any effect.

FRONTIER MEDICINE

MEDICINE–OR THE LACK OF IT–PLAYED A MAJOR role in settling the frontier West. It's an accepted fact that the informal "First Families of the West"– those on the Pacific slope of the Continental Divide–were a hardy folk, whether offspring of mountaineers, homesteaders, farmers, miners, ranchers, drifters, or whatever. They had gumption, grit, and backbone: essentials for survival in the great wide open with its attendant perils. They had no national health plan to fall back on, just native intelligence, a robust constitution, and a high threshold of pain to endure ailments and injury.

Early settlers responded to bruises, cuts, and fractures with poultices, splints, needles, and thread. Genuine doctors, when they were available, functioned on the barter system, accepting foodstuffs and products for services rendered. There are plenty of cases of fur trappers and traders who took to the mountains with their city ailments to die, only to discover years later that the rugged life agreed with them.

Just how tough and resilient these frontiersmen and women were is exemplified by Hugh Glass, a fur trapper left for dead by his companions in September 1823 after being terribly mauled by a "she grizzly." Glass–near death and despite horrific wounds that left him with arms, legs, and body torn open and neck bitten so savagely he could barely breathe–was able, with but the tatters of clothes on his back and without weapons, to claw his way from the Yellowstone River down to the Grand and ultimately the Missouri River to rejoin his astonished brigade camped at Fort Kiowa some three hundred miles away. They had long since marked him off as a fatality of the season.

Another example is Jim Bridger, the celebrated mountaineer, trapper, trader, and guide, who for years carried a Blackfoot arrowhead imbedded in his back, until the medical missionary Marcus Whitman dug it out at the fur rendezvous of 1835 on Horse Creek, a tributary of the Green River, near today's Daniel, Wyoming.

Women of the early West endured unattended childbirth and in turn later assumed the role of doctor and nurse to their offspring. Beyond that are the heroics of covered wagon women like those of the Donner-Reed party, who suffered the torment of the waterless salt desert crossing and survived the horrors of starvation and isolation in the snowbound fastness of the Sierra Nevada.

Newlywed Lucena Pfuffer Parsons, 28, was headed for California with her husband in March 1850 to settle in Oakland. The wagon train to which they attached themselves was hit by cholera. Her diary entries, as edited by historian Kenneth L. Holmes, record her thoughts; the spelling and language are preserved:

> June 23 [1850] Last night visited a very sick boy, son of the first man that died. This morning [wagon train] started early. Passt some beautifull country. All it wants to make it delightfull is a little of the arts of civilization. It has rained early all day. Encampt at 3 oclock on what I call Mud creek from the nature of the stream, having made 18 miles. The boy that was sick died about noon to day on the way coming. These are hard time for

us but harder on the sick. Nothing for their relief at all it seems. Still it rains. Very hot.

June 24 Last evening there was 3 more died out of the same family. One was a young lady & there was another child. The 3 are buried together 2 Spoffords & one Brown. Staid here all day & some of the company did up there washing. . . . Had a meeting in the afternoon to consider whether it is best to travel in such larg company or not. We are to remain as we are a short time longer & then split if the sickness continues. Passt 5 graves to day of people who had died in another company.

Mormon journals are sprinkled with cures and home recipes for treating colds, rheumatism, toothache, diarrhea, colic, and a list of other "miseries." Usually these remedies were jotted at the back of a journal, almost as an afterthought, with grandpa's favorite blend of cider.

In the late 1860s, eastern newspapers were dotted with ads extolling private convalescent homes for "veterans." It's impossible to tell how many Blue and Gray casualties suffering the agonies of war wounds were placed in these havens by well-meaning families, to be cared for . . . and innocently sentenced to a lifetime of drug addiction. Laudanum and a variety of other potions laced with opium and its derivatives were as available as laxative from the nearest apothecary—no prescription necessary, thank you.

The popular image of frontier pharmacology is a snort of "Dr. Snidely's Miracle Snake Oil" peddled at a medicine show from the back of a wagon. And while that description is stretching things a bit, the truth wasn't far off. For instance, here's a sampling of patent medicines found alongside other sundries on the shelves of a Utah general store at the turn of the century. Included are such nostrums as:

Loxol Pain-Expeller (contains 49% alcohol, capsicum, ammonia, camphor, soap, essential oils). For sore muscles, strains, sprains, bruises, neuralgia, muscular lumbago, chest cold, stiff neck due to exposure, wet feet, nonvenomous insect bites, and for hours of comforting warmth and relief from rheumatic pains. Use externally as a liniment. Price 75 cents.

Seven Barks Compound (alcohol 7%). For dyspepsia, indigestion, rheumatism. Dose: 10 to 20 drops in a wine glass full of water. Price 60 cents.

Kickapoo Worm Killer, made by the Kickapoo Indian Medicine Co. (contents 12 tablets, in the form of candy lozenges, containing santonin, hydragyri, subchloridum, podophyllin, sugar, rice flour, fat, licorice, oil, anise). For worms. Adults take 2 lozenges half hour before supper and before breakfast. Kickapoo Worm Killer is also a laxative and assists Nature in expelling worms. Price 35 cents.

Chamberlain's Colic Cholera Diarrhoea Remedy (contains 48% alcohol, 19 minims of chloroform, 1.99 grains of opium). For pain in the stomach, colic, cholera morbus, summer complaints, dysentery, bloody flux, and bowel complaint in all its forms. The wrapper also carries the aforementioned description in eight foreign languages, including Polish, Dutch, Bohemian, German, French, Swedish, Norwegian, and Italian. Price 25 cents.

Egyptian Regulator Tea (contains "Egyptian Regulator Tea made in America from the original formula"). A remedy for constipation and biliousness. Dose: an ordinary dose for an adult is a teaspoonful of the herbs and a cup of hot water taken every night. Price 35 cents per package.

The first true "drug store" in Utah was opened by William S. Godbe in the autumn of 1855 on East Temple (Main Street) near 100 South. Godbe advertised his new establishment, the Deseret Drug Store, in announcing his return from a buying trip in the East with "a valuable assortment of merchandise—drugs and medicine, chiefly botanical; soaps, oils and perfumeries, gunpowder, [percussion] caps, knives, toys, spices, jams, preserves, cordials, nuts, candies, lozenges, medical liquors." Utah was a step closer to taming its frontier.

TIMELY GULL ON THE GREAT SALT LAKE

AS GOVERNOR OF UTAH TERRITORY IN THE 1850s, Brigham Young was prepared for anything from establishing a provisional state to dealing with hostile Indians, from masterminding the systematic colonization of his domain to warding off New Mexican slave traders, from planning an effective mail service to controlling the hordes of gold rushers cutting across Utah on their way to California. But when the waters of Great Salt Lake began rising, Young found himself at sea with the problem of keeping lake islands accessible to the community as herd grounds.

One hundred and thirty years later, another Utah governor, Norman Bangerter, faced with a similar quandary, addressed the challenge by installing $60 million pumps to move the overflow lake water into the western desert. But in 1854, Brigham Young's answer was to build a boat.

The winter of 1853 saw lake levels swelling almost as precipitously as they did in 1986. Antelope Island was the community pasture for Mormon cattle, ideal for its quiet isolation and protection from marauding Indians, but that isolation was now becoming a serious handicap. The sandbar between the island and the mainland, once easily crossed on foot, was deepening under the briny overflow and increasingly difficult to ford. When conditions did not improve and the shoreline crept higher, Young ordered construction of a boat capable of ferrying livestock to the island.

Aside from the buffalo-hide "bullboats" used by fur trappers in 1825 to explore the inland sea and Captain John C. Frémont's inflatable India rubber raft of 1843, there had been but two other boats on the lake to 1853: the skiff *Mudhen*, built to explore its waters in 1848, and Captain Howard Stansbury's flat-bottom yawl, *Sally*, employed in the 1849–50 U.S. topographical survey. As historian Dale L. Morgan remarked in his fine book *The Great Salt Lake*, "it is not known what happened to either of these boats, but neither would have been of much service for ferrying stock."

Young's new vessel would be forty-six feet long and designed with the future in mind. Always the visionary, Brigham Young christened the ferry the *Timely Gull*. The boat had "a stern wheel propelled by horse power," according to the *Deseret News* for July 6, 1854. Later the *Gull* might be converted to steam. A Utahn who went east on business that fall shopped for an engine and fittings to take back with him, making it known that a boat already had been built and was awaiting a power plant. Word was that such a vessel on the lake might in high water run down the Jordan River near the city and connect the capital city with the most northern settlements. But in these early years, the Mormon settlement had better use for steam engines than an occasional ferry.

So it was that after two years service the governor in 1856 ordered *Timely Gull* fitted out as a sailboat and its "horse power" put out to pasture. As Morgan explained, "It was fortunate that the boat was ready for use by the early fall of 1854. Even during the spring, the lake had been so high as to swim a horse on the Antelope bar, and cattle taken off the island at that time had to swim the greater portion of the way. Spring brought astonishing floods, raising the Jordan to levels higher than had ever been known, and by fall, had it not been for the 'Timely Gull,' [livestock] on the island would have been marooned."

In autumn of 1854 and the early spring and summer of 1855, onslaughts of grasshoppers wreaked havoc and devastation on Mormon crops. While the lake might have served as a protective moat against the cricket infestations of 1848, the flying hoppers had little trouble reaching the islands. Great dark clouds of the insects swarmed over patches of green, which disappeared in their wake. When it became apparent the herds would have to be moved or perish from starvation, Young and others took *Timely Gull* to the island and ferried five hundred head of cattle to the mainland. These were driven to new herd

Daguerreotype of Brigham Young, 1850.
Utah State Historical Society.

grounds near Utah Lake, and the following year to Cache Valley, thus managing to stay just a jump ahead of the grasshoppers.

Valiant as its service was, *Timely Gull* came to an untimely end in 1858 when a gale swept the ferry from its moorings at Black Rock and piled it up; the derelict wreckage was visible for years. As for the lake itself, the levels dropped markedly until 1862, then once more began a sustained rise. Until then it was possible to move between the island and the mainland without swimming horses or cattle, but after 1862 barges were necessary to move the stock.

THE GREAT CAMEL EXPERIMENT

LEGENDS ARE WONDERFUL. MOST UTAHNS HAVE heard of the Bear Lake monster, an Americanized version of Nessie of Loch Ness. But not too many know of Jerry, the Arabian camel.

In September 1936, Charles Kelly, a western history buff of the first magnitude, was adding to his research notes on the Hastings Cutoff to California (his book *Salt Desert Trails* had been published a few years earlier), and he had occasion to talk to William Carter, an early Grantsville, Tooele County, resident. During the conversation, Carter's wife mentioned a dromedary that chased two frightened horses into Grantsville one Sunday in the early 1900s. She could recall no particular date. "The camel seemed tame," Kelly jotted in his notebook. "Mrs. Carter says the school children rode it and she rode it in a July 24 parade. . . . It later wandered off and was not seen again. It did not appear to be a young animal. They called it Jerry."

Kelly made no further mention of the camel, perhaps chalking the story off as folklore. But there is another possible answer; for Jerry, "a ship of the desert," was not the first such sighting in the parched hinterland of Nevada. Reports cropped up from time to time in those days, and as a matter of record, the Nevada legislature had taken the trouble to pass a law in February 1875 prohibiting camels and dromedaries from running at large on public roads in the state. The act was repealed in 1899.

The business with camels had its impetus about 1850, with the California gold rush in full swing and thousands of emigrants jamming the overland trails for a chance to settle in the land of milk and honey (and mayhaps find a lump or two of placer gold in the bargain). The Isthmus of Panama was choked with rushers who opted to steam to California.

Still twenty years in the future was the transcontinental railroad, and the U.S. military was struggling with the knotty problem of protecting its real estate in the Southwest and lower California acquired in the War with Mexico. How to move people and provisions through hostile Indian country and supply the forts spreading through southern California and the Southwest? That was the question. Pack mules and ox trains were barely adequate in the desert regions. And so was born the great camel experiment.

The military had first toyed with the notion in 1836, but it wasn't until 1848 that a recommendation came to import a few camels in a test of their worth on the American frontier. Horses are not native to America, but they flourished after being introduced by the Spanish conquistadors in 1540. There is evidence that camels may have been brought to America by a Virginia slave trader in 1701 and to Jamaica about the same time. U.S. Secretary of War Jefferson Davis proposed a military camel corps as early as 1855, but the American Southwest was not the Sahara and there was no Lawrence of Arabia on the horizon.

Still, if there was money to be made in such a venture, the private sector would eagerly pursue it. And so it did, in the form of the American Camel Company, a short-lived New York speculation which sputtered briefly in 1855, before expiring. The army then budgeted $30,000 to "purchase and import camels and dromedaries for the military." One David Dixon Porter visited England and was encouraged to seek British Army opinion of camels. He also studied the animals at the London Zoo.

Ultimately, Porter with Major Henry C. Wayne arranged for shipping thirty-three Arabian camels from Smyrna to Indianola, Texas, in May 1856. A second drove of forty-four animals arrived the following year. Major Wayne was ordered to transfer the camels to San Antonio and there to turn them over to a retired U.S. Navy lieutenant, Edward F. Beale, who had served for several years as superintendent of Indian affairs in California. It was he who brought the first California gold east, and he had explored Death Valley with Kit Carson. Beale was a believer in camels for use in the western deserts.

Secretary of War John B. Floyd, successor to Davis after the election of 1856, ordered a wagon route surveyed from Fort Defiance, New Mexico, to the Colorado River, and Beale was his choice for the task, with collateral orders to test the dromedaries as pack animals at the same time. Thus to Lieutenant Edward F. Beale fell the honor of being the first and last commander of the U.S. Camel Corps.

It was during the transfer to San Antonio that Major Wayne overheard a number of grizzled Texans comment with some cynicism on the camels, allowing that they would have a bleak future in the U.S. They "walked funny" and didn't look as if they could tote much. Wayne ordered a kneeling dromedary to be loaded with two bales of hay, each weighing three hundred pounds—more than triple what a prime mule could pack. The onlookers murmured in disbelief. "That hoss will never stand with that load!" At the major's signal, two additional bales were cinched to the beast's pack saddle—the total: 1,256 pounds! "Impossible! Not a chance in hell. Cain't be done!" Wayne nudged the camel, which obediently lurched upright and strode off with the load. The crowd broke into cheers. The dromedaries had won their first supporters.

When the grand experiment was over, Beale would prove camels could carry enormous loads, some up to a ton, and walk forty miles in a day for as many as eight to ten days without water over barren country. They could swim—and did, across the Colorado—and function in sand or snow. Their drivers swore "camels would get fat where a jackass would starve to death." On the strength of Beale's report, Secretary Floyd recommended the purchase of one thousand dromedaries for the U.S. Army, but the clouds of civil war were gathering, and the experiment was abandoned.

So what has all this to do with Jerry, the Grantsville camel? Well, Beale had turned over twenty-eight government dromedaries to the California quartermaster in 1861. The camel corps story spread throughout the West. (In this century Hollywood would treat this historical footnote dramatically in "Southwest Passage" in 1954 and as a comedy in "Hawmps" in 1976.) The California and Utah Camel Association bought some army animals in 1859 and sold them at auction to a company in Esmeralda County, Nevada,

Secretary of War John Buchanan Floyd, 1857. Utah State Historical Society.

which employed them to carry salt from a marsh there to a silver mill in Washoe County some two hundred miles distant. It was said a party of French men had rounded up twenty to thirty camels near Tucson, broke them to pack, and sold them in Virginia City, where a visiting Yale professor reported seeing camels in 1865.

The dromedaries didn't receive the same understanding care as they had in the army and suffered from the high alkali content in the region. Neglected by teamsters, some camels died, others ran off into the desert, and still others were sold to mine owners in Arizona to haul ore. Within a decade, the animals had become enough of a nuisance on wagon roads to result in the previously mentioned legislative act prohibiting them to wander at large on Nevada's public roads.

For years there were scattered reports of camels seen in various parts of the Southwest and

Nevada and even remote areas of Utah. Those reports usually were accompanied by claims that the "escaped circus animals" were frightening horses, mules, and teamsters. The teamsters, in turn, would open fire in the face of such "vicious creatures." Fortunately, the residents of Grantsville, Utah, were more curious than terrified when Jerry, the camel, visited their town.

More on Firearms in the West

GUNS HAVE BEEN AN INTEGRAL PART OF WESTERN American culture since Lewis and Clark crossed the wide Missouri in 1804. Historian Frederick Jackson Turner launched a career in 1893 when he delivered his now-celebrated frontier thesis. He suggested, among other things, that because frontier settlers fought to hold the land, the weapons they used became their legacy as did the land itself.

Novelist Owen Wister romanticized the mystique of the six-gun in *The Virginian*, and Hollywood glorified the "showdown" shoot-out through William S. Hart and John Wayne. For better or worse, that mystique is so wrapped up in the western heritage as to be inseparable from it. In Utah, for instance, firearms have been an accepted part of the state's history; although not so rambunctious a part perhaps as in later cattle towns the like of Dodge City or Abilene, Kansas, where City Marshal Wyatt Earp insisted rifles and pistols be checked like luggage while their owners were in town.

But in Great Salt Lake City, a seemingly innocuous squib like this, in the *Deseret News* of December 22, 1853, carried significant import:

COLT'S PISTOL.—The Patent Office has refused an extension of Colt's patent firearms, on the ground that he has already made $1,000,000 from the sale. The patent has four years yet to run.

An advertisement in same newspaper announced a new business in town:

WHO WANTS REVOLVERS, RIFLES, AND HOLSTER PISTOLS?

The subscriber would respectfully inform the inhabitants of this city and adjacent country, that he is putting up machinery for manufacturing the above articles in the Seventeenth Ward, opposite Ames Tannery, and will be ready to supply customers at short notice.

Those who will furnish him with produce, such as wheat, oats, corn and potatoes, onions, butter, cheese, etc. . . . immediately, shall be first served.

Tithing office prices given for all kinds of produce.

/s/ David Sabin

Keeping in mind the news item concerning the patent protections on Samuel Colt's firearms expiring in four years, consider this notation in Brigham Young's "Manuscript History" for March 21, 1857: "Commenced this morning to make revolving pistols at the public works in the new shop which ha[s] been put up from a portion of the wheelwright shop. David Sabin and William Naylor were employed at this work." Within two months, newly inaugurated President James Buchanan would approve the Utah Expedition and set its fifteen hundred troops on the march, ensuring the safe delivery of a new governor to succeed Brigham Young. After being stalled by deadly blizzards and sub-zero temperature in winter quarters near the Fort Bridger trading post, the expedition finally moved out and settled into its new quarters at Camp Floyd, west of Provo, in the fall of 1858.

When representatives of the eastern press visited Great Salt Lake City to attend the third annual Deseret Agricultural and Manufacturing Association Fair held in the Social Hall, the *New York Times* correspondent commented on one "remarkable feature" of the exhibit: "A case of Colt's pistols and rifles, manufactured at the public works of the Church, for the use of the Mormon army." All of which proves little, except that the settlers in Utah were capable and familiar enough

Social Hall, Great Salt Lake City. LDS Church Archives.

with firearms to produce, as it was subsequently learned, some five hundred Colt's patent pistols in that arsenal/shop. But just because guns were readily available didn't mean there were shooting scrapes in Zion every day. In fact a case might be made that fewer arguments reached trigger point because guns were handy. But that's an irresolvable argument.

Nevertheless, a fracas in Pioche, Nevada, in 1877 proved that pistols should never fall into the hands of newspaper editors. According to an account in the *Salt Lake Herald*, the principals in this "lively shooting affair" included one Pat Holland, said to be the traveling correspondent for the *Virginia Enterprise* and formerly proprietor of the *Pioche Record*, and George T. Gorman, current local editor of the *Record*. Trouble between the two was sparked by an article in the morning *Record* critical of its former proprietor. It seems he had written a story about the town of Pioche for the *Enterprise* and failed to mention the *Record*. The story in the *Record* was especially bitter, the *Herald*

reported, and the latter portions "highly embellished with vulgarity," giving Holland "a bad deal."

On the afternoon the article appeared, Holland worked up an elaborate poster, written by himself, with highly colored pencillings and containing language, if anything, more vulgar than that in the *Record*. He fastened it on the side of Pres Wand's Eldorado Saloon, where it remained for hours, Gorman being out of town. When Gorman returned and saw Holland's handiwork, he set out to confront the *Enterprise* correspondent.

It's fair to remark at this point that both newspapermen should have heeded the adage that the pen is mightier than the sword. For when they forsook the pen, the sword very nearly did them in. The two antagonists met about eight o'clock that evening at the doorway of the Eldorado. Both men had armed themselves with pistols. Six shots were fired, and here is how the *Herald* reported the ensuing affray:

Holland's pistol fired prematurely while pulling it from his pocket. Gorman then got in two shots. Holland's pistol now failed to fire, whereupon he coolly placed it on his knee, rearranged the trigger, and it went off, grazing his hand. The two men were within ten feet of each other for the first five shots and did all the shooting around the center post of the saloon door. Holland ran through the back door, Gorman firing one shot after him.

Besides the wound to his hand, Holland also was slightly wounded in the left side. Gorman apparently went unscathed. The town's sympathy was somewhat divided, but for the most part was with Holland. "Some loud remarks are made against the *Record*," the *Herald* correspondent remarked in closing his report. A cursory search of succeeding editions of the newspaper failed to reveal whether the two journalists reconciled their differences.

There's a curious postscript to this minor discourse on guns. For virtually every growing frontier settlement—Deadwood, South Dakota; Tombstone, Arizona; Dodge City; Abilene; Wichita; and any number of border towns in Texas—there survived an ample photographic history of its lawmen and outlaws. The Earps, Bat Masterson, James Butler Hickok, and the rest of the "legends" of the West were captured for posterity on film either wearing or posing with firearms. Not so in Great Salt Lake City or for that matter in Utah.

If portrait photographs exist of Zion's lawmen, the sheriffs and deputies during those rowdy early days—which occurred a good twenty years, incidentally, before the cattle towns and railheads—they are noticeably sans firearms. What's more, the other citizens of this wild West of the Great Basin are not seen with shooting irons, either. Perhaps it was the Mormon influence, but guns and gunsmiths notwithstanding, discretion appeared to be the watchword.

The Big Chill: The Winter of 1857–1858

There is cold weather, and then there is *cold* weather. In Salt Lake City, the record is minus thirty degrees, recorded on February 9, 1933. That's cold. For the state, the record is substantially lower: a minus sixty-nine in February 1985 at a place called Peter Sinks in Cache County.

The temperature didn't come close to falling that far in 1857 in the Fort Bridger area, but it was low enough to wreak damage and perhaps save Great Salt Lake City from being occupied by the U.S. Army. In those days Fort Bridger, mountaineer Jim Bridger's trading post, was in Utah Territory (Green River County, actually), and as Camp Scott, it became winter quarters for the Utah Expedition, the military force of some fifteen hundred troops ordered to unseat Brigham Young as governor of the territory and install Alfred Cumming of Georgia in his place.

As the soldiers—elements of the Fifth Infantry, the Tenth Infantry, the Fourth Artillery, and the Second Dragoons—made their way west from Fort Leavenworth, Kansas Territory, over the Continental Divide, through South Pass, they ran into bad weather in the vicinity of Hams Fork of the Green River, in present Wyoming, northeast of Fort Bridger. It was November and cold describes it well.

The expedition was under the command of Colonel Albert Sidney Johnston, who hadn't reached the main body yet; that wouldn't happen for a month. The troops were congregating near Fort Bridger, and supply wagons and work cattle (oxen) were at a place designated Camp Winfield on Hams Fork. Such was the situation during that first week of November 1857 as soldiers, teamsters, and supply trains struggled to rendezvous at the trading post, where they would bivouac until the mountain passes to the City of the Saints opened in the spring.

That's when winter set in hard. Not quite as bad as Jim Bridger might describe a cold snap: "When ye'd speak, the words would fall as icycles, and it were necessary to melt the icycles over a campfire afore ye could hear what was bein' said." Not quite as cold as that, but cold enough.

Camp Scott officers' tents, 1857. LDS Church Archives.

The bad spell closed in on the early morning of November 6 as Companies A and D of the Tenth Infantry joined the regiment at Hams Fork. Before the day was out, the soldiers would call this "the camp of death." Five hundred animals perished that night, and the march route was strewn with frozen carcasses of horses, oxen, mules, and abandoned wagons. Captain John W. Phelps, Fourth Artillery, noted in his log that of 103 horses to pull his cannon and caissons, more than 60 died during the night and that the Second Dragoons had lost half their animals.

Teamsters made shelters from logs and wagon covers. Private Charles A. Scott, an artilleryman, marched to camp in the teeth of a violent storm that evening and made a mental note for his diary that "horses, mules, oxen were dying in harness by the dozen." When he finally fell in an exhausted sleep in his tent, Scott did not awaken when a horse toppled over on the tent, bringing the canvas down on its occupants. "We had to crawl out from underneath this morning half froze to find the thermometer at 16 below," he wrote. "Rather a hard show for the poor horses, no shelter and nothing to feed on but sage brush and but few of them

with strength enough left to masticate it. A couple could not stand the pressure, they gave up the ghost," Scott recorded in pencil. Other diarists and letter writers would have to wait until the ink thawed before penning their thoughts. Outdoors the mud was hard as granite, the snow depth fourteen inches, with a sharp and jagged crust that resisted footfalls until the sun's rays had played across the surface for an hour or so.

The Mormons fared little better. Major Lot Smith, a young Mormon firebrand in command of a guerrilla company dispatched to harass and worry the invaders, had for some days been suffering from a severe cold, when his company of twenty-six Nauvoo Legionaires, with a baggage wagon, was ordered to duty "on the coldest day I ever experienced." Howard Spencer had volunteered to go along, but he had a terrible fever sore on his leg and was turned down. "Boys," he said, "if you ever want to get out of doing anything, just scratch your leg a little." With that he rolled up his pants leg and filled the gaping wound with hot embers from the campfire.

Smith ordered his men to mount up and head toward Fort Bridger where "the enemy" was camped. "I feared the night more than all the troops we had seen during the campaign," said the guerrilla leader who a month earlier had set aflame more than seventy U.S. government supply wagons and forced the army to go on short rations. "We had a terrible time," he recalled in later years. "The men froze faces, ears and feet. I saw that all would perish if we remained with the baggage wagon, so I told the teamsters they could shelter themselves with the blankets and we would push on to Bear River. I was mounted on a magnificent horse, but the snow was deep and the wind blew fiercely . . . the men were ordered not to stop for any reason." It was so intensely cold that the riders couldn't tell if their hats were on without feeling for them. His men had to be careful in touching their ears, which were stiff as sticks and turning black; most of their feet were frostbitten.

In the army camp, Captain Phelps had a new problem: his surviving animals, wild from the want of food, wandered in search of warmth. The officer ordered men to drive the oxen back to camp. Among them was one pitiful ox wearing a yoke which dragged its head to the snowpack.

As the morning warmed, the thermometer budged to a half-degree above the zero mark. Phelps gazed over the carcass-strewn herd ground. Two crows and a camp dog chased a rabbit through the snow. "One of the crows flew close over and behind, the other was three or four yards to the rear, and the dog followed at a distance of a hundred yards." The chase continued for some time, the officer noted. Then the rabbit disappeared. At a nearby wagon, teamsters struggled with its running gear. Some of the wheels recently greased adhered to the axles so they slipped instead of rolling. The moisture in the grease had frozen.

A correspondent for the *New York Tribune* who was with the expedition wrote his editor: "While thawing hands over a campfire, one poor old ox staggered through the brush, passed between me and an officer, directly into the blaze, in which it stood until the hair was burned from its forelegs and flesh was scorched. Then it retreated a yard or two, fell and died."

Ultimately, Colonel Johnston would send Captain Randolph Marcy with a detachment of volunteers over the mountains to Fort Massachussets in New Mexico for replacement horses and mules. Marcy succeeded, losing but one man to the elements. When Marcy returned the following June 1858, the Utah Expedition would move on to Great Salt Lake City, but by then the crisis was over. Governor Cumming accepted the seal of Utah and took over from Governor Young. The troops moved south of the city. On the eve of the Civil War, having been promoted to brigadier general, Albert Sidney Johnston took his leave of Utah. In time he would join the Confederacy and would be mortally wounded at the battle of Shiloh. The terrible winter of 1857–58 and its Camp of Death high in the mountains of Utah would disappear in the forgotten past.

TARTAR THE WAR HORSE

THIS IS THE TALE OF A WAR HORSE NAMED TARTAR. He was purchased by the U.S. Army at Fort Leavenworth, Kansas Territory, in July 1857 to serve in Battery B, Fourth Artillery. He was four years old.

Being part of the frontier army was not an easy lot for man or beast in the mid-1800s, and it was especially grueling as an artillery horse; aesthetically, the dragoons, the cavalry, even the mounted rifles, would have been better equine duty. It certainly would have seemed more dashing. In any of those branches a horse would be assigned as a mount, not a draft animal. But the artillery! The options were slim and none.

A horse likely would be chosen to pull a field piece and limber (its ammunition carriage) or a caisson; and that was exhausting business in the mountains, even for a horse. Then, of course, there was the matter of being conditioned to the roar of cannon fire (which did not include having its ears stuffed with cotton). All this is moot, however, since horses had no say in the matter. But it happened that Tartar was picked by First Sergeant James Stewart to be his mount: "There was something about the animal. . . ."

When the Fourth Artillery was assigned to duty with the Utah Expedition that July 1857, it meant a journey from Fort Leavenworth to Great Salt Lake City of some twelve hundred miles over South Pass of the Continental Divide. Tartar's first taste of action came when Stewart took him on a buffalo hunt to supply meat for the battery mess. Herds were plentiful in the 1850s, and the sergeant was anxious to test his marksmanship and courage against the celebrated American bison. "Riding up close to a young bull, I shot him in front of the shoulder. As soon as I saw he was badly hit, I tried to drive him toward the battery. But he came for me and Tartar and that settled it. "I gave him four more shots and down he went." The battery had fine steaks for dinner. After that, Stewart remarked, not a day went by that Tartar and he didn't bag a buffalo or two for the regiment.

But by October, Tartar came down with "malignant distemper" near Green River in what is now Wyoming. Since the expedition expected trouble from Brigham Young, Captain John W. Phelps, Fourth Artillery commander, ordered that Tartar be abandoned, left to fend for himself, while the expedition moved on. Winter was extraordinarily brutal on the Wyoming plains that year, as the six hundred horses, mules, and oxen the expedition lost to cold and starvation testified.

When spring finally struggled to the surface, Brigadier General Albert Sidney Johnston, commanding the expedition, was short of horses and offered a thirty-dollar bounty for each stray carrying a government brand that was returned to camp. Indians brought in the first horses, one of which Stewart recognized as Tartar. "They said they found him last fall near Green River and had used him all winter to haul tent poles," the sergeant told the aide-de-camp, Major Fitz John Porter, who paid the reward. Phelps returned Tartar to duty, remarking the horse had fared better with the Indians than other animals had with the battery.

In the summer of 1860, the eight-pounder and twelve-pounder field cannon were left at Camp Floyd west of Provo, and the men of Battery B formed into a provisional cavalry company, serving double duty as mounted infantry in keeping the mail routes open and free from Indian raids between Salt Lake City and Carson City. Tartar's usual work included forty to fifty miles a day.

Then, early in 1861, in response to the Civil War, the battery marched from Camp Floyd to Kansas, then went by rail to Washington, D.C., and the Army of the Potomac. Tartar and Stewart, now a lieutenant, found themselves at the second battle of Bull Run. In the considerable cannonading that followed, Tartar was struck by shell fragments that tore both his flanks and carried away his tail. Stewart marked Tartar off as a casualty: "I turned him into a small farmyard and left him." The next morning, the gallant horse had jumped a fence and followed the battery. Tartar, it seemed, liked the army.

At Fredericksburg, Virginia, prior to one of the most ferocious battles of the war, President Lincoln had come to review the troops. He noticed Stewart riding Tartar and commented on the horse's wound. "Reminds me of a tale," he joked. Tartar was wounded again at Fredericksburg, and from then on, not surprisingly, it was difficult to get him to stand under musket fire. "The day we reached Gettysburg," Stewart related, "Tartar was lamed by running a nail into a forehoof and did not go into battle." In the pursuit of Robert E. Lee after the fight, Tartar could not keep up the pace, and once more Stewart was forced to leave him with a farmer on the road, along with a note explaining what command he belonged to. A month later, Stewart heard Tartar was with another division. It was August 1863 before the officer located his now celebrated horse. "He had no further war wounds but served to the end of hostilities."

Tartar, who had earned his place in the army with the Utah Expedition and whose record showed service at Camp Floyd, Indian fighting on the Overland Trail to Carson City, several major engagements of the Civil War, and wounds on three occasions, now became one of the most celebrated horses in the military.

He was present at Appomattox Court House when the surrender was signed. "When I was promoted and transferred to the 18th Infantry in 1866," wrote Stewart, "I left Tartar with the battery, in the 10th year of his honorable and distinguished service." So ends the tale of this war horse.

Is That You, Pike?

THE ANTAGONISMS OF THE 1850S IN UTAH WERE painfully slow in easing, so slow some carried over to the late 1880s. A perfect example is the Pike-Spencer affair, an abrasion between Mormon settlers and the frontier army that erupted into attempted murder and murder charges that spanned three decades.

In 1859 the U.S. Army had taken possession of Rush Valley in Tooele County as a government reserve for pasture and hay supply for its horses and mules. However, a Mormon stock company, Spencer, Little & Company, owned a ranch adjacent to the reserve in the north part of the valley. Twenty-year-old Howard O. Spencer with one or two other men employed by the stock company were at the ranch on March 22 to make the spring roundup of cattle. They were stopped by a detachment of infantry from Camp Floyd and ordered off the "government's range."

Spencer argued his right to be on the property since he was one of the owners. Because of overriding agreements between territorial officials, settlers, and Brigadier General Albert Sidney Johnston on the part of the army, the question of whether Spencer was right in arguing his position was never reconciled. And the versions of what occurred next are in total conflict.

What is certain is that First Sergeant Ralph Pike, I Company, Tenth Infantry Regiment, with men of his unit, confronted Spencer and his cowboys and ordered them off the pasturage. Spencer had a hayfork in his hand and responded to Pike's words with a few of his own. They argued. Pike, a veteran of the Utah Expedition and a career soldier, later swore that Spencer attacked him with the pitchfork, while the Mormon's companions swore he was only defending himself with it.

In any case, Pike, brandishing a musket, brushed the pitchfork aside, and, swinging his weapon by the barrel, brought the gun butt down on Spencer's head with such force that the pitchfork handle was splintered into three pieces and

the rancher's skull was crushed. It's possible that the pitchfork handle actually saved Spencer's life. The soldiers carried him to the ranch house and sent for a doctor, Army Surgeon Charles E. Brewer, who pulled several pieces of shattered bone from the victim's head and skillfully patched the fracture as best he could.

Spencer, drifting in and out of consciousness, was moved to the home of relatives where it was thought he would soon die from his fearsome wounds. Incredibly, despite the loss of some brain matter, he began to recover. And with his recovery came thoughts of revenge. Under a doctor's care until June of that year, Spencer, with an ugly, livid trench high along the right side of his head, brooded about his lot in life. It was said that he and friend George Stringham in late summer discussed ways of decoying Pike from the camp to even the score.

At the same time Spencer had taken the matter to law and a grand jury indicted the sergeant for "assault with intent to kill." When the news was posted on I Company's bulletin board, Pike's comrades-in-arms were enraged. Lieutenant Louis H. Marshall, who had been in charge of Pike's detail, reported to General Johnston that Pike was blameless, that Spencer's behavior was that of "a perfect bully" who was lucky he wasn't shot instead of having his head broken.

Nevertheless, on August 11 the sergeant—accompanied by a military escort of four men, who also were to be witnesses in the case, and by Major Fitz John Porter, Johnston's assistant adjutant general—appeared before Associate Justice Charles R. Sinclair in district court in Great Salt Lake City and entered a plea of not guilty. A noon recess found the defendant with Major Porter and four soldiers in uniform strolling south on the east side of Main Street near the Salt Lake House (about 169 South Main). It was a crowded summer afternoon. Orlando F. Herron remembered there were an emigrant wagon and about two dozen men on the street. Nearby, Trumbo's Elephant Store, a favorite gathering place in the late 1850s and 1860s, was enjoying its usual steady business.

Leonard Phillips was sitting in the Salt Lake House when he spotted a crowd coming down the street. In front of them were Pike and another soldier. A man came up behind the sergeant and tapped him on the shoulder. "He said, 'Is that you, Pike?'" Phillips remembered. "Pike turned around and the man shot him in the side." The revolver muzzle was about two or three feet from Pike when it was fired, and the man who pulled the trigger stopped for an instant with the smoking pistol in his hand and stared at Pike, Phillips said. "Bill Hickman came up and said, 'Git!'; the man went over the [irrigation ditch] and ran across the street into an alley," he recalled. Phillips also noticed that George Stringham was a dozen feet or so from the gunman.

Pike, clutching his side, wobbled and cried out, "My God! I'm shot!" Phillips sprang out and caught the wounded man. He and a corporal in the crowd helped carry Pike into the Salt Lake House. Pike had been wearing a gunbelt, but his holster flap was buttoned. The bullet struck the bone handle of a Bowie knife on the belt and coursed upward, entering just above the right hip and lodging behind the ribs. A bit of bone from the knife handle also penetrated his body.

As the soldiers moved Pike to a room in the hotel, Hickman, a lawyer with the reputation of a killer and desperado, was seen with a pistol in each hand, chasing the shooter west through an alley between blocks. At the same time he was warning others away from the scene, "Keep back, I'll drop him!" Some thought Hickman was actually hindering pursuit; the shooter jumped a fence into a lumberyard where a saddled horse was tethered and, mounting up, made good his escape.

Pike lingered for two days, long enough to make a dying declaration to Justice Sinclair that Howard Spencer had shot him. Lieutenant G. A. Gordon said, "Pike, are you positive it was Spencer?" "I know it," was the reply. Pike died on August 14, despite the efforts of an army surgeon to save him. He was buried at the Camp Floyd Cemetery.

General Johnston took preliminary measures to keep the situation from becoming explosive, but

William A. Hickman, 1874. Photo by C. W. Carter; LDS Church Archives.

his order regarding the death of Pike was scarcely calming: "It is with much regret the commanding officer announces to the regiment the death of that excellent soldier, First Sergeant Ralph Pike, of Company I, late last night, the victim of Mormon assassination, through revenge for the proper discharge of his duty."

After the funeral, hell broke loose in I Company. Captain Jesse A. Gove, company commander, had always taken great pride in his men and was especially proud that among other units of the Tenth Infantry Regiment, it was conceded that the "I's have it." On the night of August 15, however, Gove lost control of his fiercely disciplined company. Lorenzo Brown, a Mormon, had quite a different view of the troops. It was the "grandest company of rascals in the command," he said, a bunch that gained for itself very justly the title of "the Forty Thieves—that being their number." That night I Company roared out of the camp, despite orders confining all soldiers to the post, and descended on Cedar Fort, a Mormon settlement some five miles distant. Whooping and hollering, they set ablaze a number of haystacks. When the townsfolk ran to extinguish the flames, they were greeted by gunfire. A horse was killed; no one else was injured.

Consternation over the raid on Cedar Fort overshadowed Pike's murder. Although soldiers always kept an eye peeled for Howard Spencer, there was no other concerted effort by Utah authorities to arrest him, and a grand jury, after issuing an indictment for murder, ignored the matter. Spencer lived in the Fourth LDS Ward in Great Salt Lake City and in 1862 joined Colonel Lot Smith's Utah volunteer battalion to protect the Overland Mail route against Indian depredations.

In 1874 Spencer moved to Kanab in southern Utah to live. His was a life of relative obscurity until August 1888 when U.S. marshals swooped down on Liberty Park in Salt Lake City to round up a number of Mormon men on warrants charging "unlawful cohabitation," one of the several legal devices used to nab polygamists. Among those snared was Howard O. Spencer. Prison Warden Arthur Pratt, who also was a U.S. marshal, slapped him not only with the cohab warrant but also with the indictment on the twenty-nine-year-old murder. Pratt also arrested George Stringham at his ranch on charges of being an accessory to murder.

Spencer posted $6,000 bail; Stringham was held on $5,000. Trial was scheduled for May 6, 1889, before Third District Court Judge J. W. Judd. A twelve-member jury, nearly all non-Mormons, was to hear the case. Spencer's lawyers sought and were granted a separate trial; Stringham was to face the music the following week.

Defense counsel LeGrand Young argued that no one actually saw Spencer pull the trigger, and even if they had, "Would it be strange if Spencer was fired by the torture of his wound, and in his demented condition grew frenzied and brought retributive justice to the boastful sergeant who had committed the cowardly assault? . . . And when Pike was brought in he was permitted to go on parade with his subordinates, an armed man flaunting in the face of his victim the position he was in, and boastful of what he had done. Would not a sane man have become uncontrollable under such circumstances? In those days men carried pistols because the law did not afford them protection." At that point, Judge Judd cut him off. "Stop that. Keep within the evidence!"

The prosecution contended there was no reasonable doubt that Spencer fired the fatal shot and argued that Stringham, Hickman, and a number of others since deceased had conspired to protect Spencer's escape from the scene of the crime. After three days of testimony, the jury brought in a verdict for acquittal.

It was a decision which sent the *Salt Lake Tribune* in orbit. In a stinging editorial, the newspaper railed at the verdict: "Hickman, [Jason] Luce, Stringham and the rest, while pretending to be trying to arrest him, were really keeping the crowd back until the murderer should escape. The whole business was as plain as sunlight. All the insanity in the brain of Spencer was there long before he received that blow on the head. He was born with the same insanity that the wolf feels when he is hungry and meets a lamb in his path."

And the *Tribune* was not alone in its disappointment. Judge Judd had a few words to say on the subject when the jury announced, "Not guilty." He quickly gaveled down an attempt at applause in the courtroom, and turning to the panel, intoned: "I want to say to you in reference to the verdict you have rendered, that you have doubtless followed your oath according to your own consciences, and you have doubtless done it honestly. But if this is not a case of murder, speaking from a practice of over 23 years, then I have never seen one in a court of justice. I am now of the opinion that [LeGrand] Young was exactly right when he said in his argument to the jury that the law and courts of justice in this country were no protection to anybody. You may now be discharged," Judd told the jurors.

Howard O. Spencer lived to be eighty. He died March 4, 1918, after an accidental fall from a bridge in Glendale, Kane County, Utah.

WRITING A BEST SELLER

THIS IS THE STORY OF A SOLDIER WHO WROTE A best seller. A *best* seller. Over the years his book has outsold any one volume by Tom Clancy, Charles Dickens, Alex Haley, James Michener, and perhaps even Louis L'Amour. This soldier was born in Robertville, South Carolina, May 2, 1837, the son of a distinguished educator and Baptist preacher in South Carolina and Georgia.

Henry Martyn Robert was appointed to the U.S. Military Academy at West Point, New York, in 1853, graduated fourth in his class in 1857, and was brevetted a second lieutenant and assigned to the Engineer Corps. As an assistant professor of natural philosophy, astronomy, and practical military engineering, he taught at the academy for a year and in 1859 was assigned to a wagon road expedition under the command of Captain Henry D. Wallen, Fourth Infantry, with a mission to mark out and open an overland route to "the frontiers of the western states"–specifically, from Fort Dalles in Oregon Territory to Great Salt Lake City in Utah Territory, a distance of some 630 miles.

Lieutenant Robert was part of the engineer detachment. Other officers assigned were First Lieutenant Robert Johnston, Company H, First Dragoons; First Lieutenant Nelson B. Switzer, Company E, First Dragoons; Second Lieutenant David C. Houston, Company A, sappers and miners; Assistant Surgeon John F. Randolph, medical staff; Brevet Second Lieutenant Joseph Dixon, topographical engineers; First Lieutenant John C. Bonneycastle, Fourth Infantry, acting assistant commissary of subsistence and acting assistant quartermaster; and Second Lieutenant Marcus A. Reno, First Dragoons, acting adjutant (who would spend the twilight of his military career defending his performance at the Battle of the Little Bighorn in 1876 under command of another West Pointer, Lieutenant Colonel George A. Custer).

The expedition, 9 officers and 184 enlisted men, armed with Sharp's carbines, sabres, and Colt's revolvers presented an imposing picture as it marched out with 154 horses, 344 mules, 121 oxen, 30 wagons, 1 ambulance wagon (light-springed), 1 traveling forge, 132 Mexican pack-saddles (*aperejo*), and 75 old-pattern cross-tree pack-saddles. Along with the necessary guides, teamsters, and civilian packers, Captain Wallen took as supplies 60 head of beef cattle and 4 months' rations for 319 men.

Wallen's command left Fort Dalles on June 4, 1859, and bent to its assignment. Several newly named landmarks were added to maps of the region, and Wallen (possibly recognizing the advantages of buttering up the Old Man) named a large salt water lake, twenty miles long and nine miles wide, after Brigadier General William S. Harney, commanding officer of the Department of Oregon. This same Harney was the original commander of the Utah Expedition sent against the Mormons in 1857 and was called "Squaw-killer" Harney–but not to his face–for a punitive attack on the Sioux at Ash Hollow, Nebraska Territory, in 1855. (He got the nickname because so many Indian women and children were slain in the fight.)

After a difficult three months on the trail, Wallen's detachment finished its assignment when it reached Camp Floyd, west of Provo, Utah Territory, in mid-August and reported to Brigadier General Albert Sidney Johnston, post commander, who resupplied the expedition and offered the camp's hospitality to Wallen's men for the four days needed to requisition provisions for the return march to The Dalles. That four days at Camp Floyd makes it possible for Utah to lay an honorary claim, at least, on Lieutenant Robert, though it wasn't until he returned to Fort Dalles and subsequently was reassigned to duty in charge of defenses at New Bedford, Massachusetts, during the Civil War period, 1862–65, that he began the book that would make him famous. According to his grandson, Henry M. Robert III, he had been transferred to New Bedford from more strenuous war duty after a flare-up of tropical fever.

Robert always had been active in church organizations and civic and educational work no matter where he was stationed. But it was without warning in 1863 that he was asked to preside over a church business meeting—and didn't know how. But he could not refuse. "My embarrassment was supreme," he later wrote, "I plunged in, trusting to Providence that the assembly would behave itself . . . [But I resolved] never to attend another meeting until I knew something of parliamentary law." That's when the odyssey began.

From a small book on another subject, he copied four or five items dealing with "rules for deliberative assemblies" and carried them on a scrap of paper in his wallet for several years. By 1867 he had achieved the rank of major and was assigned to San Francisco. He was now active in a large number of organizations in the bay area and all had the same difficulty when it came to procedure. The major then decided to compile a working outline that would serve all.

It was no simple task, and as each working draft was tried and tested, it seemed there would be new questions to answer. Army duty transfers took him to Portland, Oregon, and Milwaukee, Wisconsin, and at times impaired his research. Finally, when he hit upon a format he believed would serve the purpose, he could find no publisher willing to take a chance. So the officer put up his own money to print four thousand copies of what was to become *Robert's Rules of Order*. The two-year supply (he thought) sold in four months. That first edition, issued in 1876, was just the beginning. *Robert's Rules* has never been out of print and is sold today. It is recognized as the bible of parliamentary procedure.

Henry Martyn Robert retired from the U.S. military in 1901 with the rank of brigadier general and died May 11, 1923. His small manual of procedural rules is now in its umpteenth printing in various editions. At last count it had sold something more than 4,450,000 copies.

HORACE GREELEY GOES WEST AND SEES BRIGHAM YOUNG

THE WESTBOUND STAGE GROANED AND CLATTERED down the "utterly abominable" Emigration Canyon road just as the hot summer twilight was deepening into night over the Great Salt Lake Valley. Among the several passengers who squirmed from the coach to set an uncertain booted foot to Salt Lake City's dusty Main Street that July evening in 1859 was a lanky, cherub-faced individual wearing a rumpled road-weary white linen suit under a long white duster. A white hat of plain felt completed his outfit.

He was tall, perhaps 5' 10". A large domed head accentuated his bookish countenance. Contemporaries insisted his blue eyes lacked sparkle, and his critics complained he had no graces; his voice was high and shrill enough to inflict discomfort. He peered through spectacles large and round that clung for safety to the ears and gave him an owl-like look "much appreciated by sketch artists." This unprepossessing California-bound traveler with carpetbag in hand was Horace Greeley, editor of the prestigious *New York Tribune*, the most prominent journalist in America and perhaps the most influential newspaperman of his time, James Gordon Bennett of the *New York Herald* notwithstanding.

Greeley was on the final leg of a remarkable journey which would take him from New York to San Francisco by rail and stagecoach to "see for himself" this vast country and chronicle his experiences in a series of dispatches along the way. Horace Greeley, at forty-eight, was following his own advice to "go west, young man."

He had ended his latest letter, dated July 11, 1859, by informing *Tribune* readers that "Salt Lake City wears a pleasant aspect to the emigrant or traveler, weary, dusty, and browned with a thousand miles of jolting, fording, camping, through the scorched and naked American desert." Then, after another page of descriptive reporting, he closed with "But of the Mormons and Mormonism, I propose to speak only after studying them; to which end I remain here several days longer."

What he did not reveal was that he hoped to write firsthand about the Mormons of Utah—by interviewing their leader, Brigham Young. The New York editor was successful—through the good offices of his Mormon friend in Washington, D.C., Dr. John M. Bernhisel, Utah's delegate to Congress—in gaining an appointment with the celebrated church leader and colonizer. And while Greeley may not have realized it at the time, his account of that session would make journalism history.

(The interview was quoted extensively in its day and later mentioned in various histories, literary collections and texts, but because of its length would be edited in one way or another. It is published below in full, precisely as it appeared in the columns of the *New York Tribune* on August 20, 1859. Greeley's questions covered a wide range of subjects, from Christianity and Mormonism to slavery, the use of tithing money, the Church's notorious reputation, and polygamy.)

Being a forerunner was nothing new to this Ichabod Crane of the newspaper world. Greeley had made wearing white linen suits, long duster coats, and while felt toppers a personal trademark, along with an ever-present, slightly bowed whalebone-ribbed umbrella. Horace Greeley, if nothing else, was a sight to behold.

A decade earlier, while serving briefly as a fill-in congressman, Greeley had occasion to write Bayard Taylor, an enterprising *New York Tribune* reporter, urging him to prepare a weekly political column and "sign your own initials or some distinguishing mark at the bottom. I want everyone connected with the *Tribune* to become known to the public as doing what he does." This is seen by historians as the first encouragement by a newspaper editor to members of his staff to create "byline" journalism. Greeley himself would sign his editorials "H.G."

Everything about Horace Greeley was controversial, including the famous remark "Go west, young man, go west!" attributed to him in 1853, when in fact he was paraphrasing an Indiana editor's expression of 1851. But it is just as true that if others used the phrase before Greeley, no one

heard it. When Greeley said it, the whole country listened and thousands acted on it. His influence as a public voice was enormous and his conversation with Brigham Young received global attention. The Mormons had, the year before, been granted amnesty by President James Buchanan for their actions against Brigadier General Albert Sidney Johnston's expedition in the Utah War. The Latter-day Saints were always good newspaper copy.

James Gordon Bennett, the muck-racking editor of the rival *New York Herald*, was more than just a competitor, he was Greeley's nemesis. Both men were giants of journalism in their day. And while Greeley's two-hour talk with Brigham Young is generally conceded to be the first published formal newspaper interview, the ever-innovative Bennett had an earlier claim to that honor because of his interrogation of a prostitute and madam, Rosina Townsend, while covering the sensational Ellen Jewett murder case in 1836.

The interview with Young took place in the company of several leading church figures including Bernhisel, Heber C. Kimball, Daniel H. Wells, Albert Carrington, Elias Smith, and others, two of Brigham's oldest sons among them. To keep the question-and-answer dialogue flowing, Greeley did not attempt to transcribe the conversation, but jotted hasty notes and relied on his remarkable memory for the rest. His handwriting, while crystal clear to its creator, was the bane of journalism and had for some years been a standing joke within the craft. Several of his biographers have generously described his penmanship as "notoriously undecipherable" and extended their deepest sympathies to the *Tribune's* typographers responsible for making sense of the "frightful scrawl." Greeley's sentences had the appearance of words chasing themselves uphill. One of the newspaper's correspondents, Albert D. Richardson, who later would himself write a book about a western tour, found it necessary to prove the point by including a facsimile page of his boss's notes, along with his reaction to having witnessed Greeley writing aboard a pitching stagecoach during a rainstorm: "As the air was damp and chill . . . and the vehicle shaken with wind, I fancy *The Tribune's* printers will find Mr. Greeley's manuscript even less legible than usual."

But beyond his quaint appearance, his standoffishness, the shrill voice which irritated even the

James Ferguson, adjutant general, Nauvoo Legion. Utah State Historical Society.

most ardent listeners, and his propensity for being the enfant terrible of editorial pages, Horace Greeley was, once and forever, a crackerjack newspaperman. And because of that, the most striking element of his Brigham Young exclusive can be found in the concluding paragraph of his now famous dispatch XXI from Salt Lake City, in which he offered his thoughts on the interview.

Especially noteworthy, in light of 1990s issues, was Greeley's perceptiveness and his ability to get to the heart of a story. The journalist remarked to the church leader as their conversation drew to a close his disappointment with Mormonism's "degradation of (or, if you please, the restriction) of Woman to the single office of child-bearing and its accessories." It was a point no editor, newspaper, journal, or public figure pounced on or reacted to. Greeley almost casually had fired off a telling shot, which went all but unnoticed by his readers. He wrote:

I have not observed a sign in the streets, an advertisement in the journals, of this Mormon metropolis, whereby a woman proposes to do anything whatever. No Mormon has ever cited to me his wife's or any woman's opinion on any subject; no Mormon woman has been introduced or has spoken to me; and, though I have been asked to visit Mormons in their houses, no one has spoken of his wife (or wives) desiring to see me, or his desiring to make her (or their) acquaintance, or voluntarily indicated the existence of such being or beings.

That, Greeley concluded, was polygamy in essence: "Let any such system become established and prevalent, and Woman [sic] will soon be confined to the harem."

An Overland Journey

*****

Two Hours With Brigham Young

Salt Lake City, Utah, July 13, 1859

My friend Dr. [John M.] Bernisel, M.C. [Mormon Church], took me this afternoon, by appointment, to meet Brigham Young, President of the Mormon Church, who had expressed a willingness to receive me at 2 P.M. We were very cordially welcomed at the door by the President, who led us into the second story parlor of the largest of his houses (he has three), where I was introduced to Heber C. Kimball, Gen. [Daniel H.] Wells, Gen. [James] Ferguson, Albert Carrington, Elias Smith, and several other leading men in the Church, with two full-grown sons of the President. After some unimportant conversation on general topics, I had come in quest of fuller respecting the doctrines and polity of the Mormon Church, and would like to ask some questions bearing directly on these, if there were no objections. President Young avowed his willingness to respond to all pertinent inquiries, the conversation proceeded substantially as follows:

H.G.–Am I to regard Mormonism (so-called) as a new religion, or as simply a new development of Christianity?

B.Y.–We hold that there can be no true Christian Church without a priesthood directly commissioned by and in immediate communication with the Son of God and Savior of mankind.

Such a church is that of the Latter-Day Saints, called by their enemies Mormons; we know no other that even pretends to have present and direct revelations of God's will.

H.G.–Then I am to understand that you regard all other churches professing to be Christian as The Church of Rome regards all churches not in communion with itself–as schismatic, heretical, and out of the way of salvation?

B.Y.–Yes, substantially.

H.G.–Apart from this, in what respect do your doctrines differ from those of our Orthodox Protestant Churches–the Baptist or Methodist, for example?

B.Y.–We hold the doctrines of Christianity, as revealed in the Old and New Testaments–also in the *Book of Mormon*, which teaches the same cardinal truths, and those only.

H.G.–Do you believe in the doctrine of the Trinity?

B.Y.–We do; but not exactly as it is held by other churches. We believe in the Father, the Son, and the Holy Ghost, as equal, but not identical–not as one person. We believe in all the Bible teaches on this subject.

H.G.–Do you believe in a personal devil–a distinct, conscious, spiritual being, whose nature and acts are essentially malignant and evil?

B.Y.–We do.

H.G.–Do you hold the doctrine of Eternal Punishment?

B.Y.–We do; though perhaps not exactly as other churches do. We believe it as the Bible teaches it.

H.G.–I understand that you regard Baptism by Immersion as essential.

B.Y.–We do.

H.G.–Do you practice Infant Baptism?

B.Y.–No.

H.G.–Do you make removal to these valleys obligatory on your converts?

B.Y.–They would consider themselves greatly aggrieved if they were not invited hither. We hold to such a gathering together of God's People as the Bible foretells, and that this is the place and now is the time appointed for its consummation.

H.G.–The prediction[s] to which you refer have, usually, I think, been understood to indicate Jerusalem (or Judea) as the place of such gathering.

B.Y.–Yes, for the Jews–not for others.

H.G.–What is the position of your Church with respect to Slavery?

B.Y.–We consider it of Divine institution, and not to be abolished until the curse pronounced on Ham shall have been removed from his descendants.

H.G.–Are there any slaves now held in this Territory?

B.Y.–There are.

H.G.–Do your Territorial laws uphold Slavery?

B.Y.–Those laws are printed–you can read them for yourself. If slaves are brought here by those who owned them in the States, we do not favor their escape from the service of those owners.

H.G.–Am I to infer that Utah, if admitted as a member of the Federal Union, will be a Slave State?

B.Y.–No; she will be a Free State. Slavery here would prove useless and unprofitable. I regard it generally as a curse to the masters. I myself hire many laborers and pay them fair wages; I could not afford to own them. I can do better than subject myself to an obligation to feed and clothe their families, to provide and care for them, in sickness and health. Utah is not adapted to Slave Labor.

H.G.–Let me now be enlightened with regard more especially to your Church polity [government]; I understand that you require each member to pay over one-tenth of all he produces or earns to the Church.

B.Y.–That is a requirement of our faith. There is no compulsion as to the payment. Each member acts in the premises according to his pleasure, under the dictates of his own conscience.

H.G.–What is done with the proceeds of this tithing?

B.Y.–Part of it is devoted to building temples and other places of worship; part to helping the poor and needy converts on their way to this country; and the largest portion to the support of the poor among the Saints.

H.G.–Is none of it paid to Bishops and other dignitaries of the Church?

B.Y.–Not one penny. No Bishop, no Elder, no Deacon, or other church officer, receives any compensation for his official services. A Bishop is often required to put his hand in his own pocket and provide therefrom for the poor of his charge; but he never receives anything for his services.

H.G.–How then do your ministers live?

B.Y.–By the labor of their own hands, like the first Apostles. Every Bishop, every Elder, may be daily seen at work in the field or the shop, like his neighbors; every minister of the Church has his proper calling by which he earns the bread of his family; he who cannot or will not do the

Expulsion of Mormons from Far West, Missouri. Illustration by C. B. Hancock; LDS Church Archives.

Church's work for nothing is not wanted in her services; even our lawyers (pointing to Gen. Ferguson and another present, who are the regular lawyers of the Church) are paid nothing for their services; I am the only person in the Church who has not a regular calling apart from the Church's service, and I never received one farthing from her treasury; if I obtain anything from the tithing-house, I am charged with and pay for it, just as anyone else would; the clerks in the tithing-store are paid like other clerks, but no one is ever paid for any service pertaining to the ministry. We think a man who cannot make his living aside from the Ministry of Christ unsuited to that office. I am called rich, and consider myself worth $250,000; but no dollar of it was ever paid me by the Church or for any service as a minister of the Everlasting Gospel. I lost nearly all I had when we were broken up in Missouri and driven from that State; I was nearly stripped again when Joseph Smith was murdered and we were driven from Illinois; but nothing was ever made up to me by the Church, nor by any one. I believe I know how to acquire property and how to take care of it.

H.G.—Can you give me any rational explanation of the aversion and hatred with which your people are generally regarded by those among whom they have lived and with whom they have been brought directly in contact?

B.Y.—No other explanation than is afforded by the crucifixion of Christ and the kindred treatment of God's ministers, prophets, saints in all ages.

H.G.—I know that a new sect is always decried and traduced—that it is hardly ever deemed respectable to belong to one—that the Baptists, Quakers, Methodists, Universalists, &c., have each in their turn been regarded in the infancy of their sect as the offscouring of the earth; yet I cannot remember that either of them were ever generally represented and regarded by the older sects of their early days as thieves, robbers and murderers.

B.Y.—If you will consult the cotemporary [sic] Jewish accounts of the life and acts of Jesus Christ, you will find that he and his disciples were accused of every abominable deed and purpose—robbery and murder included. Such a work is still extant, and may be found by those who seek it.

H.G.—What do you say of the so-called Danites, or Destroying Angels, belonging to your Church?

B.Y.—What do you say? I know of no such band, no such persons or organization. I hear of them only in the slanders of our enemies.

H.G.–With regard, then, to the grave question on which your doctrine and practices are avowedly at war with those of the Christian world–that of a plurality of wives–is the system of your Church acceptable to the majority of its women?

B.Y.–They could not be more averse to it than I was when it was first revealed to us as the Divine Will. I think they generally accept it, as I do, as the will of God.

H.G.–How general is polygamy among you?

B.Y.–I could not say. Some of those present [heads of the Church] have each but one wife; others have more: each determines what is his individual duty.

H.G.–What is the largest number of wives belonging to any one man?

B.Y.–I have fifteen; I know no one who has more but some of those sealed to me are old ladies whom I regard rather as mothers than wives, but whom I have taken home to cherish and support.

H.G.–Does not the Apostle Paul say that a bishop should be "the husband of one wife"?

B.Y.–So we hold. We do not regard any but a married man as fitted for the office of bishop. But the Apostle Paul does not forbid a bishop from having more wives than one.

H.G.–Does not Christ say that he who puts away his wife, or marries one whom another has put away, commits adultery?

B.Y.–Yes; and I hold that no man should ever put away a wife except for adultery–not always even for that. Such is my individual view of the matter. I do not say that wives have never been put away in our Church, but that I do not approve of the practice.

H.G.–How do you regard what is commonly called the Christian Sabbath?

B.Y.–As a divinely appointed day of rest from secular labor on that day. We would have no man enslaved to the Sabbath, but we enjoin all to respect and enjoy it.

*****

Such is, as nearly as I can recollect, the substance of nearly two hours' conversation, wherein much was said incidentally that would not be worth reporting, even if I could remember and reproduce it, and wherein others bore a part; but as President Young is the first minister of the Mormon Church, and bore the principal part in the conversation, I have reported his answers alone to my questions and observations. The others appeared, uniformly to defer to his views, and to acquiesce fully in his response and explanations. He spoke readily, not always with grammatical accuracy, but with no appearance of hesitation or reserve, and with no apparent desire to conceal anything, nor did he repel any of my questions as impertinent. He was very plainly dressed in thin summer clothing, and with no air of sanctimony or fanaticism. In appearance he is a portly, frank, good-natured, rather thick-set man of fifty-five, seeming to enjoy life, and be in no particular hurry to get to heaven. His associates are plain men, evidently born and reared to a life of labor, and looking as little like crafty hypocrites or swindlers as any body of men I ever met. The absence of cant or shuffle from their manner was marked and general, yet, I think I may fairly say that their Mormonism has not impoverished them–that they were generally poor men when they embraced it, and are now in very comfortable circumstances–as men averaging three and four wives apiece certainly need to be.

If I hazard any criticisms on Mormonism generally, I reserve them for a separate letter, being determined to make this a fair and full exposé of the doctrine and polity in the very words of its Prophet, so far as I can recall them. I do not believe President Young himself could present them in terms calculated to render them less obnoxious to the Gentile world than the above. But I have the right to add here, because I said it to the assembled chiefs at the close of the above colloquy, that the degradation (or, if you please, the restriction) of Woman to the single office of child-bearing and its accessories, is an inevitable consequence of the system here paramount. I have not observed a sign in the streets, an advertisement in the journals, of this Mormon metropolis, whereby a woman proposes to do anything whatever.

No Mormon has ever cited to me his wife's or any woman's opinion on any subject; no Mormon woman has been introduced or has spoken to me; and, though I have been asked to visit Mormons in their houses, no one has spoken of his wife (or wives) desiring to see me, or his desiring me to make her (or their) acquaintance, or voluntarily indicated the existence of such a being or beings.

I will not attempt to report our talk on this subject, because, unlike what I have above given, it assumed somewhat the character of a disputation, and I could hardly give it impartially; but one remark made by President Young I think I can give accurately, and it may serve as a sample of all that was offered on that side.

It was in these words, I think exactly: "If I did not consider myself competent to transact a certain business without taking my wife's or any woman's counsel with regard to it, I think I ought to let that business alone."

The spirit with regard to Woman, of the entire Mormon, as of all other polygamic systems, is fairly displayed in this avowal. Let any such system become established and prevalent, and Woman will soon be confined to the harem, and her appearance on the street with unveiled face will be accounted immodest. I joyfully trust that the genius of the Nineteenth Century tends to a solution of the problem of Women's sphere and destiny radically different from this.

H.G.

A Lengthy Gallows Soliloquy Impedes Swift Justice

STANDING IN THE SHADOW OF THE HANGMAN'S noose, the condemned man was asked if he had any last words. As a matter of fact, he did, and it was about his right to choose between being beheaded, shot, or strung up. Thomas H. Ferguson had thought about it along the mile or so from the county jail as he rode handcuffed and ankle shackled in the same wagon with his coffin to the place of his impending demise. A small detachment of Utah militia ordered out for the occasion by the governor joined U.S. Marshal Peter K. Dotson and his deputy, J. F. Stone, who, with Sheriff Robert T. Burton and City Marshal J. C. Little, made up the escort to Great Salt Lake City's north bench, where, a few hundred yards above South Temple and just east of City Creek Canyon, a temporary gallows had been constructed.

Believing it was Utah Territory's first execution under a "regular judicial sentence," officials made every effort to have it carried out properly and with decorum. But memories were a little skewed in that respect. It was not the first legal execution in Utah. Five years earlier two Goshute Indians–Long Hair and Antelope–were indicted on murder charges by a grand jury, convicted in district court after a trial in which they were represented by court-appointed counsel, then hanged near the Jordan River two weeks later, with few spectators other than Lieutenant Colonel Edward Jenner Steptoe and his detail of cavalry acting as official escort.

Now, as the grim procession wound its way to the place "prescribed by law," it attracted a growing number of spectators, who surrounded the scaffold to hear what the doomed man would say. There for the better part of an hour, Ferguson, convicted of shooting his employer, Alexander Carpenter, in an argument, looked out over the three thousand or so faces collected to watch his execution that autumn morning and told them just what he thought of his trial and sentencing.

The day was October 28, 1859, little more than a month since his arrest for the killing–the law did not drag its feet in those frontier times. But while swift justice may have been laudable in the eyes of many, Ferguson had encountered some other problems. The judge, for one. The Honorable Charles E. Sinclair, associate justice of the Territorial Supreme Court of Utah, Ferguson claimed (and most of the town agreed), was a drunk who had sentenced him to be executed on a Sunday. Moreover, Ferguson complained, he had been deprived of his right under the law to choose the method of his execution:

I was tried by the statutes of Utah Territory which give a man the privilege of being shot, beheaded or hung, but was it given to me? No, it was not!

All Judge Sinclair wanted was to sentence someone to be hung, then he was willing to leave the Territory, he had too much whiskey in his head to know what day he sentenced me to be executed on, and would not have known, if it had not been for the people of Utah laughing at him and telling him it would be on a Sunday. A nice judge to send to any country.

I am not afraid to die, but I would have liked it better if I had had a fair trial; and I would have felt better if Gov. Cumming had commuted my sentence to the penitentiary . . . . I hope the next judge . . . will be a temperate judge, capable of tending to business.

He could not have known then, but his "last words," delivered in a rambling half-hour, more in desperation than purpose, may have been a record of sorts for gallows soliloquy. The condemned man thus spoke his piece, the noose was adjusted around his neck, the knot snugged beneath and behind his ear, a cap pulled down to cover his face, and, at thirty-eight minutes past noon, the executioner cut the rope securing the gallows' trap. Thomas H. Ferguson, with a fall of several feet, was launched into eternity. He was pronounced dead a few minutes later and "immediately buried near the gallows."

Public executions were the rule in Utah—as they were throughout most of the West—until well into the 1870s. John D. Lee of Mountain Meadow massacre infamy was in March 1877 shot by firing squad at the scene of his crime, the last prisoner in Utah to be executed in public. Most of the early executions were meted out by firing squad and a few by hanging, but there is no official record of beheadings, although Nelson Slater, an aggrieved California emigrant who spent the winter of 1850–51 in Great Salt Lake City, did claim another emigrant was pursued by the sheriff and two others who believed the stranger was part of the Illinois mob that assassinated Joseph Smith. Slater, who published a whole catalog of complaints against the Mormon citizenry of Utah Territory once he was safely in California, said the posse "came up to [the emigrant], and without trial, judge, or jury, they cut off his head." Presumably the perpetrators used Bowie knives or the celebrated swords of the Nauvoo Legion to commit the heinous deed. Slater did not elaborate further.

It is true, however, that Utah law on the books in 1852 allowed those condemned to death their choice of the three—bullet, rope, or blade. Utah's death penalty punishment was predicated on strong Mormon feelings concerning the atonement of sins by shedding an offender's blood, but because execution by firing squad satisfied that contingency, the third alternative was erased when the laws were updated in 1878. It seems more than coincidence the change in statutes did not come until after the death of Brigham Young in August 1877. He had been an unrelenting voice from the pulpit and in private arguing for the shedding of blood to atone for sins. At the same time, a law was written to eliminate public executions, specifying such punishments must be meted out within the walls or yard of a jail or some "convenient private place" in the district. This also appears to be a result of the Lee execution, in which the prisoner in secrecy was transported by horse-drawn carriage for two days almost one hundred miles from the Fort Cameron post guardhouse, on the outskirts of Beaver City in south central Utah, to Mountain Meadow to be shot.

The *San Jose Patriot*, commenting in 1876 on Utah's peculiar criminal law, remarked not on the option for beheading, but that "in capital convictions the culprit has the right to select the manner of the three methods," namely, shooting, hanging, or decapitation. The California newspaper reflected that "although this favor is granted to criminals, they seldom take advantage of the statutory right, probably because in that solemn extremity human nature cares little for such preferences." Thomas H. Ferguson's last utterances on earth that October day in 1859 proved otherwise.

MARK TWAIN IN UTAH

IT'S TIME FOR A LIGHTER LOOK AT UTAH HISTORY, time to turn to Samuel Langhorne Clemens. His alter ego, Mark Twain, got an immense amount of mileage from Utah and the Mormons, using anecdotes about them in his lectures and books until he was all but buried in cash folks paid for such entertainment.

Twain had a way with words, but more often than not he was disposed never to let the facts stand in the way of a good story. In *Roughing It*, his account of travel through the West, for instance, he tells of an Indian attack on a mail coach in 1856 in which the stage driver and conductor perished

> . . . and also all the passengers but one, it was supposed; but this must have been a mistake, for at different times afterward on the Pacific Coast I was personally acquainted with a hundred and thirty-three or four people who were wounded during that massacre, and barely escaped with their lives. There was no doubt of the truth of it — I had it from their own lips. One of these parties told me that he kept coming across arrow-heads in his system for nearly seven years after the massacre; and another of them told me he was stuck so literally full of arrows that after the Indians were gone and he could raise up and examine himself, he could not restrain his tears, for his clothes were completely ruined.

To set the record straight, Twain erred in the date. He can be forgiven because he was writing from a distance in time. *Roughing It* was published in 1871, and he may have been suffering from spasms of CRS (Can't Remember Scat). There was, indeed, such a mail coach massacre, but it was perpetrated by Sioux in November 1854. Three of the four passengers aboard were killed, including the conductor, a fellow named John Jamison. The lone survivor, one Charles A. Kinkead, partner in Livingston & Kinkead mercantile company of Great Salt Lake City, was struck by a half-dozen arrows but recovered. The Indians rifled the mail pouches, tore open the letters, and took $10,500 in gold—the company receipts—from him before vamoosing.

Twain took a liking to Jack Slade, the notorious Sweetwater Division superintendent for the Overland Stage. Well, it might not have been a liking, exactly, but Slade did provide the humorist with so much material Twain could scarcely not be beholden. That he relished writing about Slade the mankiller, Slade the desperado, Slade the most bloody, is evident in his earliest anecdotes concerning the gunman, whose mortal remains now lay buried in the Salt Lake City Cemetery. Here is how Twain introduces Slade to his readers:

> One day on the plains he had an angry dispute with one of his wagon-drivers, and both drew their revolvers. But the driver was the quicker artist, and had his weapon cocked first. So Slade said it was a pity to waste life on so small a matter, and proposed that the pistols be thrown on the ground and the quarrel settled by a fist fight. The unsuspecting driver agreed, and threw down his pistol—whereupon Slade laughed at his simplicity, and shot him dead!

Violence was the rule in Slade's world, Twain insisted. And the author-lecturer reveled in stories about Slade's run-in with Jules Beni, the station keeper who had treated him to the entire contents of a double-barrel shotgun. When Slade recovered and eventually trapped his nemesis, he tied him to a corral gate, and commenced to exact his revenge. Twain wades into the fray with quill poised:

> In the morning Slade practiced on him with his revolver, nipping the flesh here and there, and occasionally clipping off a finger, while Jules begged him to kill him outright and put him out of his misery. Finally, Slade reloaded, and walking up close to his victim, made some characteristic remarks and then dispatched him. . . . Slade detailed a party and assisted at the burial himself. But first he cut off the dead man's ears and put them in his vest pocket, where he carried them

for some time with great satisfaction. That is the story as I have frequently heard it told and seen it in print in California newspapers. It is doubtless correct in all essential particulars.

So what would happen if Twain should meet the protagonist of his tales? He tells of stopping at a stage station for breakfast with "a half-savage, half-civilized company of armed and bearded mountaineers, ranchmen and station employes":

The most gentlemanly-appearing, quiet and affable officer we had yet found along the road in the Overland Company's service was the person who sat at the head of the table, at my elbow. Never youth stared and shivered as I did when I heard them call him SLADE!

Here was romance, and I sitting face to face with it!—looking upon it—touching it—hobnobbing with it, as it were! Here, right by my side, was the actual ogre who, in fights and brawls and various ways, had taken the lives of twenty-six human beings, or all men lied about him! I suppose I was the proudest stripling that ever traveled to see strange lands and wonderful people.

He was so friendly and so gentle-spoken that I warmed to him in spite of his awful history. . . . The coffee ran out. At least it was reduced to one tincupful, and Slade was about to take it when he saw that my cup was empty. He politely offered to fill it, but although I wanted it, I politely declined. I was afraid he had not killed anybody that morning, and might be needing diversion. . . .

We left him with only twenty-six dead people to account for, and I felt a tranquil satisfaction in the thought that in so judiciously taking care of No. 1 at that breakfast table I had pleasantly escaped being No. 27.

When he wasn't waxing melodramatic with gunslinging desperadoes the like of the inestimable Jack Slade, Twain the newspaperman-steamboat captain tweaked the Mormons. Scarcely had he put Slade's station behind him, than Twain rambled on about "taking supper with a Mormon 'Destroying Angel.'" Here was fodder for his cannon. Salvo upon salvo, who could ask for anything more?

Destroying Angels as I understand it, are Latter-Day Saints who are set apart by the church to conduct permanent disappearances of obnoxious citizens. I had heard a deal about these Mormon Destroying Angels and the dark and bloody deeds they had done, and when I entered this one's house I had my shudder all ready. But alas for all our romances, he was nothing but a loud, profane, offensive, old blackguard! He was murderous enough, possibly, to fill the bill of a Destroyer, but would you have any kind of an Angel devoid of dignity? Could you abide an Angel in an unclean shirt and no suspenders? Could you respect an Angel with a horse-laugh and a swagger like a buccaneer?

During his brief stay in Great Salt Lake City, Twain had the opportunity of discovering "valley tan," a potent potable absorbed in some quantity by a fellow traveler named Bemis, who it seems had made one trip too many to the flagon from which this fiery liquid issued. The fact that Bemis had gone to bed with his boots on led Twain to fear that something he had eaten had not agreed with him:

But we knew afterward that it was something he had been drinking. It was the exclusive Mormon refresher, "valley tan." Valley tan (or, at least, one form of valley tan) is a kind of whisky, or first cousin to it, and is of Mormon invention and manufactured only in Utah. Tradition says it is made of (imported) fire and brimstone. If I remember rightly no public drinking saloons were allowed in the kingdom by Brigham Young, and no private drinking permitted among the faithful, except they confined themselves to "valley tan."

As you can see, Twain was easily misled. During the period in which Twain, with his brother Orion Clemens, journeyed west in July 1861 and through various peregrinations in Carson City and Virginia City, Nevada, in 1862, and then wandered in the various mining centers of the West in 1864, Utah was occupied by remnants of Brigadier General Albert Sidney Johnston's Utah Expedition and later by troops of Brigadier General Patrick E. Connor's command. Which is to say there were saloons all over the place. In fact, Main Street south of 200 South after 1859 was familiarly known as Whiskey Street. And valley tan certainly was not the refreshment of choice; Orrin Porter Rockwell called it liquid strychnine, and other frontiersmen had more imaginative names for this paralyzing intoxicant.

Exaggerations aside, Twain had nothing but praise for the City of the Saints:

Brigham Young. Photo by C. R. Savage; LDS Church Archives.

Next day we strolled about everywhere through the broad, straight level streets, and enjoyed the pleasant strangeness of a city of fifteen thousand inhabitants with no loafers perceptible in it; and no visible drunkards or noisy people; a limpid stream rippling and dancing through every street in place of a filthy gutter; block after block of trim dwellings, built of "frame" and sunburned brick—a great thriving orchard and garden behind every one of them, apparently—branches from the street stream winding and sparkling among the garden beds and fruit trees—and a grand general air of neatness, repair, thrift and comfort, around and about and over the whole. And everywhere were workshops, factories, and all manner of industries; and intent faces and busy hands were to be seen wherever one looked; and in one's ears was the ceaseless clink of hammers, the buzz of trade and the contented hum of drums and fly-wheels.

The armorial crest of my own State consisted of two dissolute bears holding up the head of a dead and gone cask between them and making the pertinent remark, "United, We Stand—(hic)—Divided We Fall." It was always too figurative for the author of this book. But the Mormon crest was easy. And it was simple, unostentatious, and

fitted like a glove. It was a representation of a Golden Beehive, with the bees all at work!

Yes, Twain had stumbled on a mother lode of material. In the Mormons he had discovered the perfect foil for his humor—well, almost perfect. The U.S. Congress was high on his list of targets; he was once able to glean enough for a book and a lecture tour out of one day in the Senate gallery. A perfect goldmine! he exulted. Still, the Mormons proved his *bona fides*. And he loved the ruffians.

It is a luscious country for thrilling evening stories about assassinations of intractable Gentiles. I cannot easily conceive of anything more cozy than the night in Salt Lake which we spent in a Gentile den, smoking pipes and listening to tales of how Burton galloped in among the pleading and defenseless "Morrisites" and shot them down, men and women, like so many dogs. And how Bill Hickman, a Destroying Angel, shot Drown and Arnold dead for bringing suit against him for a debt. And how Porter Rockwell did this and that dreadful thing. And how heedless people often come to Utah and make remarks about Brigham or polygamy, or some other sacred matter, and the very next morning at daylight such parties are sure to be found lying up some back alley, contentedly waiting for the hearse.

But say what you may about Mark Twain, he was never above making himself the butt of his own stories. Take the time he and Orion, newly appointed secretary of Nevada, paid a "state visit" to the king—Brigham Young—himself:

He seemed a quiet, kindly, easy-mannered, dignified, self-possessed old gentleman of fifty-five or sixty, and had a gentle craft in his eye that probably belonged there. He was very simply dressed and was just taking off a straw hat when we entered. He talked about Utah, and the Indians, and Nevada, and general American matters and questions, with our Secretary and certain government officials who came with us. But he never paid any attention to me, notwithstanding I made several attempts to "draw him out" on federal politics and his high-handed attitude toward Congress.

I thought some of the things I said were rather fine. But he merely looked around at me, at distant intervals, something as I have seen a benignant old cat look around to see which kitten was meddling with her tail. By and by I subsided into an indignant silence, and so sat until the end, hot and flushed, and execrating him in my heart for an ignorant savage. But he was calm. His conversation with those gentlemen flowed on as sweetly and peacefully and musically as any summer brook. When the audience was ended and we were retiring from the presence, he put his hand on my head, beamed down on me in an admiring way and said to my brother:

"Ah—your child, I presume? Boy, or girl?"

That Brigham, what a card.

HERE LIES JOSEPH SLADE

JACK SLADE IS ONE OF THE WEST'S MANY PARAdoxes. He was the Overland Stage Company's most feared enforcer, protecting the route from road agents and keeping the coaches on schedule. Yet, on the occasion of his death, Slade missed his connection with the Overland Stage and was fated to spend eternity in Salt Lake City. A terror to outlaws, Slade was, by all accounts, a loving husband and loyal friend, but when drunk, he became an uncontrollable, sadistic bully.

Joseph Alfred "Jack" Slade came from a respected family in Clinton County, Illinois, served in the 1846–48 Mexican War, and earned a reputation as a tough man on the frontier. His story begins in 1858 when Overland Stage hired him to superintend the Sweetwater Division of the mail line from St. Joseph, Missouri, to Salt Lake City. The division ran from the "Upper Crossing" of the South Platte River to Rocky Ridge on the east slope of the Continental Divide.

Station keeper at the Upper Crossing was Jules Beni, a sullen, bear-like French Canadian also reputed to be the leader of a band of cutthroats in the vicinity. The town of Julesburg at the Upper Crossing was founded by Beni, and it had become a rendezvous for traders, Indian fighters, buffalo hunters, adventurers, bandits, and desperadoes who rode into town to divide their loot and squander it riotously. Beni's high-handed acts with company livestock and the constant feuds arising from them brought Slade and Beni into open rupture. Jules would not submit to the authority of the division agent, and Slade would not brook Jules's interference.

Beni "sequestered" some of the livestock, and Slade recovered it for the company. That brought matters to a crisis. It was a day in the early spring of 1859 when Slade chanced to be at the Upper Crossing station. He, the hired hands, and Beni were all in the corral engaged in conversation. After a few moments Jules walked away from the group and entered his adobe quarters. Slade meanwhile headed for the bunkhouse to get something to eat.

As he was about to enter, one of the hands spotted Beni emerging from the adobe with a pistol. "Look out, he's going to shoot!" Slade, unarmed, turned at the warning and was struck by three shots from Jules's revolver. He staggered but did not fall. With a curse, Beni reached within the open door for a double-barrel shotgun. He fired both charges into Slade's slumping body. "There's an empty crate in the barn. You can bury him in it," Beni said and walked away.

But in the dramatic tradition of every wild West yarn ever spun, witnesses that day claimed a bloody, bullet-torn Jack Slade breathed through smashed lips and told would-be grave diggers not to bother, that he did not intend to die, but would live to even the score with Beni. And he did.

He was taken into the bunkhouse, his wounds treated, and in a few weeks he was removed to the family home in Carlisle, Illinois, where he eventually recovered to return to his duties on the stage line. The company hands, however, had decided to settle things their own way. While Slade was being doctored, they agreed the world would be better rid of cowards. They tossed a rope over a beam trussed between two large freight wagons, put a noose around Beni's neck, and pulled him up. It was at this moment that Ben Ficklin, general superintendent of the line, rode into the station—in time to cut Jules down before life was extinct. Hearing the story of Slade's shooting, Ficklin, because there was no legal tribunal at hand, ordered Beni to leave the country or be hanged by an informal court. He took the offer and fled. But he hadn't reckoned on Slade's terrible vengeance.

It came in August 1861, two years after the shooting scrape. Slade was riding east on the stage from Rocky Ridge to his home at Horse Shoe, some forty miles west of Fort Laramie in present Wyoming. He had heard Jules Beni was driving stock out of Denver and would be crossing the Sweetwater Division. Slade had been told, too, that if Beni saw him first, he likely would be ambushed. So Slade and a small party of Overland hands waited for Beni and in a running gunfight shot and wounded him.

There are various accounts of what took place next, Slade's friends denying them, and his enemies swearing they were true. But popular history holds that Slade ordered Beni tied to a corral fence and spent the better part of a day drinking and shooting the unfortunate captive to death by degrees. When he satisfied himself that Beni's murderous attack on him had been repaid, he put an end to it with a fatal shot, and in a final act of vengeance cut off the dead man's ears. The Overland Stage Company, which employed him, and a military tribunal at Fort Laramie, the nearest for fifteen hundred miles, exonerated Slade after he reported the shooting.

He became more troublesome than ever after that. His reputation blackened with each succeeding tale, such as how he responded to emigrant complaints seeking lost or stolen livestock by confronting a rancher he suspected of rustling and opening fire through a doorway, killing three ranch hands and wounding a fourth. Stories of hanging men and of innumerable assaults, shootings, and beatings ultimately took their toll with the Overland Company. His violent behavior—he was fond of shooting canned goods off grocery shelves—brought about his discharge from the line.

Such was the reputation he took with him to Virginia City, Idaho Territory, in the spring of 1863. There were problems in that part of the country that were to have a devastating effect on Jack Slade. A gang of desperadoes had been successful in robbing gold shipments with impunity in the region and had reached a point at which a vigilance committee had been organized to deal with the situation. It had been discovered that the leader of the outlaws was the sheriff, Henry Plummer, himself. And the vigilantes set out to correct the matter. They began hanging men suspected of being in league with the Plummer gang. And on January 14, 1864, strung up five at once.

After the summary executions, the vigilantes, considering their work accomplished, having freed the territory of highwaymen and murders, established a provisional court to try future offenders by judge and jury. Jack Slade found himself high on the list of community undesirables. It had become a common occurrence for him to take Virginia City by storm; he and his friends would gallop through its main streets, "shooting and yelling like red devils, firing their revolvers, riding their horses into stores and destroy the goods within," while insulting all who stood in their way. Slade had never been accused of murder or even suspected of robbery in the territory. His lawlessness while drunk and his defiance of civil authority led to the belief that as he had killed men in other places, he would, unless he was checked in his wild career, commit the same deeds in Virginia City.

After one of his all-night carouses had made the town a pandemonium—and presumably he had displayed his now infamous shriveled "Jules's ear" to patrons of the saloons he frequented—a warrant was issued for his arrest on disturbing the peace charges. Slade reacted in expected fashion. He seized the writ, tore it into bits, stamped on it in fury, and set out with a loaded Derringer in search of the judge. The vigilance committee went into emergency session.

One of its principal men was John Xavier Beidler (known simply as X. Beidler among friends), who in his own career had been a store clerk, prospector, pack train operator, freighter, deputy U.S. marshal, and stagecoach shotgun guard and was known for having backbone, despite being scarcely taller than a rifle. On one occasion in Kansas, Beidler was with a party that chased a gang of border ruffians into a blacksmith shop. For want of lead, the posse loaded a small howitzer with printer's type and fired. Those not killed, he said, "had to pick the type from the bodies of their comrades, and that is the way they first learned to read."

Of Slade, Beidler said, "We communed on many occasions as friends. He was an honest man and did not like a thief, but he was a very dangerous man when drinking." And Slade had been drinking a great deal. With him on the loose and threatening to shoot the deputy and the judge, Beidler made one last effort to avoid what he knew was coming. He asked Slade's friend Jim Kiskadden to take Slade home, that a party of miners were headed for town with the intention of carrying out the vigilance committee's order.

Slade reluctantly turned his horse around and began riding out, when he spotted his quarry near a store. With a gun in each hand, he began an insulting tirade against the judge, the deputy, and the store owner, P. S. Pfouts, who also was the president of the vigilantes. At that moment, the miners hove into view with Captain James Williams, a vigilante, at their head. The sight sobered Slade immediately; his only response, "My god!" Williams informed him he had just one hour to live, and if he had any business to attend to, "he had better do it." Beidler later remarked that if Slade had ridden out when he was told, he would not have been hanged.

A group was sent to find a place of execution and decided on an empty beef scaffold. A noose was thrown over it, and Beidler said, "When Slade's hour expired . . . he expired with it." Standing on the boxes beneath the scaffold with the rope around his neck, he pleaded for his life. The crowd responded, "Time's up." Williams ordered, "Do your duty," and boxes were kicked away, plunging Slade into the abyss of death, for having disturbed the peace of Virginia City.

When Virginia Slade, who had been summoned from the ranch some dozen miles distant, rode into the city, she discovered to her horror she was too late. Her husband had been removed to a nearby store, his clothing arranged and prepared for burial. It was March 11, 1864. The bereaved widow cursed the town, took her husband's body home in a tin-lined coffin, filled, it was said, with a keg of whiskey. She swore he would never be buried in this "damned territory," and shipped the remains to Salt Lake City with instructions for the coffin to be transferred to an eastbound stage for Illinois.

By the time the roads cleared and the stage reached Utah, it was mid-July, and Virginia Slade's instructions had become confused. Slade's body was transferred to the Salt Lake City Cemetery and buried in the Stranger's Lot, "to be removed to Illinois in the fall." But no one ever came for Jack Slade. And today his remains—and the whiskey that proved his undoing—still await the stage for Carlisle.

CREATING CAMP DOUGLAS

UNITED STATES TROOPS ORDERED TO UTAH FROM California during the Civil War were intended to protect the overland trail from Indian depredations, but they instead made it their business to keep a sharp eye on Brigham Young and the Mormons. The founding of Fort Douglas in 1862 on the east bench of Salt Lake City by Colonel Patrick E. Connor and his California Volunteers was the last thing Young wanted, and the incident is riddled with ironies long forgotten in the century and more since.

For instance, when Shoshoni war parties had raided the overland mail route between the North Platte and Fort Bridger with relative impunity that spring, and it had become apparent that President Abraham Lincoln would have to take action, Young wired Washington: "The militia of Utah are ready and able . . . to take care of all the Indians . . . and protect the mail line." It was Young's idea that his offer would be seen as a logical answer to the situation and no federal forces would be necessary—what with the Union husbanding its troops to face Southern armies. But Brigham Young was no longer governor of Utah and could not deal directly with the federal government. He had been replaced by Alfred Cumming, who, in turn, had resigned in 1861 to join the Confederacy.

Patrick Edward Connor. Utah State Historical Society.

John Dawson of Indiana was then appointed chief executive of the territory. He had barely settled in before becoming embroiled in a scandal that sent him packing just six weeks into his term. Next up was Stephen Harding, another Indianan, who arrived in July 1862 just as private citizen Young was wiring Abraham Lincoln his offer to provide militia. Lincoln was well aware of the church leader's power and influence. He understood that while Young had not been governor since 1857, the mantle of that office rested invisibly, but securely, on Brigham's shoulders. The Mormon people would listen only to him. And President Lincoln also knew that Young knew it.

Lincoln authorized him to raise, equip, and arm one company of cavalry for ninety days. Young acted within an hour of receiving his answer. The commander of the militia company was to be Lot Smith—the shrewd guerilla leader of the recent Utah War, that standoff between Brigadier General Albert Sidney Johnston's Utah Expedition and the Mormon Nauvoo Legion that resulted in the establishment of Camp Floyd west of Provo. (Camp Floyd, its name changed to Fort Crittenden because Secretary of War John B. Floyd had defected to the South, was by 1862 deactivated.) The irony in Lot Smith's appointment was its complete turnaround from the days

Camp Douglas, Utah Territory. Photo by C. W. Carter; LDS Church Archives.

when he raided and burned government supply wagons near Fort Bridger. Now he was charged with protecting U.S. property at all costs.

In the long run, Young's ploy failed, for feisty Patrick E. Connor was on the march for Great Salt Lake Valley and nothing would prevent it. There was a bit of a fuss that October as Connor's five companies of infantry and two troops of cavalry entered Fort Crittenden. That was where the citizens of Great Salt Lake City wanted the flinty Irishman to station his command, but Connor had no intention of being forty miles from civilization. There were rumors that the dread "Danites," the so-called Destroying Angels, would prevent Connor from crossing the Jordan River on the outskirts of the city, thus keeping the federal force at a distance.

The challenge—though nonexistent—suited Connor just fine. He had been looking for an excuse to justify marching his men more than seven hundred miles on outpost duty. The colonel let it be known he would cross over the Jordan "If hell yawned below him." He crossed the river that

afternoon without incident, and the following morning struck out due north for the city. But let T. B. H. Stenhouse, who was there, describe the scene: "On the 29th of October, 1862, with loaded rifles, fixed bayonets and shotted cannon, Colonel Connor march the Volunteers into Salt Lake City, and proceeded 'to the bench,' directly east of the city. There, at the base of the Wasatch Mountains, they planted the United States flag, and created Camp Douglas." In a footnote to his book, *The Rocky Mountain Saints*, Stenhouse remarked, "Connor could not possibly have selected a better situation for a military post, and certainly no place could have been chosen more offensive to Brigham. The artillery have a perfect and unobstructed range of Brigham's residence, and with their muzzles turned in that direction, the Prophet felt awfully annoyed."

Connor named the new camp after recently deceased "Little Giant" Stephen A. Douglas. The following January, Connor ordered his command into the field to punish Indians in the Bear River area near present Preston, Idaho. What ensued was a massacre of Shoshonis with the toll numbering from 224 to 350, depending on the source. Connor lost 14 dead and scores wounded; he gained a promotion and a reputation as an Indian fighter.

It was after word later arrived at Camp Douglas that Connor had been promoted to brigadier general for his Bear River campaign that exuberant members of his regiment loaded the howitzers with powder and wadding and fired an eleven-gun salute in his honor, rudely awakening Brigham Young. Although express riders were dispatched to rally available fighting men to protect their leader from what they perceived as an "unprovoked military bombardment," the record is silent regarding Young's comments on learning the true cause of the artillery barrage. Fort Douglas stands much as it did 135 years ago, mute testimony to Utah's frontier heritage.

THE DISAPPEARANCE OF JOHN BAPTISTE

THE VIOLENT DEATHS OF THREE MORMON DESPERADOES at the hands of the law caused a considerable stir in Great Salt Lake City in 1862, yet it was mild compared to the shock value of the aftermath, which began with the arrest of a serial grave robber and ended with the discovery of a headless skeleton three decades later.

A posse had tracked Lot Huntington, John P. Smith, and Moroni ("Rone") Clawson to Faust's Mail Station, twenty-two miles west of Fort Crittenden (old Camp Floyd). Huntington was wanted on charges of assaulting former Governor John W. Dawson at Ephraim Hanks stage station in Mountain Dell between Little and Big Mountains east of the city three weeks earlier and additional charges of stealing a cash box from an Overland Mail Company employee two weeks later. Smith was also named in the theft of the cash box. Clawson was charged with participating in the beating of the governor.

All three were headed for California when the posse, led by Orrin Porter Rockwell, caught up with them. Huntington resisted and Rockwell killed him. The other two surrendered. Back in the city, Rockwell turned his prisoners over to police and was tending to his team of horses when gunfire exploded down the street in the direction the outlaws had been taken. At the scene minutes later he found a policeman standing over the bodies of Smith and Clawson. "They tried to escape," the constable explained.

Both outlaws were laid to rest in the city cemetery, and since no one claimed Clawson's body, he was buried in potter's field at city expense. A few days later relatives arranged for his reburial in the family plot in Draper. Then, the unthinkable. When the coffin was opened, the body was naked.

George Clawson, a bitter and indignant brother of the deceased, poured out his anger to Henry Heath, a Salt Lake policeman. "That's a terrible thing to do–to bury a man like that." Momentarily taken aback, Heath rejoined with: "No such thing! No pauper ever had better or cleaner burial clothing than 'Rone.' I bought them myself!" There could be but one answer, and neither man could bring himself to put it in words. But Heath could, and did, begin an investigation, one that would send a wave of horror through the Mormon community. With Probate Judge Elias Smith's blessing, Heath with several other officers questioned cemetery sexton, Jesse C. Little, who gave them the name of John Baptiste, for nearly three years the cemetery's gravedigger.

Baptiste's wife answered the door of their home on Third Avenue. John was at work, she said, but the officers were welcome to come inside and talk. "There were numerous boxes of clothing stacked around," Heath recalled in an 1893 interview with the *Deseret News*. "Imagine our shock and surprise when we discovered these were the funeral robes of people buried in the city cemetery for several years past." The discovery held a special horror for Heath, who but a short time before had buried "an idolized daughter . . . I feared that her grave, too, had been desecrated and that her funeral shroud was among the motley, sickening heap of flesh-soiled linen we found in the grave-digger's hut."

Heath's "investigation" took a desperate turn. He and his fellow officers set out for the cemetery, but the grim-faced policeman now had murder in his heart: "In my breast rankled the unconquerable determination to kill him there and then should my suspicions be confirmed." Confronting the man, Heath accused him outright of grave robbing, and a terrified Baptiste fell to his knees and sobbed that he was innocent. "Liar!" Henry Heath, shouting, "We found the clothes," became uncontrollable in his rage.

"I choked the wretch into a confession while he begged for his life as a human being never plead before. I dragged him to a grave near my daughter's and pointing to it, inquired: 'Did you rob that grave?' His reply was 'Yes.'

"Then directing his attention to the mound which covered my child's remains I repeated the question with bated breath and with the firm resolve to kill him should he answer in the affirmative.

"'No, no, not that one!'

"That answer saved the miserable coward's life."

If it is true that bad news travels fast, word of Baptiste's arrest flashed like lightning through the city and its environs. The boxes of funeral clothing along with a cache of jewelry and other baubles found in the suspect's home were brought to the county courthouse to be displayed in hopes of identifying the owners. The business of putting Baptiste safely behind bars was another matter. Constables had difficulty getting him to the county jail in one piece. Had the people gotten to him, he would have been lynched outright, an officer remarked. Another officer recognized the broadcloth Prince Albert suit Baptiste was wearing. A storekeeper named Alexander Carpenter, deceased these two and one-half years from the lethal effects of a bullet fired by one Thomas H. Ferguson, was the last owner of that particular suit—in fact, he had been buried in it.

Baptiste's interrogation now began in earnest. Wilford Woodruff made note in his journal that Baptiste admitted plundering graves for more than two years but that he could not accurately estimate how many he had robbed. He said the devil was in him, which I think was true, Woodruff added. "He said his only motive was to sell the clothing," Woodruff wrote.

Police took the man to the cemetery to identify individual graves he had looted, but so many spectators gathered that Baptiste refused to continue after having identified but a dozen. They will kill me, he said, pointing to the muttering crowd. Take me back to jail. He was bundled off in a wagon to screen him from "excited, indignant people" and returned to his cell. This ghoul, who dug graves by day and prowled without conscience among the dead at night, greatly feared death itself.

Policeman Albert Dewey described him as "the most singular human being I ever knew in my life." He hoarded the clothes of the dead about his premises as a miser would his gold, Dewey said. It was not true though that Baptiste sold his plunder to secondhand dealers, contradicting Woodruff's observation; actually the grave robber seldom disposed of any and kept careful watch over his "ill-gotten gains." Baptiste used his victims' coffins for kindling in the winter, Dewey added.

The personal effects were exhibited at the courthouse; long lines of citizens streamed passed the piles of clothing. "There lay the grave clothes of fifty persons or more, some 20 pairs of little children's stockings [60 pairs of children's shoes] and clothing of all ages, male and female which that man had stripped from the bodies of Saints & Sinners," Woodruff confided to his journal. Woodruff also was apprehensive that he might discover something of his own deceased child among the remnants on display.

Baptiste's background was as addled as his behavior. In the 1860 census, his place of birth was listed as Ireland, while Woodruff marked him as having been born in Venice, Italy, in 1814; and Heath, who interrogated Baptiste, said he was a Frenchman who came to America from Australia. "Killing is too good for him," was Brigham Young's response when told of the ghoul's arrest and the extent of his crimes. It was to be a prophetic observation.

Elias Smith, editor of the *Deseret News* as well as probate judge, had written of Baptiste in his journal for January 27: "The monster was arrested and placed in jail, otherwise the populace would have torn him to pieces, such was the excitement produced by the unheard of occurrence." Then, on February 1: "I had Baptiste out of his cell and heard his statements as to how he came to engage in the business of robbing the dead and his confession as to the extent to which he had carried the operation . . . he had robbed many graves, but how many he could not or would not tell."

Here then was a quandry for the judge. What Baptiste had done and confessed to was a heinous crime, a despicable crime, no question of that. Woodruff at one point—as the parent of a recently deceased child—had fumed that Baptiste had committed one of the most "Damnable, diabolical, satanical, hellish sacrileges . . . ever known or recorded in the history of man." Some guessed he had violated as many as three hundred graves. But fury and anger aside, Baptiste had committed a felony, not a capital crime. Despite the outraged populace, the grave robber had done nothing punishable by death under the law.

With Elias Smith's brief journal note, John Baptiste disappears from the record, public and private—at least from recoverable accounts. To comfort his troubled flock, Young, speaking in the Salt Lake Tabernacle a week later, reassured them that Baptiste's crimes "did not injure the dead in the morning of the resurrection . . . all of the dead will be clothed in the morning of the resurrection no matter how they are buried. As to the punishment of the man Baptiste, to shoot or hang him would not satisfy my feelings at all." What Young suggested was banishment: "I would make him a fugitive and a vagabond upon the earth. That would be my sentence."

The church leader had already spoken of the matter in private. He told Woodruff that Baptiste ought to be branded as a robber of the dead and "cropped" and placed on Miller's (Fremont) Island—turned out of the community and told if he ever came back he would be killed. That would be a fitting sentence, Young said. Here again the story becomes confused. Dewey was one of the police assigned to take Baptiste to the island. "We had to promise we wouldn't kill him." The "branding," according to Dewey, took the form of an indelible ink tattoo across the forehead: Branded For Robbing The Dead.

Dale L. Morgan wrote that Heath remembered Baptiste was kept in jail three weeks, but Morgan thought it was more likely three months. Dewey recalled in later years that the prisoner was taken to the island in "early spring when the lake was very low." Dewey also insisted there was no "ball and chain or gyves [shackles]" of any kind. The question of mutilation was not raised. It is significant, however, that Wilford Woodruff, who, as a confidante of Brigham Young, was in a position to know of such things, would mention that Baptiste had been "cropped." That phrase to a cattle rancher means to earmark, or notch the ears; but it had yet another more sinister connotation on the frontier. There are historians who speculate that Baptiste lost more than pieces of his ears to the knives of vengeful Utahns.

The police took him to Antelope Island, where it had been arranged that boatmen would convey Baptiste five miles north to Fremont Island. There the surrounding lake water was deeper and the ghoul was less likely to make an easy escape. The island served as a pasture for cattle, and, according to Dewey, two Davis County stockmen, Henry and Dan Miller, had constructed a shanty and stocked it with provisions for herders. In August, Dan Miller visited the island and discovered that Baptiste had helped himself to some provisions and torn down the cabin, apparently to build a raft. He also had killed a two-year-old heifer.

At that point, Morgan says, Baptiste vanishes from the realm of ascertainable fact. He simply disappears. But that disappearance leaves behind a "whole train of provocative possibilities." Nearly thirty years would pass before a party of duck hunters found a human skull at the mouth of the Jordan River where it empties into the Great Salt Lake Lake. The hunters brought their grisly find to the city and gave it to R. G. Taysum, a *Salt Lake Herald* writer, who reported the discovery. An unsuccessful search was made for the rest of the skeleton. Three years later, John Winegar Jr., hunting in the same area, stumbled across the arms, legs, ribs, and vertebrae of a human skeleton, but no skull. Around one of the leg bones was an iron clamp and chain; at the end of the chain, an iron ball.

In a mildly sensational account, the *Herald* recounted—not too accurately—the gist of the 1862 episode and stated the skeleton was "undoubtedly" that of Baptiste. This seemed to aggravate the rival *Deseret News*, which huffed, "it is better to hear and shudder over facts than fables." Then, quoting "reliable sources," the *News* went on to publish interviews with the two retired policemen, Heath and Dewey, who in turn concluded that since Baptiste was not shackled, the skeleton probably was that of a penitentiary prisoner who may have escaped in irons years after Baptiste's banishment. However, use of the ball and chain was not that prevalent, even in the territorial penitentiary, and escapes in shackles rare. More likely is the possibility that the skeleton was indeed that of Baptiste, who may have made it to the Jordan outlet on a makeshift raft before he perished of exhaustion or drowning. As for the skull, it could have been knocked free in later years by floating debris on the river.

More strange is the total absence of a public record on the prisoner. A painstaking search of Salt Lake County probate court minutes and docket books as well as county probate files and the territorial penitentiary warden's office records fails to disclose even a mention of the man. As Morgan cogently remarked in his *The Great Salt Lake*:

> The whole episode is almost unparalleled in Mormon history. The *Deseret News* of 1862 had absolutely nothing to say of Baptiste—nothing but the stenographic report of Brigham's sermon. . . . What of the people who thronged the courthouse; what of the furor that gripped the city? How was it that a newspaper could pass such matters by?
>
> And how is it Baptiste could be jailed—for weeks, admittedly; for months, almost for a certainty—and leave no trace in the criminal records? How could he be given a judicial hearing and not leave so much as a shadow upon the records of the court?
>
> And who, finally, could take upon himself the responsibility for sentencing a man, without trial, to be marooned upon a desert island?
>
> Folklore and history alike have turned their face from Baptiste. His story itself has almost sunk from sight. He is a presence on a lost page of history, the only specter of the Great Salt Lake.

Artemus Ward and Another "Wilde" Visitor to Utah

As the crossroads of the West, Salt Lake City in the nineteenth century found itself playing host to some odd celebrities—from comics to tragedians, even the occasional aesthete. But for individuality none could match Artemus Ward and Oscar Wilde.

Ward, the stage name for Charles Farrar Browne, has been described as Abraham Lincoln's favorite funny man and Mark Twain's mentor. He was irrepressible, simply incapable of letting a straight line pass unmolested. He was a newspaperman.

Though he made his reputation by creating the persona of a semiliterate sideshowman he called Artemus Ward, Browne actually was a young man of considerable elegance, intelligence, and sophistication. By the early 1860s he was editor of New York's *Vanity Fair*. And it can be said he was the first of the stand-up comedians. He came to prominence while writing a regular column for the *Cleveland Daily Plain Dealer* in which he conceived the character of Artemus Ward, describing his fictional adventures in letters from various towns and cities visited by a sideshow. In a blizzard of bad grammar and misspellings, "Artemus" would write of touring with "wild beests, snaiks and wax figgers."

Browne himself was described by a Cleveland contemporary as "young, tall, slender, and cheerful in manner." Another said he was "tall and thin, his face aquiline; his carriage bouyant, his demeanor joyous and eager." But his mood would vary as a roller coaster, from high-flying exuberance to such fits of depression he was sometimes afraid to be left alone at night. In essence, a typical journalist.

His newspaper columns were so popular that in 1861 he was persuaded to take to the stage as a lecturer and by November of that year had thought out the approach for Artemus Ward as a speaker. His "monologue" was not so much what he said, but how he said it. And though there is no written transcript of that fateful debut in Boston, it is enough to say the audience—surprised by this serious young man who seemed to have such difficulty lecturing—was kept in a constant roar of laughter.

By 1864 Artemus Ward was in huge demand both as a writer and lecturer. He was a show business celebrity. His humorous writings were widely circulated. In 1862, however, he wrote about Brigham Young and the Mormons an entirely fictional spoof that convulsed its readers and added to Ward's celebrity. Because Ward had not actually been to Utah, that satire would come back to haunt him.

As the Civil War battled on, Ward hit upon the notion of a western tour. He persuaded his business manager, E. P. Hingston, to accompany him to California (by steamer via the isthmus of Panama) then return overland "across the Plains and do the Mormons as we return." Against his better judgment, Hingston agreed. And the dead of winter 1863–64 found the two easterners in a stagecoach, armed to chattering teeth against hostile Paiutes who were burning overland stations, bound for Great Salt Lake City.

It was a precarious journey, but the intrepid travelers made it through safely. Then Ward heard that "a certain humorous sketch of mine, written some years before, had greatly incensed the Saints . . . and my reception at the new Zion might be unpleasantly warm." Hingston strolled the city to get a sense of the atmosphere and returned to their Salt Lake House rooms, "thanking God he never wrote against the Mormons himself." There is a prejudice against Artemus Ward, Hingston reported gloomily, and advised the performer to stay indoors. "He has heard that the Mormons thirst for my blood and are on the look out for me. Under these circumstances, I keep in."

They contacted T. B. H. Stenhouse, an Englishman and Latter-day Saint who had Brigham Young's ear. Stenhouse, an old newspaperman himself, allayed Ward's anxiety "in regard to having my swan-like throat cut by the Danites, but thinks my wholesale denunciation of a people I had never seen was rather hasty." Stenhouse read

aloud a paragraph which Ward had written, and to which the Saints objected: "I girded up my Lions [sic] and fled the Seen. I Packt up my duds and left Salt Lake, which is a 2nd Soddum and Germorer, inhabited by as theavin' & onprincipled a set of retchis as ever drew Breth in eny spot on the Globe." Ward swallowed hard and pleaded that it was a purely burlesque sketch, that the strong paragraph should not be interpreted literally at all. "The Elder didn't seem to see it in that light, but we parted pleasantly."

After a bout with mountain fever which put him down for two weeks, Ward asked for and was granted an interview with Brigham Young to seek approval for a performance in the Salt Lake Theatre. Young made no allusion to the Mormon story Ward had written, and the okay was given for a "comic oration." What he said is not reported (the *Deseret News* was in the throes of a periodic newsprint shortage and suspended publication from December 1863 through March 1864). But Ward noted that the performance was a sellout and mentioned that among his box office receipts for the night were

4 bushels of potatoes,
2 bushels of oats,
2 hams,
1 live pig (Hingston chained him in the box office),
1 wolf-skin,
1 firkin of butter,
and so forth.

Artemus Ward and the Mormons parted company in mid-February, and Ward returned to the East, to write more about his visit to Zion. Charles Farrar Browne died while on tour in England March 6, 1867, at the age of thirty-three, the victim of apparent pulmonary tuberculosis.

Utah's reception for Dublin-born British writer Oscar Wilde in 1882 was somewhat less frenetic. Wilde (born Fingal O'Flahertie Wills) had gained a reputation for brilliant wit, studied aestheticism (sensitivity to art and beauty), which was to dominate his life, and was a minor celebrity when he made his American tour. His success with novels (*The Picture of Dorian Gray*) and plays (*The Importance of Being Earnest*) came later. As did his notorious lawsuit against the marquis of Queensbury for libel and subsequent prison term at hard labor for homosexuality.

Billed at the Salt Lake Theatre April 10, 1882, Wilde was to speak on the subject: "Art Decoration, Being the Practical Application of the Aesthetic Theory to Every-Day Home Life and Ornamentation." Salt Lakers who attended the performance didn't know what to make of the lecturer. And the *Salt Lake Herald* reporter who covered the event devoted more than two columns of front page space to saying as much. It was not a rave review.

The large attendance at the lecture, he said, was due to curiosity. Wilde, he said, is on the whole a jolly good fellow, sharp as a whip, and has enough sense to know how the ducats can best be seduced from the astute American. His costume struck the journalist as "not entirely favorable." Wilde was dressed in "a black velvet coat somewhat approaching the conventional claw hammer in style, black velvet vest, ruffles at the throat, breast and wrists, black knee breeches, black stockings, and low pumps with pointed toes and silver buckles." The lecture delivery was "as odd and unpleasant to the ear as his appearance to the eye." His style was no more monotonous than the delivery, and there was a total absence of gesture, though he occasionally pulled out his handkerchief or affectionately disturbed his long straight tresses, remarked the critic.

In closing his fifty-minute lecture, Wilde told his audience, "Let there be no flower in your meadows that does not wreathe its tendrils around your pillars; no little leaf in your Titan forests that does not lend its form to design; no curving spray that does not live forever in carven arch or window of marble; no bird in your air that is not given the iridescent wonder of its color, the exquisite curves of its flight, to make more precious the preciousness of simple adornment; for the voices that have their dwelling in sea and mountain are not the chosen music of liberty only, or the sole treasure of its beauty." Commented the critic, "a mere recognition of the close of the lecture was conveyed by the brief and short-lived applause."

And so, in another time, did Artemus Ward and Oscar Wilde make their marks in Utah.

THE DESERET ALPHABET

IN 1869, YOUNGSTERS IN THE UTAH PUBLIC SCHOOL system were being taught a second written language. It wasn't Spanish and it wasn't Latin. It was Deseret.

The new language had an alphabet of thirty-eight characters and was an outgrowth of a frustrating effort by the board of regents of the University of Deseret (today's University of Utah) to simplify English. Failing that, the regents decided instead to "invent an entirely new and original set of characters." The Deseret Alphabet was the result.

Just why the project was undertaken at all is still a matter of some dispute, but at least one western historian has theorized that greatly expanded missionary activity on the part of the Church of Jesus Christ of Latter-day Saints in the 1850s may have precipitated for Brigham Young, governor of Utah and president of the church, a pressing need for revision of the language. Alone in the Great Basin save for the occasional trapper and trading post, the Mormon settlements were swelling with converts from Norway, Sweden, Denmark, Germany, and France, as well as from that "greatest mission field of all, the British Isles," wrote the late scholar and historian Dale L. Morgan. "These converts presented difficult problems of assimilation. If they were to be knit into the Kingdom of God, they should have to learn to speak and write a common language," Morgan said. And that's what Young set out to do.

In October 1853 the board of regents appointed a committee of three–Parley P. Pratt, Heber C. Kimball, and George D. Watt (an accomplished Pitman shorthand reporter or "phonologist")–to "prepare a small school-book in characters founded on some new system of orthography whereby the spelling and pronunciation of the English language might be made uniform and easily acquired." In the simplest of terms, the committee was to streamline English.

Three months later the committee reported a setback; it had despaired of reworking English and instead had opted to "invent an entirely new and original set of characters." An impossible task? Not so. By January 19, 1854, the *Deseret News* was able to report the university regents, in company with the governor (Brigham Young) and heads of departments, were adopting a new alphabet of thirty-eight characters. With minor variations, the final version was the alphabet determined for use in the schools.

But "language" was little more than a code. For an individual to be proficient in Deseret would require a measure of proficiency in English since it was based on the sounds found in English grammar. And it was crude, this "shorthand language." For instance, the Deseret characters (which cannot be reproduced by a conventional typewriter) for the First Reader's initial lesson are translated "Lesn I" and, for the heading, "L u urn [Learn] to [to] ur e d [read] woo el [well]." The *ur* in the third word is to provide the "r" sound in English. The *e* is given an "ee" sound, and the *d* is a "d". Makes one wonder why the regents and Brigham Young pursued this as they did.

Nevertheless, the regents met in February 1868 and voted to petition the legislature for $10,000, then to send a practical printer to the East and have fonts of type cast and cut for the alphabet, and to "publish and import this season, spelling books, primers, readers, &c., to be introduced immediately among our children, and so continue from year to year, until we have published in that alphabet the cream of all knowledge relating to theology, science, history, geography, and all necessary educational works."

By April Orson Pratt was engaged in preparing the first and second readers to be printed in Deseret. The slim volumes—*The Deseret First Book* ran to thirty-six pages and the *The Deseret Second Book* to seventy-two—were illustrated with engravings from *Willson's Readers* (with permission from the publisher). *Willson's Readers* were gaining popularity across America, though they had not yet outperformed *McGuffey's Readers* in 1868. In total, twenty thousand copies of each Deseret reader were printed.

Brigham Young told church members at the LDS General Conference in October that thousands of the primers were on their way to public schools. They were offered for sale in Utah at fifteen cents and twenty cents each. (In the 1960s the LDS Church sold remaining copies of the primers for twenty-five cents each, and today the two little books in good condition will cost at least $130 a set from rare book dealers.) But the books did not take hold. For nearly twenty years Brigham Young strove to persuade his followers that the new alphabet would restore purity to the language, yet there was the inherent flaw in its inception, having been developed as it was to a degree from Pitman shorthand and by individuals unfamiliar with the nuances of orthography and unprepared for the complexities of language. Explaining this "genuine difficulty," Morgan pointed out that the alphabet could be learned, "but except in communication it was functionless. It provided no access to the literature of the world, and provided no substitute for that literature."

More cynical was the editorial comment some ten years earlier in a *San Francisco Globe* issue of December 15, 1857, after a sample of Deseret had crossed the paper's desk:

> The Mormons . . . are a progressive people. They not only want more wives than is wholesome, but more letters to their Alphabet. Letters written with this Alphabet are as incomprehensible as the movements of woman or the hieroglyphics of the Chinese and the Egyptians.
>
> The Mormon alphabet consists of about 40 letters, which have been so arranged and named to cause the greatest possible annoyance to outsiders. The Saints not only wish to convert Utah into an oyster, but to close the shell against all knives except those found in the vicinity of Great Salt Lake. The Mormons wish to isolate the "generation of vipers" which are to succeed them. For this reason they wish to get up a new alphabet, a new spelling book, and a new language. The idea is ingenious, but it will not succeed. To get a new language in this country is as difficult as to bore a hole through the Rocky Mountains with a leather auger.

In the long run, for all the effort and money that had gone into creating the new language, it was as troublesome to meld into the mainstream as the metric system in the 1990s. For schools the alphabet was impractical, and the general public

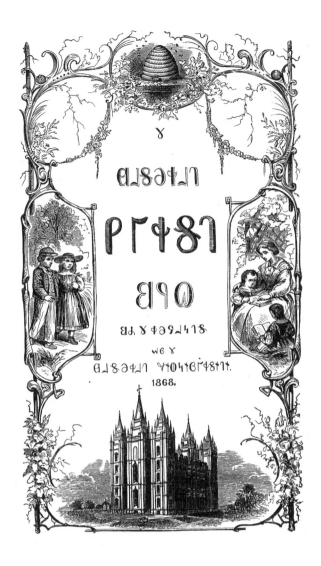

The *Deseret First Book* and *Deseret Second Book* readers, which employed the Deseret Alphabet.

was entirely disinterested. And as the years passed, the characters of Deseret disappeared even from the occasional lesson feature in the *Deseret News*. In all the project resulted in two school primers, *The Deseret First Book* and *The Deseret Second Book*; a 116-page volume of *The Book of Nephi* (published in 1869); a 443-page edition of *The Book of Mormon* (also printed in New York in 1869); and some seventy-two articles in the *Deseret News* from February 1859 through August 1864.

In July 1877 Orson Pratt was sent to England to investigate the possibility of printing Mormon scriptures in Pitman. With Brigham Young's death that August, Pratt was called home. As Dale Morgan put it, "Mormon experimentation in alphabetic and orthographic reform never again lifted its head."

PART III

It was a time for celebration when the Central Pacific met the Union Pacific at Promontory Summit, but Brigham Young chose not to show. Utah State Historical Society

9

Brigham Young and Hard Times Ahead

Pioneer Era Fades as Full Assault on Polygamy Begins
1869–1877

As moguls of the Central Pacific and Union Pacific railroads puffed and postured in ceremonially hammering the final spike linking the transcontinental track at Promontory Summit north of Ogden, they also were knocking down the barrier known as the western frontier. Just as surely as America was opened by rail from the Missouri River to Sacramento that sunny May 10, 1869, the overland "plains-travel" era faded, and from that day on immigrants to Utah would no longer be considered pioneers as covered wagons gave way to rail cars. There were other major changes in the decade ahead; not the least of which were the unrelenting attack on the Mormon practice of polygamy and the death in 1877 of Brigham Young.

For now dignitaries representing East and West attended the "last spike" ceremonies, but Utah's chief executive, Governor Charles Durkee, and the territory's most prominent citizen, Brigham Young, were conspicuous by their absence. Durkee, governor since 1865, was in feeble health and had been in the East during the early part of 1869. He returned to Utah on the eve of the ceremonies, but the fatigue of travel prevented him from participating. Young on the other hand had decided to visit the southern settlements in April and, though invited to join the Promontory festivities, chose not to return to Salt

Lake City until May 11. Critics believe he snubbed the Promontory ceremony and simultaneous doings in Salt Lake City because the railroads had chosen not to route the track through the capital, taking it instead north of the lake. If, indeed, Young ignored the spike-driving ceremony because of petulance, his failure to participate is all the more tarnished in the annals of this historic event.

However glorious the realization of coast-to-coast rail travel and transportation seemed, the connection between West and East now loomed as an ominous two-edged blade. For almost a year, church authorities had made it clear "that those who redeemed the country from the wilderness and had labored to bring it prosperity, had a right to protect what they had built." To that end, Mormons pledged among themselves to strictly buy from each other and to ignore Gentile merchants. Young well understood that Utah-owned companies would now have to compete on their own home ground with eastern manufacturers. If the businesses were to survive, then the cost of production had to be lowered in order to be competitive.

To the Mormon leader's way of thinking, the place to start was by cutting wages across the board. He urged representatives of all the trades to present to their fellow workers the idea of reducing

Brigham Young. Photo by C. W. Savage; LDS Church Archives.

excommunicated for apostasy. But before that, they took the side of the workers by criticizing what was perceived to be an effort to "fix wages" by the men who "paid the wages and not the men who received the wages."

Young's plan was to reduce the pay of common laborers to one dollar a day, and that of skilled laborers (mechanics, masons, carpenters, and painters), who had been earning as much as four dollars a day, to a dollar fifty. Tullidge, in fact, complained that an editorial in the *Deseret News* threatened to bring Chinese labor to Utah if "working men did not come to terms." LDS Church historian Brigham H. Roberts brushed that aside, however, saying the *News* editorial had been misinterpreted. He also offered a rather vague explanation that the proposal to bring the trades into a lower wage scale seemed to have been left "to the adjustment of natural trades forces."

On the heels of this opposition came an article in *Utah Magazine*, apparently written by a group of rebel merchants and Mormon elders, clamoring for the opening of Utah mines "for the social redemption of the Territory." That corked it. Brigham Young was furious. At a session of the School of the Prophets, the malcontents and reformers were called to task for their opposition to Young's leadership, a step in their expulsion from the church. The School of the Prophets, according to historian Roberts, was "a select gathering of the brethren of the priesthood, meeting regularly through these years to be taught in the doctrine of the gospel and in the policies of the church. Admission was by card and the sessions confidential. Here questions of practical affairs as well as of theological importance were freely discussed and instruction and council given according to the wisdom of the assembly or the presidents thereof."

Young's proposed cutback does not seem to have been discussed again publicly; but because it came from him, the idea enjoyed a certain added clout. The implication is that employers used the opportunity to exercise a measure of restraint in setting pay scales. Utah has always been below the national average in wages.

With the appearance of the *Salt Lake Daily Tribune* in the spring of 1871, the citizens of Utah were treated to the liveliest (many would call it vicious) exchange of editorial insults between the

wages. It was a proposal that would affect the way of life in Zion into the next century, and against Brigham Young it and the Mormon economic monopoly stirred the bold opposition of some of the most able and brilliant men in the community life of Utah, prominent members of the LDS Church who also were its intellectuals.

Four among them—William S. Godbe, E. L. T. Harrison, Eli B. Kelsey, and Henry W. Lawrence—subsequently founded the *Salt Lake Daily Tribune and Utah Mining Gazette*. Also caught up in the dissent were their friends and associates: historian-author Edward W. Tullidge, newspaperman T. B. H. Stenhouse, and Ogden merchant W. H. Shearman. These men, too, became involved in varying degrees with the *Mormon Tribune* and the *Salt Lake Weekly Tribune*, both liberal cause newspapers, precursors of the daily, which made its debut April 15, 1871. In the end, they were editors of the *Tribune* and the *Deseret News* since the *Valley Tan* closed up shop in February 1860. To this mix was added the pro-Mormon *Salt Lake Herald*, seen as a buffer between the *News* and the *Tribune*.

Now that Utah was readily accessible by railroad, and an opposition newspaper voice to Brigham Young was making itself heard throughout the territory, antipolygamy forces stepped up efforts to eliminate the practice within the LDS Church. Unfriendly congressional legislation increased. The antichurch Liberal political party was born, said Brigham Roberts, and its first heartbeat had come from the Godbe-Harrison-Kelsey-Shearman-Tullidge revolt, the so-called Godbeites. The onslaught from Congress took the form of the Cullom Bill, a cruel measure that aimed at severely punishing bigamy by destroying families created by such marriages. Even the *Missouri Republican*, never a friend of the Mormons, complained of the bill's sweeping unfairness:

> The superfluous wives of Young and his followers are declared concubines and their offspring bastards and both women and children are literally turned out of doors and consigned to the cold charities of the world. The punishment of these comparatively innocent parties is actually more severe than that inflicted upon the more guilty. The male polygamist may escape scot free by simply giving up his female companions, but in any event [the wives and children] are reduced to pauperism at once, and forced to beg, starve, or do worse.

The *New York World* recognized that if the Cullom Bill passed, it could mean war:

> If we force them into a hostile attitude, the Mormons can give us a very disagreeable, a very wearisome, and tremendously expensive war. . . . The government should not forcibly interfere with polygamy or Mormonism at all.

And the *New York Times* editorialized:

> The whole Mormon population of Utah Territory does not much exceed 100,000 and in a very few years [because of the railroad] this little band will be outnumbered by the crowd of Gentiles who will surround Salt Lake. There will be no need then to make laws against polygamy, and until then there will be no use in doing so."

William S. Godbe, prominent Utahn and dissident Mormon. Utah State Historical Society.

The Cullom Bill passed the House but died in a Senate committee; perhaps the avalanche of similar opinion from throughout the country had buried it.

In another maneuver to quash polygamy in Utah, members of Congress acted on the notion that, since Mormon women were held in bondage by plural marriage, this "degrading" practice could be eliminated by giving them additional power. Reasoned Congress, the way to do this was by granting women suffrage. With it, the women of Utah would soon vote their way to freedom. But bills did not come to a vote in either house because members of Congress became suspicious when Utah's delegate expressed hearty support of the measure. Back home, acting governor S. A. Mann took the opportunity and signed a suffrage bill, allowing Utah women to become the first in the nation to vote. Utah's new chief executive, appointed by President Ulysses S. Grant, was J. Wilson Shaffer. He wasn't in favor of enfranchising Utah women and intended to wire Mann to veto the bill, but failed to do so.

In the latest batch of federal appointees were individuals from Illinois, Alabama, New York, and Michigan—politicians from all over the country thrown into Utah to decide what was good for Utahns. This continual turnover of outsiders in positions of authority proved a constant source of frustration to the citizens and business leaders of the territory. Once more the territory was to become an arena for the same old fight by Utah citizens to determine the right of local self-government versus federal impingement on that right.

Shaffer tangled almost immediately with Chief Justice Charles C. Wilson over judicial matters; then the governor set out to dismantle the Nauvoo Legion, embroiling himself in a sharp exchange of letters with Lieutenant General Daniel H. Wells over the legality of Shaffer's action. Shaffer's intended suppression of Mormon influence in Utah was successful in regard to the legion; the thirteen-thousand-man militia ceased to drill after the governor's order, and seventeen years later it was annulled by Congress as well. Shaffer's health failed. He had suffered from tuberculosis, and he died in October 1870.

Scarcely had Shaffer's casket been placed on the train for burial in his home state of Illinois than Vernon H. Vaughn, secretary of the territory, was appointed to fill the gubernatorial vacancy. Vaughn, an Alabaman, held the office until March, when George L. Woods, whose term as governor of Oregon had recently expired, was named to the high office in Utah. Historian H. H. Bancroft pointed out that Woods was a Missourian by birth and a pronounced anti-Mormon by nature. Utah, it seemed, was in for more rough sailing.

This political bickering reached the point of absurdity in July of 1871 when Salt Lake City's citizens held rival Independence Day celebrations—one for Mormons and the other for non-Mormons. And for a year or more the pressure to "get Brigham Young" was pronounced. He was indicted on charges of "lewdly and lasciviously associating and cohabiting with women, not being married to them." This in connection with his plural wives. It was a variation of an 1852 law to punish adultery, and it was invoked to fight the institution of polygamy "in the person of Brigham Young."

While that case was pending, R. N. Baskin, newly appointed acting U.S. District Attorney and a fiercely rabid anti-Mormon, succeeded in indicting Brigham Young on charges of murder in the death of Richard Yates during the so-called Utah War of 1857–58, based on the confessions of the notorious William A. Hickman. But after months of contentious maneuvering in the courts, all indictments issued in the territorial courts during the previous eighteen months were quashed by the U.S. Supreme Court because jury selection was deemed unlawfully drawn and invalid. One hundred and thirty-eight defendants and prisoners were released, Young and his co-defendants—Salt Lake City mayor Daniel H. Wells, former territorial attorney general Hosea Stout, and W. H. Kimball—among them.

By the mid-1870s the courts in Utah had become so embroiled in politics that Grant-appointed officials were accusing each other openly in eastern newspapers of corruption in Utah. What followed was a round of resignations and repercussions. One Utah judge, Cyrus M. Hawley of Illinois, had been charged with bigamy in his home state; another, Judge O. F. Strickland of Michigan, "bought his appointment" to the bench. Both jurists resigned. In 1874 Congress passed the Poland Bill, which, though less drastic than many others proposed, did sharply curb the jurisdiction of Mormon courts. And in the fall of the year John Doyle Lee was arrested in southern Utah after nearly twenty years on the dodge and, after an abortive first trial, was executed for his role in the Mountain Meadow massacre of 1857.

It was not until the early 1880s that the body blow was struck on the issue of Mormon plural marriage, with the passage of the Edmunds Act (1882), which disenfranchised polygamists, added to the crime of polygamy unlawful cohabitation, and provided for legal action against violators. As Dale Morgan aptly described it, "U.S. deputy marshals began 'polyg hunts' the length and breadth of the territory. The polygamists were forced into hiding, some even going to Canada or Mexico in hope of finding a haven, but the raids kept a constant flow of [such] cases moving into the courts. The penitentiary was filled with resisting Saints." Then came the *coup de grace*. It was called the Edmunds-Tucker Act. Designed to smash the Mormon Church to a floor stain, it dissolved the church as a corporation, and allowed the federal government to confiscate the church's property. It was the death blow.

Crowds pack Second South during Brigham Young's 1872 trial on murder charges. The courtroom was on the upper floor of the livery stable. Utah State Historical Society.

Brigham Young was not on hand to suffer it. He died August 29, 1877, "in the gabled Lion House." The strain of directing the ordinary business of the church, coupled with the warfare in the courts, had taken its toll. On August 23 he was seized with the illness that would later prove fatal: Doctors of the day called it *cholera morbus,* but it is thought to have been appendicitis. Brigham Young likely died of a ruptured appendix.

To the end he displayed the organization that ruled his life. He had prepared strict instructions regarding his burial:

> I want my coffin made of plump 1¼-inch redwood boards, not scrimped in length, but two inches longer than I would measure, and from two to three inches wider than is commonly made for a person of my breadth and size, and deep enough

to place me on a little comfortable cotton bed with a good suitable pillow in size and quality. My body dressed in my Temple clothing and laid nicely into my coffin, and the coffin to have the appearance that if I wanted to turn a little to the right or left I should have plenty of room to do so; the lid can be made of crowning.

> At my interment I wish all my family present that can be conveniently, and the male members to wear no crepe on their hats or their coats; the females to buy no black bonnets, nor black dresses, nor black veils.

Twenty-five thousand people paid their last respects to the Lion of the Lord as he lay in state in the Salt Lake Tabernacle. An era ended for Utah in a private cemetery on 1st Avenue, a half-block northeast of the Eagle Gate.

The Lion House, ca. 1890, home of the Brigham Young family. Photo by C. R. Savage; LDS Church Archives.

Unveiling of the Brigham Young Monument in Salt Lake City in 1897. Photo by C. R. Savage; LDS Church Archives.

10

War on Polygamy

Federal Vengeance Finally Wears Down Mormon Doctrine
1877–1890

In the decade of the 1880s, Utah became industrialized and the federal government attacked Mormon polygamy with a vengeance, jailing women as well as men in its relentless crusade to crush the practice. Electricity and telephones came to the territory, railroads continued to make Utah the hub of the West, and Congress passed the Edmunds-Tucker Act, the death blow to Mormon plural marriage as a church doctrine. The territory's population in 1880, according to the census, stood at 143,963. Utah's growing pains were audible and visible.

Fort Cameron, the U.S. military post near Beaver, was closed, and its buildings sold at auction. The post, having served its primary function as a place to hold John D. Lee during the trials for his role in the Mountain Meadow massacre and in the months before his ultimate execution in 1877, was deactivated and dismantled.

Eli Murray, the territory's eleventh governor, arrived in Salt Lake City with his family in February 1880, and by the fall of the year made his presence felt with a monumental thump in the form of a report of conditions in Utah to the secretary of the interior in Washington. In essence, the governor decried the enactment of laws against polygamy without enforcing them. Murray, a Kentuckian who had joined the Union Army at the age of nineteen when the Civil War broke out,

left the service at the end of hostilities as a brigadier general. Now, as the new chief executive of Utah, he had already aroused some snickering animosity because of his reputation as the "most handsome man in Kentucky." When his appointment was announced, the *Deseret News* smirked editorially, "We trust his excellency will have something more than this [his manly good looks] to recommend him to the position of governor. *'Pretty men' are not appreciated in the west.*"

But Murray surprised the public by suggesting that existing antipolygamy laws should be either strictly enforced or repealed. With repeal, he said, officers of the United States should be recalled, non-Mormons removed from the territory, and the country turned over to the LDS Church. Murray's plea had the expected effect of provoking newspaper editorial comment. When he described Mormon polygamy as a practice punished as criminal in every part of the republic but that "flourishes unchecked in Utah," the *Deseret News* snapped peevishly: "Our marriage system does *not* exist in any other part of the United States, therefore *it cannot be punished there as criminal.* Common bigamy and 'Mormon' plural marriage, as has been repeatedly demonstrated have nothing in common. . . . The law against it was framed specially to prohibit and punish a religious ordinance, and was aimed directly and solely against The

Utah Governor Eli Murray. LDS Church Archives.

Church of Jesus Christ of Latter-day Saints, as is well known, and not denied by anyone but sophists and quibblers."

So once again Utah and its appointed officials were at loggerheads, and with each succeeding collision the federal government added another weapon to its antipolygamy arsenal. It would only be a matter of time before the battle became overwhelmingly one-sided; Utah and the Mormon Church were certain to be the losers. Until that day, however, polygamists fought desperately to ward off the inevitable.

Meanwhile, progress, though plodding, was inexorable. Salt Lake City streets, which had been lighted by oil lamps since November 1869, made the change to gas in June 1873, and in September 1880 the first electric lights blazed in the city. When hydroelectric plants went into operation in Salt Lake City, Provo, and Ogden, the Rocky Mountain Electric Light Company gave way to Utah Power & Light Company.

In the general elections that year (1880), George Q. Cannon walloped Allan G. Campbell for Utah's congressional seat, but Governor Murray refused to issue an election certificate to Cannon, a polygamist. Cannon protested and left for the nation's capital; Campbell picked up the election certificate and followed. Once in Washington, Cannon produced a declaration of results of the election, which attested that he had received the greater number of votes, and the chief clerk of Congress entered the Mormon's name as Utah's delegate. After a year of bickering and acrimonious debate in and out of Congress, the House of Representatives denied Cannon and Campbell and declared the delegate's seat vacant.

Finally, in October 1883, John T. Caine was elected to succeed Cannon and to fill his unexpired term as well as the full term for the 48th Congress. It was a position Caine would hold for the next ten years. Without a voice on the floor of Congress in the first years of the decade, Utahns could only watch as those who would crush polygamy labored to fashion legislation that would forever stifle the remaining "relic of barbarism."

From this distance in time and in light of the 1990s attitude toward "consenting adults," the venom spewed by the phenomenon of Mormon polygamy is difficult to understand. This "peculiar institution," as it was described by non-Mormons, inspired such hatred during the half-century of its official existence that it seriously occupied armies and presidents of the United States. Not all individuals viewed the matter with the biting good humor of Mark Twain, who recalled in *Roughing It*:

> Our stay in Salt Lake City amounted to only two days, and therefore we had no time to make the customary inquisition into the workings of polygamy . . . I had the will to do it. With the gushing self-sufficiency of youth I was feverish to plunge in headlong and achieve great reform here—until I saw the Mormon women.
>
> My heart was wiser than my head. It warmed toward these poor ungainly and pathetically "homely" creatures, and as I turned to hide the generous moisture in my eyes, I said, "No—the man that marries one of them has done an act of Christian charity which entitles him to the kindly

Perrigrine Sessions and his polygamous families in front of their (above) adobe house and (below) brick house. LDS Church Archives.

John Taylor, third president of the Mormon Church. LDS Church Archives.

applause of mankind, not their harsh censure—and the man that marries sixty of them has done a deed of open-handed generosity so sublime that the nations should stand uncovered in his presence and worship in silence.

The Edmunds Bill, introduced by Senator George F. Edmunds of Vermont, was an amendment to the antibigamy law of 1862, and it further defined the crime of polygamy—every person who has a husband or wife living who thereafter marries another, whether married or single, and any man who simultaneously, or on the same day, marries more than one woman . . . is guilty of polygamy. The penalty was a $500 fine and five years in prison or both. Edmunds's amendment went further. It excluded polygamists or those engaging in unlawful cohabitation from jury duty and made it sufficient cause for challenge if any juror *believed* in polygamy. Polygamists also were denied voting rights through an oath administered by registration officers and were denied the privilege of holding elected office.

As a result of the Edmunds Law, anywhere from twelve to fourteen thousand polygamous Mormons—citizens of Utah—were disenfranchised. The U.S. Supreme Court, however, in October 1884 declared such a test oath to be null and void. Mormon authorities, though, believed the real motive of this antipolygamy crusade was the political control of Utah by the "crusaders" and that polygamy was the smokescreen used to "hide the brutal villainy and outrageous hypocrisy of the whole infamous plot."

Life in Utah otherwise was as nearly routine as it could be under the circumstances. John Taylor had succeeded to the presidency of the LDS Church upon the death of Brigham Young and in 1882 had moved into a newly renovated Gardo House. Amelia Folsom Young, twenty-fifth wife of the deceased president, had lived in the mansion on South Temple and State Streets for about a year before selling her "life interest" in the structure that by now was known as the Amelia Palace. She moved to a smaller home at First South and First West. Because church authorities felt their president should have a residence befitting his position, they invested $15,000 in completing the Gardo House and furnishing it to his tastes. Taylor was not to enjoy his new digs for long because the Edmunds Act kept him moving, one step ahead of federal marshals. He and apostle Cannon decided to "visit" southern Utah.

Liberty Park was officially opened to the public in balmy May of 1882, but the winter that followed was nasty. Those who could find a thermometer on January 19, 1883, discovered the mercury at 35 below! The Denver and Rio Grande Western Railroad completed its link between Salt Lake City and Denver that March. And the notorious desperado William A. Hickman died in bed near Lander, Wyoming, on August 21.

When police captain and city marshal Andrew Burt was shot to death in downtown Salt Lake City, an angry mob hanged the perpetrator from a stable rafter at the rear of the city jail on August 25, 1883. The *Salt Lake Tribune* lamented:

> It was done under the noon day sun and in the shadow of the temple of the Saints. We do not believe that there has been a parallel to the case in history. Mobs have hung men repeatedly, but never before that we remember of have the

View of the Wasatch Mountains from Liberty Park. LDS Church Archives.

policemen who had this prisoner in charge, first beaten him into half insensibility; and then turned him over to the mob. This is not a question between Mormon and Gentile; it is one in which the good name of the city government is at stake.

Had the same thing happened in the office of the U.S. Marshal, we would demand the Marshal's instant dismissal and that of his deputies. Now, in the name of the law which was yesterday so cowardly insulted by officers sworn to uphold it, we call upon the city authorities to vindicate their claim and the claim of their people that they are a law abiding people and that they stand ready to punish unfaithfulness on the part of those in whom they repose official trust.

The territorial legislature, in an effort to escape the "repeated assaults" upon the rights of the people to local self-government, tried again to obtain statehood. Thus on December 11, 1883, Delegate Caine presented a bill for the admission of Utah as a state. It was referred to the committee on territories, which is to say it was relegated to the wastebasket.

Prosecutions under the Edmunds Law—funded by the federal government—went from a lope to a full gallop. Women alleged to be polygamous wives were hauled into court and jailed for contempt when they refused to answer "indelicate" questions "respecting sexual associations with their supposed husbands." A mass meeting of more than two thousand LDS women gathered in the Salt Lake Theater, "representing the wives, mothers, sisters and daughters of the whole territory of Utah," protested this course of action in the administration of antipolygamy laws.

About the same time, a man named Edward M. Dalton was arrested in Parowan on charges of unlawful cohabitation. He escaped the deputy marshal who arrested him and some months later returned to his Parowan home. The deputy and a partner spotted Dalton driving livestock through town, yelled "Halt!" and then shot and mortally wounded him. The shooting was deemed justifiable and the deputy was acquitted of any wrongdoing.

It was this temper of the crusade to exorcise polygamy that convinced John Taylor and George

$800 REWARD!

JOHN TAYLOR.   GEORGE Q. CANNON.

To be Paid for the Arrest of John Taylor
and George Q. Cannon.

The above Reward will be paid for the delivery to me, or
for information that will lead to the arrest of

JOHN TAYLOR,

President of the Mormon Church, and

George Q. Cannon,

His Counselor; or

$500 will be paid for Cannon alone, and
$300 for Taylor.

All Conferences or Letters kept strictly secret.

S. H. GILSON,
22 and 23 Wasatch Building, Salt Lake City.

Salt Lake City, Jan. 31, 1887.

A wanted poster for the arrest of John Taylor and
George Q. Cannon. *Salt Lake Tribune* Centennial
Archives.

Q. Cannon that discretion was the better part of
valor. Taylor, his counselors, and several apostles
had only recently returned from an extended trip
to Mormon settlements in Arizona and southern
Utah when, speaking to an audience in the Salt
Lake Tabernacle, he related the "outrages" that
were being visited upon church members. He
asked, "Would you resent these outrages and break
the heads of men engaged in them, and spill their
blood? No, avoid them as much as you can. . . .
Would you fight them? No, I would take care of
myself as best I can, and I would advise my
brethren to do the same."

With that, Taylor, Cannon, and others "went
into retirement." They went underground. For all
intents and purposes, they disappeared from public view, surfacing only rarely for a secret meeting
with trusted individuals and directing the affairs of
the LDS Church by general epistles to the membership. It was humiliating to run and be accused

of deserting their flocks at a crucial time, but
faced with a choice of fleeing or the alternative–
imprisonment–they scrammed. So it went until
U.S. Marshal E. A. Ireland posted a $500 reward
for the arrest of Cannon and a lesser amount for
the aging Taylor, presumably to belittle the church
leader's importance.

Many Mormons went into exile, some to
Canada and others to Mexico, a few to Hawaii.
LDS missionaries around the world were jailed,
beaten, even murdered. Ultimately there were
more than a thousand convictions of polygamous
Mormons for bigamy, polygamy, unlawful cohabitation, adultery, and incest. Since "cohabs" frequently were indicted on two or more counts or
were imprisoned more than once, the actual number of Mormon men convicted was in the neighborhood of nine hundred.

Federal officials had devised a system of
indictment for separate offenses, so sentences could
be "pyramided" even to life imprisonment. Cannon
was singled out for special attention because it was
widely believed he was actually in charge; Taylor at
seventy-eight was conceded to be slowing down.
Cannon was headed for Mexico when he was
nabbed by a sheriff at Humboldt railroad station in
Nevada. The lawman had been tipped that Cannon
was en route to San Francisco to catch a steamer
south. The fugitive was returned under arrest to
Salt Lake City, where he subsequently pleaded
guilty and was fined and sentenced to a term in the
territorial prison. There Cannon, with a dozen fellow polygamists, sat for one of the most famous
group photographs in Mormon history–the celebrated "prison stripes" portrait.

While the infighting continued to rage
between local authorities who were Mormons and
Utah federal officials who were non-Mormons,
some important events occurred that would have a
profound influence on the territory's future. The
first was a setback for the anti-Mormons. Governor
Murray, who had been in the forefront of maneuvering to neuter Mormon influence, vetoed the
general territorial appropriations bill in 1886. It virtually blocked the administration of government in
Utah in all departments. Four days later, President
Grover Cleveland, now convinced that Murray
was unworthy of confidence, fired the governor. A
number of other federal officials joined the ranks of
the unemployed in ensuing months. Murray's

Polygamists in prison, ca. 1889. George Q. Cannon is the white-bearded man sitting at center. Photo by C. R. Savage; LDS Church Archives.

replacement was Caleb Walton West of Kentucky. The new governor offered the forty-nine Mormon elders in prison under the Edmunds Law an amnesty of sorts if they would agree to refrain from "unlawfully cohabiting" in the future. The answer was a resounding refusal. West withdrew with a sour opinion of Mormon polygamists.

The second important event was the death of President John Taylor, exhausted from two and a half years in "retirement," living on the run. Taylor died in Kaysville, Davis County, July 25, 1887. His successor was Wilford Woodruff.

The antipolygamy crusade was now entering its final, feverish venal stages. In February 1887 the Edmunds-Tucker Act was passed; it became law March 3. The law

- —disincorporated the LDS Church and, by reviving a property limit of $50,000 for a religious organization, initiated forfeiture proceedings against the church, resulting in confiscation of most of its property;
- —abolished female suffrage;

- —dismantled the Perpetual Emigration Fund Company (the system by which the church was able to bring foreign converts to Utah);
- —abolished the Nauvoo Legion; and
- —required a test oath for all citizens desiring to vote, hold elective office, or serve on juries.

Property amounting to more than $800,000 was placed in the hands of a receiver pending an appeal to the U.S. Supreme Court.

The Mormon Church was all but bankrupt as it entered the decade of the 1890s. Drastic action was necessary to save what was left. Woodruff, since his succession to the church presidency, was also on the run and in hiding to avoid prosecution for polygamy. But on September 25, 1890, he took the only option open and published in the *Deseret News* his manifesto, or "Official Declaration," against new polygamy. Woodruff's statement, in essence, explained that

Inasmuch as laws have been enacted by Congress forbidding plural marriage, which laws have been

Wilford Woodruff, ca. 1888, the fourth Mormon president, who issued a manifesto advising church members to obey laws against polygamy. LDS Church Archives.

pronounced constitutional by the court of last resort, I hereby declare my intention to submit to those laws, and to use my influence with the members of the church over which I preside to have them do likewise.

. . . And I now publicly declare that my advice to the Latter-day Saints is to refrain from contracting any marriage forbidden by the law of the land.

The manifesto was ratified by the church membership on October 6, 1890, and Mormons officially abandoned plural marriage as an essential church practice. It did not go down easily with many of the faithful, who asked with some bitterness, why? Why was it not done sooner and the suffering of past years avoided? The answer came from George Q. Cannon on October 18, 1890: "We have waited for the Lord to move in the matter."

The way was now open to deal for statehood and self-rule.

11

Statehood at Last

Amid Jubilation and Bunting
Utah Is Dubbed the Forty-Fifth State of the Union
1890–1897

In the decade preceding the turn of the century, Utah and its citizens experienced an easing of the suffocating pressure applied by the federal government in its crusade to smash Mormon plural marriage. That relaxation was a consequence of the Wilford Woodruff Manifesto discouraging the practice of polygamy in the LDS Church. The doctrine did not go gently, but it did go. It was a time in which President Benjamin Harrison also would issue a manifesto—his offered amnesty to polygamists. That same year, 1893, members of the Church of Jesus Christ of Latter-day Saints dedicated their Salt Lake Temple forty years after construction of the edifice began in Great Salt Lake City. And, of course, it was the decade in which Utah's dream came true and its half-century struggle for statehood became reality.

Meanwhile, the territory was progressing in other directions as well. Public-school funding came wholly from local taxes until 1874, a scant revenue derived from taxing citizens who had little cash. In some cases, the taxes were paid in produce or livestock, and that did not permit building schoolhouses. There were still no high schools in Utah as late as 1884, but a comprehensive school law passed in 1890 by the legislature made all common schools free.

Sir Richard Burton, during his visit to Utah in 1860, had some colorfully cogent observations on Mormon education, which, he concluded, was "of course, peculiar." The famous adventurer and linguist reflected that Utah's climate "predisposes indolence." Mormon youngsters, he allowed, had special qualities:

> At 15, a boy can use a whip, an axe or a hoe—he does not like the plow—to perfection. He sits a bare-backed horse like a centaur, handles his bowie-knife skillfully, never misses a mark with his revolver and can probably dispose of half a bottle of whiskey. It is not an education I would commend to the generous youth of Paris and London, but it is admirably fitted to the exigencies of the [Utah] situation.
>
> Mormons have discovered, or rather have been taught by their necessities as a working population in a [territory] barely 12 years old, that the time of school drudgery may profitably be abridged. A boy, they say, will learn all that his memory can carry during three hours of book work and the rest had far better be spent in air, exercise and handicraft.

Burton's views notwithstanding, higher education strengthened its position during the decade. The University of Deseret, revived in 1867, struggled through to 1892, when its name was changed to the University of Utah, and it soon included schools of law, medicine, education, and mining. Brigham Young Academy had

Salt Lake City, looking southwest from Prospect Hill, ca. 1888. Photo by C. R. Savage; LDS Church Archives.

been established in Provo in 1875 but would have to wait until 1903 to become Brigham Young University. The Presbyterian Church founded Salt Lake Collegiate Institute in 1875 (later to become Westminster College), while the Catholics established St. Mary's Academy; and Utah Agriculture College was founded in Logan in 1888 as a product of a federal land grant act. As for mission schools, the Presbyterian Church established forty-nine in the territory, the Methodists forty-six, the Congregationalists thirty-eight, and the Baptists thirteen.

Utah's population reached 210,779 by the 1890 census, and as the territory came in closer harmony with the national scene, 1891 saw Republican and Democratic Parties organized in Utah, while the Mormon People's Party, which had so staunchly fought the Liberals, was dissolved. The Liberal Party would disband in 1893.

Once President Harrison had officially pardoned polygamists, the way was clear to press again for self-rule—work was begun on Utah's seventh attempt at admission into the Union. Governor Caleb West, in his annual report to the secretary of interior for 1893, now strongly urged passage of an enabling act allowing Utahns to for-

mulate a constitution; he also recommended the return of LDS Church property, which the Edmunds-Tucker Law had escheated. "There is left, neither reason nor excuse, in my judgment for taking from the Mormon Church and people their property, and it ought to be restored to them," the governor said. West's use of the word "escheated" was, in the eyes of many citizens, merely an available legal term to describe the act of outright confiscation. Nevertheless, the return of nearly a half-million dollars in personal property was more than welcome to an almost-bankrupt Mormon populace.

The year 1894 saw Utah's legislature pass a law mandating an eight-hour working day in the territory. And in March 1895, the 107 members of Utah's constitutional convention convened in the civil courtroom of the new Salt Lake City-County Building at Fourth South and State Streets. It was a diverse group indeed, those 107 delegates. Their task was arduous, especially since they were faced with addressing sensitive issues such as separation of church and state—a particularly prickly question in Utah—and woman suffrage. If nothing else, the delegates brought a wide range of experience to the job at hand. Several had served in previous

Salt Lake City, southeast view. Photo by C. R. Savage. LDS Church Archives.

constitutional conventions and were familiar with the infighting and political maneuvering that marked such events. The convention was steeped in talent. There were former legislators, mayors, county selectmen, county attorneys, probate judges, justices of the peace, lawyers, businessmen, merchants, manufacturers, and civic leaders by the score. Many had been active in the Mormon People's Party and the Liberal Party.

Utah's then twenty-seven counties all had a voice, and a sharp eye was peeled for potential problems such as water rights, the school system, a realistic homestead law, and collateral headaches. Blurred by a century of hindsight, the perspective of Article I, Section 4, a 134-word guarantee of religious liberty stricter than that found in the First Amendment to the U.S. Constitution, became controversial in the 1990s, when it was argued the 1895 delegates overdrew the constitutional line between church and state. (In 1992, the paragraph was targeted for change in a failed effort by those who supported prayer in public meetings.) Yet it was framed by men who represented the extreme and mainstream factions of nineteenth-century society in Utah.

A unique situation existed in 1895 to ensure a less turbulent atmosphere for convention delegates. Recognizing that the Woodruff Manifesto indeed met conditions for admission to the Union, non-Mormons and their supportive newspaper voice, the *Salt Lake Tribune*, both opponents of polygamy and ecclesiastical control of politics, reached a delicate armistice with the LDS Church

and came out for statehood. In this way, the national press was robbed of fodder to fuel antagonism over Utah's latest try at self-rule.

With the adjournment of the convention on May 8, 1895, after sixty-six days of vigorous debate and compromise, preparations were made for election of state officers, and all the other requirements being met, President Grover Cleveland signed the proclamation declaring the admission of Utah into the Union on an equal footing with the original states "is now an accomplished fact!" The date was Saturday, January 4, 1896.

Salt Lake City exploded in celebration: cannons, bells, whistles, and general jubilation. Precisely at 9:13 A.M., the superintendent of Western Union Telegraph Company had rushed frantically from his Main Street office brandishing a double-barrel shotgun, the contents of which he discharged skyward in two resounding reports. A small boy, witnessing the unusual scene from a distance, dove for cover, assuming a holdup was in progress. Meanwhile, two blocks away, at 133 South West Temple, Benjamin Midgely was raising the first forty-five-star American flag over the *Salt Lake Tribune* building. Utah was a state in the Union at last!

As the news spread through the city, merchants began decorating their stores and buildings with national emblems, bunting, and flags. According to the *Deseret News*, George M. Scott and Cunningham & Company had installed temporary but effective steam whistles outside their respective

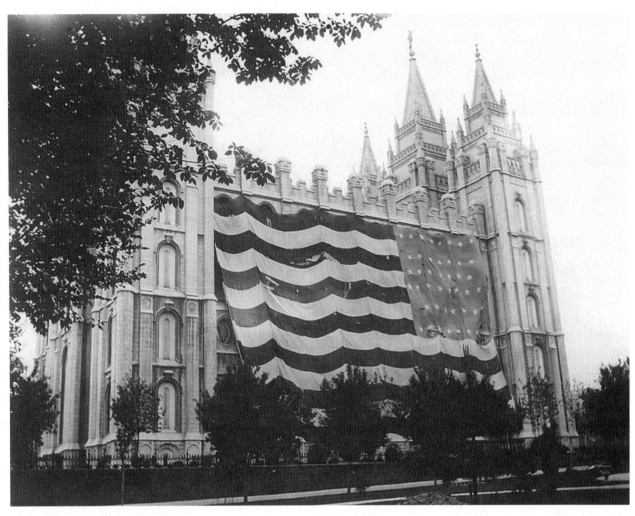

In haste to salute Utah's admission to the Union, workers reversed the flag between the east and west towers of the Salt Lake City LDS Temple. University of Utah Marriott Library.

businesses and blared their approbation. Workers hastily strung the Stars and Stripes between the east and west towers of the Salt Lake LDS Temple. And just before noon, a Utah National Guard artillery battery assembled at the capitol and fired a salute of twenty-one guns followed by ringing bells and hooting steam whistles; a half-dozen "bombs" boomed on a downtown street corner and rattled windows for half a block. All this amid enthusiastic cheering from the gathering throng of Utah celebrators. The *Deseret News* also noted that one Bill Bingley and his "shotgun brigade" kept things popping with repeated volleys opposite Browning Bros. store, while a youngster nearby joined with a vigorous toot on his tin horn.

On inaugural day, the following Monday, citizens crowded the Salt Lake Tabernacle for ceremonies that would invest the new state with its first slate of elected officers. Inside, the tabernacle dome was festooned with an American flag measuring 132 feet by 78 feet and made from 1,296 yards of bunting so weighty it took eight men to carry it. Through the cutout shape of the forty-fifth star, five 32-candlepower electric lights beamed downward on the audience.

The statehood proclamation was read by Joseph L. Rawlins, the territorial delegate who maneuvered the enabling act through Congress. Chief Justice Charles S. Zane administered the oath to the state officials, headed by Heber M. Wells, the new governor. Wells was the son of Daniel H. Wells, third mayor of Great Salt Lake City and commander of the Nauvoo Legion during the Utah War.

As historian Richard D. Poll remarked, Utah already had a larger population than five of her sister states; of its residents, eight of ten were

The east side of East Temple (Main Street) in Salt Lake City, ca. 1900. Photo by C. R. Savage; LDS Church Archives.

American born and nine of ten were Mormons. "Apart from approximately 3,000 Indians, mostly on reservations, the 571 Negroes and 768 Chinese counted in the 1895 territorial census were the largest racial minorities." Few of the new state's residents lived in cities, though the fifty thousand populating the capital enjoyed many of life's urban amenities. Power and telephone lines prevailed in the downtown area; the city boasted a university and eight academies, a limited distribution of natural and manufactured gas, sixty-eight miles of street railway, three daily newspapers, three theaters and two businessmen's clubs, a recently completed gravity sewage system with seven miles of mains, and the three-year-old resort Saltair, perched on piles in Great Salt Lake, further evidence of progress.

But as progress moved from the heart of town, it marched on unpaved streets. As Poll pointed out,

> Twenty-seven years as a railroad center had brought Ogden 15,000 inhabitants, 10 miles of street railway, two academies, one of the first

hydro-electric projects in the United States, and some of the most eventful Saturday nights to be found outside the mining camps.

Provo with only 400 students in its Brigham Young Academy and the Geneva steel plant not even dreamed of, was a quiet county seat with 6,000 people; its street railway was only six miles long, but it was steam-powered. Logan, with 5,000 inhabitants, was beginning to orient its life around its eight-year-old land-grant college.

As for the rest, the towns of Utah were either unpaved and unexciting farming centers, whose chief buildings revealed the industriousness and occasionally the artistic imagination of the pioneers, or unpaved and uninhabited mining camps, which might be gone tomorrow but were notoriously here today.

As Utah moved forward, the Uinta Forest Preserve, the first national forest in the state, was established in 1897, and the legislature created the Utah Art Institute to sponsor fine arts. The horizons for this spanking new forty-fifth state were bright and beckoning as the new century dawned.

The original Salt Palace in Salt Lake City. Photo by C. R. Savage; LDS Church Archives.

Edmund family log cabin. Photo by George Edward Anderson. Utah State Historical Society.

R. Woodward, Springville, Utah, 1900. Photo by George
Edward Anderson. Utah State Historical Society.

12

A New Century

From Statehood to Host for the 2002 Winter Olympics

Utah's entry into the new century was greeted by a colossal roar. A cataclysmic explosion ripped through a coal mine at Scofield, Carbon County, killing two hundred workers in the most devastating mine disaster to that time in U.S. history. A dynamite blast that ignited dense coal dust throughout Winter Quarters No. 4 was blamed for the calamity. It was a horrible debut to the 1900s, and residents of the fledgling state could only pray the catastrophe was not a howl of dire portent.

With federal confiscation of property no longer a threat to the Church of Jesus Christ of Latter-day Saints because of Wilford Woodruff's manifesto renouncing polygamy as a doctrine, the state's economy began to pick up. Utah already could boast of a score of millionaires by 1902, most of whom amassed their fortunes through mining ventures. Among the monied could be found the names of Daniel C. Jackling, Thomas Kearns, Samuel Newhouse, Jesse Knight, David Eccles, William Jennings, Joseph Walker, S. H. Auerbach, A. W. McCune, and Elizabeth Bonnemort.

Reed Smoot was elected to the U.S. Senate but immediately became snarled in a four-year struggle to gain his seat. His opponents contended that being a Mormon apostle would conflict with his duty to defend the Constitution as a senator. Smoot ultimately won the fight and went on to serve until 1932, becoming dean of the Senate.

The Lucin Cutoff was completed across the Great Salt Lake in 1903, and three natural bridges

Reed Smoot, Mormon apostle and United States senator from Utah. LDS Church Archives.

Rainbow Bridge, 1947. Utah State Historical Society.

"discovered" in southern Utah that year were set aside in 1908 as Natural Bridges National Monument.

The American Party, a new anti-Mormon political organization, carried the Salt Lake City municipal election in 1905 and 1907 but was trounced in 1911 and disappeared from the political scene.

Mining burgeoned with the exploitation of low-grade copper deposits in Bingham Canyon and by 1917 produced ore valued at more than $100 million. The first oil wells were discovered at Virgin in 1907. The Western Pacific Railroad was completed between Salt Lake City and San Francisco the following year, and important dinosaur discoveries near Jensen, Uintah County, were declared a national monument in 1915 and enlarged in 1938.

More and more of Utah's scenic wonders came to light in these growth years of statehood, and the care and maintenance of these resources became a prime concern. In 1909, Nashja Begay, a

Paiute, led an expedition to Rainbow Bridge, a work of nature so astonishing it was declared a national monument before a year had passed.

Recognizing that water has always been the lifeblood of Utah, historians have noted that Elias Adams may have been the first Utahn to realize the value of water storage. He built a dam some three miles east of Layton in 1852 and filled it with water from Adams Canyon. Some sixty years later, Strawberry Reservoir, Utah's first large reclamation project, was completed, allowing water to be diverted from the Colorado River to the Great Basin.

Beginning in 1915, Utah's administration took offices in the new State Capitol in Salt Lake City. Unfortunately, it was coincidental to the unwelcome glare of international notoriety brought on by the impending execution of Joseph Hillstrom, a Swedish immigrant and labor organizer for the Industrial Workers of the World (IWW). Hillstrom, a balladeer and songwriter, also was known as Joe Hill. He was convicted of killing a Salt Lake grocer and his teenage son in a January 1914 robbery. The IWW claimed Hill was framed and began an international outcry that involved the Swedish consul and President Woodrow Wilson in unsuccessful efforts to commute Hill's death sentence; he died before a firing squad on November 19, 1915.

By 1919, passage of the Volstead Act blanketed the nation with prohibition, and a new word, *bootlegging*, was introduced into the language. Ironically, Utah, which had extended prohibition throughout the state as early as 1917, cast the deciding vote in 1933 to repeal the act, recognizing it to be too unpopular, too expensive, and too unenforceable to continue.

As it completed its first quarter of the new century as a full-fledged state, Utah added newly discovered scenic wonders to its array of tourist attractions: Arches was declared a national monument, as was Hovenweep Prehistoric Indian Ruins. Bryce Canyon, Timpanogos Cave, Cedar Breaks, and Capitol Reef soon followed.

An era of land-speed records began on the Bonneville Salt Flats in the mid-1920s with Ab Jenkins setting twenty-four-hour endurance marks and with a clutch of speed records established by names such as Sir Malcolm Campbell, George Eyston, John Cobb, Tommy Thompson, Athol Graham, Craig Breedlove, Art Arfons, Gary Gabelich, and Stan Barrett. These daredevils etched not only their own names in the history books, but that of Bonneville's famous speedway as well.

KSL radio began broadcasting in 1921. In the late 1920s, Utah native Philo Farnsworth was working on a scientific invention that would earn him the title of the father of television.

William Posey, chief of a small tribe of Paiutes that roamed southeastern Utah at the turn of the century, was mortally wounded in 1923 by a posse in the Comb Wash region of San Juan County. Old Posey was, by some accounts, the last "hostile" Indian killed in the United States.

Heavy industry came in 1926 when Columbia Steel Corporation first operated its blast furnace at the new plant in Ironton, Utah County. Smelting, the state's single most important industry, geared for increased production in the years immediately preceding the start of World War II. By 1940, construction was under way on Wendover Air Base

and Hill Field, which in time would become Hill Air Force Base, Utah's largest employer. Utah General Depot and Remington Small Arms plant construction soon followed. In the months after the Japanese attack on Pearl Harbor, work was begun on Kearns Army Base, Dugway Proving Ground, Tooele Ordnance Depot, Deseret Chemical Depot, Bushnell General Hospital (which would in postwar Utah become the Intermountain Indian School), Clearfield Naval Supply Depot, Topaz War Location Center, and the Geneva Steel Works (later to be purchased by U.S. Steel Corporation). Fort Douglas was named headquarters for the Ninth Service Command, and Utah Oil Refinery expanded to meet the war effort. In succeeding years, defense industries burgeoned with the addition of Thiokol and Hercules and reclamation projects including Glen Canyon, Flaming Gorge, and the Central Utah Water projects.

In this time, many GIs and war workers became enamored of the state as a place to live and rear families. They stayed on after Japan's surrender, and a majority of these new residents located in Tooele County and along the Wasatch Front, boosting Utah's population more than 138,000 during this period. It was a tremendous time for home builders and subdivisions. It also was the dawn of the atomic age, and heavy emphasis was placed on the development of nuclear energy; that in turn saw the astonishing uranium boom in southern Utah, the growth of uranium mining in the region, and the attendant frenzy in Salt Lake City money markets over penny uranium stocks. The greater Aneth Oil field was discovered in 1956, and mineral extraction from the brines of the Great Salt Lake brought a large new industrial profile to the lake.

With the election of General Dwight D. Eisenhower as president of the United States, two Utahns were appointed to high office in the federal government. Ivy Baker Priest was named U.S. treasurer and Ezra Taft Benson was named secretary of agriculture. Both appointees served from 1953 to 1961.

And on the darker side, two airliners collided in flight over the Grand Canyon, killing 128 passengers and crew in 1956. For its newspaper coverage under the pressure of deadline, the *Salt Lake Tribune* won a Pulitzer Prize. Six years later, the *Deseret News* won a similar award for its coverage of the murder of Jeanette Sullivan, 41, and the kidnapping of her daughter, Denise, 15, at Dead Horse Point.

Utah came into its own as a travel hub when its municipal air terminal became the Salt Lake City International Airport in 1968. And ironically, Utah, known as the crossroads of the West with the completion at Promontory Summit of the first transcontinental railroad in May 1869, experienced a steady decline in rail passenger service because of automobiles and airlines. Congress's creation of Amtrak in 1970 was of little help, and by the late 1990s passenger railroading in Utah, as well as the nation, seemed headed for extinction.

Medicine and medical research began making great strides in Utah in the 1960s. Willem J. Kolff, who developed the first artificial kidney using parts of a washing machine and sausage skins in his native Holland in 1944, while it was under German occupation, immigrated to the United States after the war and joined the University of Utah faculty in 1967. He brought with him research on an artificial heart. At the university, Kolff surrounded himself with students and colleagues who shared his interest in artificial organs, including Robert Jarvik and William DeVries, who were instrumental in the first permanent human implant of an artificial heart in Barney Clark at University Hospital December 2, 1982. Kolff at 84 is still actively engaged in artificial-organ research and has received major awards in his field. He was named one of the "100 Most Important Americans of the 20th Century" by *Life* magazine.

Utah's laboratory of dreams in the 1990s did produce a nightmare called cold fusion. It bubbled into a tempest in a test tube. The latest frontier being blazed in medical science is genetics research at the University of Utah. Spurred in part by the LDS preoccupation with genealogy, it is growing like the proverbial Mormon family.

Not to be outdone by the great strides being made in the sciences and industry in Utah, the state's cultural scene enjoyed a revitalization with the construction of a new arts complex in 1979 that included a new Symphony Hall (renamed after famed Utah conductor Maurice Abravanel), the Salt Lake Art Center, the Salt Palace, and Capitol Theatre. Committed first and foremost to acoustic excellence, ground was broken for the concert hall in March 1977, a decade to the day after a similar ceremony launched the initial Salt Palace construction project on West Temple between First and Second South. Restored, the Capitol Theatre on Second South was completed and opened in October 1978, and the art museum occupied by the Salt Lake Art Center opened in May 1979.

It wasn't art in 1957 when West Jordan's Gene Fullmer slugged his way to the middleweight championship of the world, but the tenacious mink rancher who had classic bouts with Sugar Ray Robinson and Carmen Basilio is the only Utahn in the International Boxing Hall of Fame.

The 1970s was the dawn of discovery for major sports in Utah. It was a time of evolution for professional basketball from the American Basketball Association's Utah Stars (1970–75) to the National Basketball Association's Utah Jazz (1979–). Sam Battistone and Larry Hatfield transferred the New Orleans Jazz to Salt Lake City in 1979, largely due to the success Denver's Bill Daniels experienced with the Utah Stars, who won the ABA championship in 1971. But Battistone and Hatfield sold the franchise to Salt Lake automobile dealer Larry Miller, whose enthusiasm as a fan and team owner led him to construct the $66 million Delta Center (19,900 capacity) at 301 South West Temple as an alternative to the Salt Palace, which seated only 12,000. In 1992, two members of the Utah Jazz–Karl Malone and John Stockton–were named to the U.S. basketball squad competing in the Olympic Games. The team went on to win the gold medal. Malone and Stockton were named to the team again for the 1996 games in Atlanta.

Dan Meyer brought professional ice hockey to Utah with the Salt Lake Golden Eagles of the Western Hockey League. The team changed hands when the eccentric Charlie Finley, owner of the Oakland A's baseball team, bought the Golden Eagles. He sold them to Utahns Art Teece and Thayne Acord. Larry Miller eventually bought the team and sold the twenty-five-year-old franchise to Detroit interests in 1994. The professional game returned in 1995 when Denver businessman David Elmore brought in the Utah Grizzlies on the promise of a $35 million West Valley arena of their own. During its rather shaky quarter-century career, ice hockey brought five championships to Utah–1975, 1980, 1981, 1987, and 1988.

On the other side of town and a sporting world away, baseball claimed its place in the hearts of Utah fans, a love affair itself almost a century old, harking to the days in 1879 when the city would close its doors to watch its Deserets thump the visiting San Francisco Athletics 22 to 15, and cheer the losers for committing "only 12 errors." Triple A baseball was first played at Community Park on Ninth South and West Temple in Salt Lake City; then Derks Field (named for *Salt Lake Tribune* sports editor John C. Derks) at Thirteenth South and West Temple would host teams known as the Bees, the Padres, and the Gulls. In 1987, the national spotlight turned on a Pioneer League rookie team known as the Salt Lake Trappers, who established an all-time minor-league record by winning twenty-nine consecutive games in one season. Derks gave way to Franklin Quest Field, a city-funded $20 million facility housing the Triple A Salt Lake Buzz, baseball's refugee from Portland, owned by Joe Buzas. In 1994, the team's first year, Utah fans set a Pacific Coast League attendance record of 715,000.

Recognition of Utah's Catholic bicentennial was marked by the largest liturgical service in the state's history, a solemn Mass celebrated by Bishop Joseph Lennox Federal in the Salt Palace on September 26, 1976, and attended by more than thirteen thousand faithful. It commemorated the advent of the 1776 Dominguez-Escalante expedition from Santa Fe into what is now Utah.

On June 9, 1978, the LDS Church struck down a 148-year-old policy excluding blacks from its priesthood, the result of a "revelation from God." A letter to church leaders from President Spencer W. Kimball and his two counselors, N. Eldon Tanner and Marion G. Romney, noted that for some time members of the church had been expecting such an announcement and that it had come after many hours of supplication for divine guidance to just that effect. Accordingly, "all worthy male members of the church may be ordained to the priesthood without regard for race or color."

As Utah grappled with growing pains, a more sinister element of its history could not be ignored. The bad men of this century were discovering new ways to horrify and outrage society. In 1976, Gary Mark Gilmore, a troubled, self-destructive parole felon with thirteen years in reform schools and prisons under his belt, journeyed to Provo to find himself. In so doing, he robbed and killed two people and was sentenced to die under a restored death-penalty law. Thirty-six-year-old Gilmore challenged Utah to make good its threats to put him to death: "Firing squad," said he, "I did it and I deserve to die. Kill me if you have the guts . . . or let me go!" And thus began a bizarre legal battle waged by capital-punishment opponents to save Gilmore from himself, in spite of himself. On January 17, 1977, little more than nine months from the day he was paroled from Marion, Illinois, a firing squad at Utah State Prison exacted the full measure of the law from Gilmore, the first to be executed in a decade. The aftershock was great. Books were written, movies made, and strident voices cried, "Murder, most foul." After a few months, the furor spent itself.

While the Gilmore charade was playing out for the nation, a monster was loose. A psychopath named Theodore Robert Bundy was murdering women and girls in a homicidal odyssey across the United States. The handsome one-time law student is believed to have assaulted, raped, and killed at least thirty-six victims in Washington, Colorado, Utah, and Florida before he was caught. His arrest in Granger, Utah, on a traffic violation ultimately led to charges of attempted kidnapping, and authorities began to peel away the layers of his depraved forays. (He confessed to killing eight Utah women, but none of the bodies were ever found.) In succeeding months, he was jailed in Colorado and escaped, finally to be captured in Florida after a savage spree in which two college women and a twelve-year-old child were killed. Bundy, after a sensational court trial, was sentenced and executed in Florida's electric chair on January 24, 1989, ten years after his conviction.

And there was the owlish Mark W. Hofmann, returned Mormon missionary and rare-book and manuscript dealer, who killed two people with homemade bombs to cover his tracks in a document scam. He mishandled a third bomb and almost killed himself. His nefarious schemes involved rare books and manuscripts, items of historical significance to the LDS Church. Hofmann flummoxed document experts, the Federal Bureau of Investigation, the highest Mormon authorities, scholars, businessmen, and historians before he was unmasked as a forger, thief, confidence man extraordinaire, and killer. His arrest, trial, and last-minute plea bargain made international headlines. The baby-faced criminal forever tainted the field of historical documents with his deceits. He currently is serving a life sentence at Utah State Prison for the two bomb murders.

A string of unusually wet years attributed to the weather phenomenon known as El Niño triggered widespread flooding and earthflows in Utah in the mid-1980s. The wet spell also caused the Great Salt Lake to rise to a modern historic high of 4,211.85 feet above sea level. The high water submerged the evaporation ponds of two mineral-extraction companies, forced Southern Pacific and Union Pacific railroads to raise and reinforce their tracks, and threatened to spill over Interstates 80 and 15. Utah spent $60 million to build giant pumps to transport excess waters to the barren west desert. The pumps started operating in 1986, just about the time the weather reversed itself and a drought lowered the lake level significantly on its own.

It was also in 1986 that I-80 was completed in Utah and four years later the final segment of I-15 linked the state to the massive transportation network that promised swift and unimpeded travel from coast to coast and border to border. A massive rebuild of I-15 through Salt Lake County began in the mid-1990s with hopes of being ready for the 2002 Olympics in Utah.

In the 1980s and 1990s, Utah's business profile began a sharp turn upward as a computer-friendly state with a multibillion-dollar future when it became home to such electronic heavyweights as Evans & Sutherland, WordPerfect, Novell, Iomega, Megahertz, and Micron Technology.

Then in 1995, Salt Lake City—after two previous unsuccessful efforts—was awarded the International Olympic Committee bid to be host of the 2002 winter games. Thus Utah, after struggling so long and so hard to enter the twentieth century as forty-fifth state in the Union, will greet the next century playing host to the world for the XX Winter Olympiad.

Sketches

BRIGHAM YOUNG'S FAVORITE WIFE

AS FORCEFUL AND DOMINANT A FIGURE AS WAS Brigham Young, when it came to marriage he was as vulnerable as the next man. The story goes that some husbands are forever henpecked; others are assuredly lords of the manor; Brigham, it seems, was some of both.

As an exponent of polygamy, the Mormon prophet had more to answer to than most men. The quantity and quality of the Mmes. Young had made a handsome and lucrative career for professional wits of the period like Artemus Ward and Mark Twain. Ward once remarked in a lecture, "I undertook to count the longstockings, on the clothesline in [Brigham's] backyard one day, and I used up the multiplication table in less than a half an hour." After his 1864 visit to Utah, Ward said, "I saw his mother-in-law while I was there. I can't exactly tell you how many there is of her—but it's a good deal. It strikes me that one mother-in-law is about enough to have in a family—unless you're very fond of excitement."

The precise number of Brigham's wives remains a matter of debate for some scholars, but insofar as the church record is recoverable, he is credited with twenty-seven spouses and fifty-six children. (One popular anecdote of the day held that a geography teacher asked her class to name the principal means of transportation in Utah. A boy answered, "Baby carriages.")

Amelia Folsom was wife no. 25 and had the reputation of being his true love, much to the chagrin and mortification of the youthful Ann Eliza Webb Dee Young, no. 27 on the list. When Amelia became part of the Young family in January 1863, she did not immediately move in with her sister-wives. In the only interview she ever granted a journalist, she told *Salt Lake Tribune* reporter

Eugene Traughber that she remained at home for three weeks, after which she "took up residence at the Lion House. His wives and children all lived there, and each wife, including myself, had her separate room. At that time, there were 75 of us in the family, including the hired help." Amelia also dropped Harriet as her first name, since there were two other Harriets wed to the church leader.

In his 1894 copyrighted story, Traughber told how he found "the former queen of Mormon society" in the "Junior Gardo," a handsome and comfortable two-story house at 6 South First West street in Salt Lake City. Armed with a letter of introduction from Apostle George Q. Cannon, the

Amelia Folsom Young, plural wife of Brigham Young. Utah State Historical Society.

newspaperman called on a cold winter day and was granted an audience. "An interview is almost as difficult to obtain from Mrs. Amelia Young as from the President of the United States, as she is daily besieged by curious tourists, both in person and by letter, and when admitted these morbid curiosity-seekers always subject their hostess to humiliating and often insulting questions and comments." Traughber was careful not to make that mistake in framing his questions.

He described Amelia as "tall and symmetrical of form, dignified and graceful of manner, and a brilliant conversationalist. The silvery locks which tell of the fifty and five years of her eventful life, are mingled with the threads of gold, reminiscent of the beauty of former years, and the large blue eyes have lost nothing of their fire and expressiveness." It was easy for him to believe she had been the most popular of Brigham Young's wives, he said.

Brigham was in the habit of meeting incoming parties of pilgrims, Traughber said, and in October 1860 when the Folsoms reached the outskirts of the city in a company of Mormon immigrants, the church president and his first counselor, Heber C. Kimball, came out in a carriage to welcome them. "Amelia Folsom was then 22 years of age, and in full bloom of her beauty, while Brigham was 59," Traughber wrote. "Beautiful women were not plentiful in this then desert valley, the number of men greatly predominating in the small settlements." It seems, the newspaperman continued, to have been a well-established case of love at first sight.

If other writers are to be believed, Traughber was guilty of understatement. M. R. Werner, a Brigham Young biographer, insists the church leader was lovesick: "Amelia could play the piano, and she could sing *Fair Bingen on the Rhine*. He was captivated by both her appearance and by her accomplishments; none of his other wives was so tall, so handsome, and so refined, and none of his other wives could sing *Fair Bingen on the Rhine*." Then there was Fanny Stenhouse, an English convert who came to Utah in 1857 with her Mormon husband, newspaperman T. B. H. Stenhouse. In her unfriendly book, *Tell It All*, she writes that she was personally acquainted with nineteen of Brigham's wives and well remembered Amelia's arrival in Zion. Her opinion of their romance? "One thing is very certain—he was as crazy over

Ann Eliza Webb Young, plural wife of Brigham Young. Utah State Historical Society.

her as a silly boy over his first love, much to the disgust of his more sober brethren, who felt rather ashamed of the folly of their leader."

Amelia's version is less colorful. The courtship, she said, began immediately after her arrival in Great Salt Lake Valley, and it lasted for two years, until August 1862, "when we were engaged." The marriage took place the following January.

Traughber's questions, phrased in nineteenth century idiom, lend an odd tone at this distance in time. "Did President Young employ peculiar methods of courtship?" he asked.

"I think not," she responded, "I was aware that he was the husband of a number of wives—I did not care to know how many—but that did not effect our courtship in the least. President Young was naturally dignified, but was always at ease with company."

The Gardo House, ca. 1885. Photo by C. R. Savage; LDS Church Archives.

After the marriage, was she immediately accepted into the "family?"

"No," Amelia replied, "I remained at home three weeks, when I took up residence in the Lion House. . . . We all dine at the same table, over which President Young presided. Every morning and evening all gathered in the large room for prayers, and here also my husband presided. I afterward took up quarters in the Beehive House, but returned to the Lion House later, and remained there until the death of President Young, August 29, 1877."

But in her notorious expose of polygamy Brigham Young-style, *Wife No. 19* (the title implied she was the nineteenth living spouse), Ann Eliza complained that Amelia had established certain ground rules before becoming another Mrs. Young. Among them was the condition that she did not have to live as did the other wives. From the day of their marriage, it became clear that Amelia ruled the roost. For instance, Ann Eliza said, in the dining room Amelia and Brigham sat by themselves while the rest of the family occupied a large table, and the couple shared delicacies which were not served to the rest of the general multitude.

"Polygamist, as he professed to be, he is, under the influence of Amelia, rapidly becoming a monogamist in all except the name," she said. Clearly, Amelia was his favorite, Ann Eliza sniffed. Amelia had jewelry, fine clothes, and a carriage of her own, and she played the piano. She also was allowed to travel. Whenever they went to the theater, she occupied the seat of honor next to her distinguished husband in the box, while the other wives sat in the special row of chairs reserved for them in the parquet.

Ann Eliza pointed out that when Amelia was ensconced in her "beautiful new elegantly furnished house," Brigham very nearly deserted the Beehive, except during business hours, spending most of his time at Amelia's. That home, the Gardo House, was Amelia's pride and joy, her palace. She planned it herself, as she did the Junior Gardo which became her residence after Brigham's death.

As for being his favorite, Amelia skirted the question with Traughber. "I can't say he had any favorites. He was equally kind and attentive to all in his lifetime, and left each surviving wife an equal legacy. I was absent from home at long intervals during the 15 years of my married life, having visited several times in the East, and having taken an extensive tour of Europe."

Then Traughber asked the question: "Do you still believe in polygamy?"

"Certainly I do. If polygamy was once right it is still right. There is no reason why a polygamous marriage may not be as happy as the ordinary marriage, if it is entered understandingly."

That was not quite the way Ann Eliza felt about it when she fled Utah and slapped Brigham with a major divorce action. In *Wife No. 19* she reveals that Brigham wanted their marriage to be kept as secret as possible out of concern that federal officers would find out. But it was Amelia's reaction he feared. "She had raised a furious storm a few months before when he married Mary Van Cott . . . and he did not dare so soon encounter another such domestic tornado."

"Amelia and I rarely spoke to each other," Ann Eliza said. "Since Amelia's marriage she ruled Brigham with a hand of iron. She has a terrible temper and he has the benefit of it," she further remarked. "On one occasion he sent her a sewing machine, thinking to please her; it did not happen to be the kind of a one which she wanted; so she kicked it down stairs, saying, 'What did you get this old thing for? You knew I wanted a Singer.' She got a Singer at once."

Once Ann Eliza bolted and dragged Brigham Young's name through the courts in the late 1870s, newspapers around the world played hob with the story. After seven years of polygamous marriage, she charged Brigham with neglect, cruelty, and desertion and asked for huge alimony. "He is worth $8 million," she announced, "and has an income of $40,000 a month!" Balderdash, retorted the church leader, his fortune did not exceed $600,000 and his income was but $6,000 a month. He offered to pay her $100 a month to settle.

When she refused, he retaliated by pointing out his marriage to the former Miss Webb was not legal because in the eyes of the law he was the husband of Mary Ann Angell (first wife)—unless, of course, the courts recognized Mormon plural marriage, something they had stubbornly refused to

Daguerreotype of Mary Ann Angell Young, first wife of Brigham Young. LDS Church Archives.

do for, lo, these past thirty years! Ann Eliza, Brigham railed, was nothing but an extortionist and that was that.

The case dragged on through the courts, but in the end it was found that Ann Eliza was not legally married to Brigham Young, so there could be no divorce—and no alimony. A judge attempted to force Brigham to pay $9,500 alimony in arrears while the suit was being adjudicated, but he refused. Ann Eliza settled for $100 a month and court costs, Brigham's original offer.

NO LOVE LOST ON LAWYERS

EARLY SETTLERS IN UTAH DIDN'T TELL LAWYER jokes—at least there don't seem to be any recorded in diaries and journals of the day. Nevertheless, frontier lawyers shared a commonality with their 1990s counterparts: they weren't the most popular professionals in the community. In fact, one might even conclude that a cardsharp stood higher on the ladder of respect.

Much of that was a result of Brigham Young's inherent dislike of attorneys-at-law. Pettifoggers, he called them. (Webster's definition: A lawyer who handles petty cases, especially one who uses unethical methods in conducting trumped-up cases. A trickster, cheater, quibbler.) In February 1856 when the first scent of a Mormon reformation was in the air, Young took to the podium in the Salt Lake Tabernacle and began blistering lawyers. It wasn't the first time, but it was the most vehement since leaving Nauvoo, Illinois, a decade earlier.

His peevishness with the profession dated back that far. After Joseph Smith, the Mormon prophet, was assassinated, Young had become a target as well, not only for bullets and blades, but for "vexatious" lawsuits as well. In mid-March 1845 he was especially aggravated, and in a Sunday sermon he shouted, "I swear by the God of heaven that we will not spend money in feeing lawyers. All the lawsuits that have been got up against the [Latter-day] Saints have been hatched up to fee lawyers . . . . I would rather have a six-shooter than all the lawyers in Illinois."

But what raised his ire that February eleven years later was a growing tendency of church members to hang around the county courthouse and encourage one another to file suit. It was Young's opinion that Mormons did not need lawyers, they needed to use common sense. So, he enlightened his Tabernacle audience on the subject: "Keep away from court houses; no decent man will go there unless he goes as a witness, or is in some manner compelled to . . . . We have the names of those who attended that court room, and we will send those characters on long missions, for we want to get rid of them, and we do not care if they apostatize or not."

Young's solution, according to his counselor Heber C. Kimball, was to send thirty or so to sell their possessions and go with their families as soon as weather permitted to raise cotton on the Rio Virgin in southern Utah; another company of forty-eight to the Grand River to strengthen that settlement, make farms, and build mills; some thirty-five or forty to Salmon River country; thirty to Carson Valley; another thirty to the lead mines at Las Vegas; and eight to the East Indies. "These are all good men, but they need to learn a lesson," Kimball remarked.

Again in 1866, Young, speaking at the Bowery on Temple Square in Great Salt Lake City, said, "It would appear that [lawyers] think a civilized community cannot live long together without contention and consequent lawsuits. . . . The law is made for the lawless and disobedient, not for the good, wise, just and virtuous. Law is made for the maintenance of peace, not for the introduction of litigation and disorder." Young had some curious notions about legal professionals, not the least of which was that they should work for free:

> I am now taking the liberty of discharging a duty I owe to the lawyers in telling them what their duty is. They read the law; they do so or should understand the law of the United States, of the states and of the territories and cities in which they live, and whenever they have an opportunity of telling people how to live in a way to avoid litigation, it is their duty to do so.
>
> Then, if they wish to get a living, instead of picking people's pockets as is too commonly the case, let them have their stores, and bring on goods and trade, buy farms and follow the healthy and honorable profession of farming, and raise their own provisions, and stock . . . and

when their services are wanted in the law, give as freely as we do the Gospel.

The years did little to mellow the church leader on the subject. As he grew older, his opinions in the matter solidified as if etched in granite. In 1871, again in the Tabernacle, he reflected on "the mining business":

> I want to say to you miners: Do not go to law at all; it does you no good, and only wastes your substance. It causes idleness, wickedness, vice and immorality.
>
> Do not go to law. You cannot find a courtroom without a great number of spectators in it; what are they doing? Idling away their time to no profit whatever. As for lawyers, if they will put their brains to work and learn how to raise potatoes, wheat, cattle, build factories, be merchants or tradesmen, it will be a great deal better for them than trying to take the property of others from them through litigation.

Young did not lambaste the legal profession on a whim; the 1870s were a time when the law was doing its utmost to clap him in irons at the very least or, as his biographer Edward W. Tullidge phrased it, "consign him to the gallows." He made good use of defense counsel himself, in those days.

The U.S. was trying desperately to tie him into the Mountain Meadow massacre through John D. Lee; Young was charged with lewd and lascivious cohabitation with his plural wives, and he had been indicted for murder, based on the confessions of the notorious killer William A. Hickman, described variously by his contemporaries as "one of the most remarkable scoundrels that any age ever produced . . . a human butcher . . . an assassin." It is bitter irony that Hickman, when not actively leading a gang of cutthroats known as "Hickman's Hounds," was a practicing attorney. In truth, it can be said, he was a criminal lawyer. And of course, there was the matter of the divorce case filed against Young by Ann Eliza Webb, his celebrated *Wife No. 19* (the title of her sensational "tell all" book). That affair alone cost Brigham Young some $24,000 in legal and other fees, according to Tullidge. All of the indictments were eventually set aside by the U.S. Supreme Court.

At one LDS conference session, Young told this anecdote: "I feel about lawyers as Peter of Russia is said to have felt . . . when asked his opinion concerning them, he replied that he had two lawyers in his empire and when he got home he intended to hang one of them."

TROLLEY SONG: CLANG, CLANG, CLANG, WHINNY

BROWSING THROUGH CENTURY-OLD NEWSPAPERS, diaries, documents, and journals for clues to life in Utah "back then" can be addictive. It can also be frustrating for what it does not reveal and satisfying for what it does turn up. For those who remember the Salt Lake City street cars of the 1940s, there is particular joy in discovering that the trolley song of 1872 would probably have included this line: Clang, clang, clang, whinny!

It was the first week of June 1872 when the vanguard of the city's new street cars was actually fitted on the track down Main Street "for the purpose of having the curves spiked in their proper places." The track was nearly complete to the Eagle Emporium on First South, and workmen were busy along East Temple (Main) preparing the road for ties. The clang, clang, clang, of course, would be the trolley's bell, warning of its approach, and the whinny refers to the method of locomotion. The city's trolleys in 1872 were horse drawn and remained that way until the late 1880s when they went electric. It was in 1891 that the Eagle Gate was rebuilt for a greater height and width to accommodate trolley cars.

Yes, to the history buff, the trivia divulged by newspapers of the period is absolutely delightful in its variety. Remember when there were drinking fountains on every street corner of the downtown area? That began in the summer of 1877, according to the *Deseret News:*

Mr. David James has put in, for the city, a temporary drinking fountain, a few yards west of the south gate of the Temple Block, near the outer edge of the sidewalk. It will, in a few weeks, be replaced by a neat iron one, which has been ordered from the east.

Similar fountains to that which is to take the place of the temporary one mentioned, will be placed at different points in the central parts of the city; one near Walker Brothers' corner, another about a block east of the City Hall, another near the Eagle Emporium, and another in the vicinity of the Z.C.M.I building.

And so marked the debut of the city's unique and celebrated system of public drinking fountains, which endured well into the mid-twentieth century.

In July of that same year, territorial surveyor general Jesse W. Fox, and A. K. Gilbert, Esq., the latter of Major John Wesley Powell's exploring expeditions, were out west, on the shores of the Great Salt Lake. "They took with them a quantity of granite from the Temple Block, and established a [survey] monument to indicate the rise or fall of the waters of the Lake. It is situated on the brow of the mountain immediately south of the Utah Western track, opposite Black Rock, and is 35 and 51/100 feet above the present level of the water. . . . Since the first settlement of Utah the waters of the Lake have risen about 14 feet," the *News* explained.

Because the *Deseret News* was the official organ of the Church of Jesus Christ of Latter-day Saints, its pages were for the most part crammed with information aimed at its Mormon readers. So it was not unusual that apostle George Q. Cannon, the paper's editor in 1868, might turn his pen toward matters of the soul. On February 12, he elected to discourse on young men who avoided matrimonial ties. Writing under the headline "Marry and Be Happy," the editor expounded on these "incorrigible bachelors," haranguing,

> they have been reasoned with, joked with, and almost threatened with fine, to urge them to marry; but so far, in vain. Reason, eloquence, wit, and threats are all alike, unavailing, they do not marry.
>
> Should they still persist in their celibacy we would be inclined to favor the revival of the Spartan custom of treating bachelors. It is said

that at a certain festival at Sparta, the women were enjoined to flog old bachelors around an altar, that they might be constrained to take wives!

> The publicity of such a proceeding might, possibly, have the effect to shame our bachelors into compliance with the first law given to man. If the fear of the first flogging would not do it, probably the dread of a repetition might cure their obstinacy.

After a full column of type in this vein, Cannon closed with, "Seriously, we advise our young men to marry. 'Marriage is the mother of the world and preserves kingdoms, and fills cities and churches, and Heaven itself.'" A perusal of subsequent issues of the newspaper failed to uncover any additional reflections on whipping the singles set.

Frequently the newspapers in the city tossed civility aside and minced few words in their editorial positions. Consider this item in the *Salt Lake Tribune*'s "City Jottings" column for September 12, 1874: "The bull's eye sign on Z.C.M.I. comes down today." It was the paper's way of adding its two cents to the fact that the "All-Seeing Eye," symbol of Mormon unity (church members trading only with church members), would no longer adorn Mormon businesses. Later in the column, the *Tribune* remarked with characteristic sarcasm when dealing with Mormon topics: "As the Profit commanded the Mormon merchants, a few years since, to have signs placed before their stores with 'Holiness to the Lord' painted thereon, wouldn't it be a fair stand-off for the Profit to give these merchants credit for same, on tithing, now that those signs have become worthless, and are encumbering the backyards of the aforesaid merchants?"

There really was no telling what would set off a tirade in those bygone days. If the *Tribune* was irked by the All-Seeing Eye, how distressed must Erastus Snow have been to tee off on sewing machine salesmen, during a church sermon in Provo in June of 1877? "I was told," he said, "that Sanpete County owed for sewing machines alone from $40,000 to $50,000 and . . . in Cache Valley $40,000 would not clear the indebtedness for sewing machines! The irrepressible sewing machine agents have ravaged our country, imposing themselves on every simpleton in the land, forcing their goods upon him." Warming to the subject, the Mormon apostle plainly did not

Z.C.M.I. Department Store, Salt Lake City. LDS Church Archives.

approve of such expensive luxuries: "Tens of thousands of dollars are lying idle in the houses of the Latter-day Saints today in this article alone; almost every house you enter you can find a sewing machine noiseless and idle, but very seldom you hear it running; and all of which were purchased at enormous figures, and now the patent rights having expired, they can be bought for less than half the prices paid for them."

In 1882, the *Millennial Star*, published in Liverpool for the benefit of British Mormons, took note that "Another effort is being made to raise oysters in the Great Salt Lake. Mr. House of Corinne, is the projector of the enterprise, at the mouth of Bear River. A former attempt to cultivate the bivalves at the mouth of the Weber, proved abortive on account of the intense saline properties of the Lake and other minor causes." Hmmph, salty oysters, indeed.

A year later, the *News* in its May 21 edition included two brief items that piqued interest. The first was a report that "No fewer than 17 boys were

arrested yesterday [a Sunday] in the act of playing baseball in the southern part of the city. . . . Justice Spiers . . . obtained a promise from them that they would cease breaking the Sabbath; and admonished them that if they were brought before him again on the same ground, he would not be so lenient, but would have them appropriately punished. Marshal Burt expressed an intention of putting a stop to the practice of which these boys are accused."

The other story was datelined Lodi, Ohio, and disclosed that "Mrs. Ann Eliza Young, of Mormon fame, 19th wife of [the late] Brigham Young, was married at 1 o'clock this p.m. in this city, to Moses R. Denning, prominent banker of Manistee, Michigan. The ceremony was performed at the residence of Dr. A. E. Elliott, and Rev. E. A. Stone, of Gallion, Ohio, officiated. Mrs. Young's son witnessed the ceremony. There were a large number of guests present, among whom were some of the most prominent citizens of this vicinity. Mr. and Mrs. Denning will make their home in Manistee. They left on the 3:30 train for Toledo."

After reporting the arrest of youthful Sabbath-breakers in 1883, the *News* in 1886 took notice with some concern that "There are now in the city some six brothels, 40 tap rooms, a number of gambling houses, pool tables, and other disreputable concerns, all run by non-Mormons." Civilization was taking its toll on Salt Lake City.

A LYNCHING AT NOON

SAM JOE HARVEY WAS A SWARTHY EX-SOLDIER, about thirty-five, tall and well-built, whose fondness for a scrap earned him the nickname of "U.S. Harvey." He was known to have spent some time in and around Pueblo, Colorado, and in the early fall of 1883 meandered from the plains to Salt Lake City.

Harvey was thought to be Negro, Creole, Mexican, "or a mixture," according to the *Salt Lake Herald*, and for a few weeks at least he established himself as a bootblack in front of Hennefer & Heinau's barber shop in the city. For reasons never quite clear, Sam Joe Harvey was on the prod. He complained of having been robbed in Ogden, and he was suspicious of everyone. Even those who knew him couldn't explain his behavior on the morning of August 25, 1883. A few said he was insane.

Whatever it was that set him off, Harvey wound up gunning down a captain of police and severely wounding the city watermaster; all this in broad daylight. It so infuriated the citizenry that a mob formed and within a half-hour lynched the shooter. A somber *Salt Lake Tribune* editorialized that the lynching "was done under the noon day sun and in the shadow of the temple of the Saints. We do not believe there has been a parallel to the case in American history. Mobs have hung men repeatedly, but never before that we remember of have the policemen who had the prisoner in charge, first beaten him into half insensibility and then turned him over to the mob. This is not a question between Mormon and Gentile; it is one in which the good name of the city government is at stake."

Events began with a telephone call to police at city hall from F. H. Grice, owner of a restaurant on the east side of Main Street between First and Second South, next door to the old Salt Lake House hotel. City Marshal Andrew Burt was the only officer on hand at the lunch hour when Grice complained that this fellow Harvey had threatened him with a pistol at the restaurant and disturbed his patrons. He wanted him arrested. Burt was also captain of police and had been talking to Charles H. Wilcken, the watermaster, when Grice's telephone call came; Wilcken went with Burt to collar Harvey.

As watermaster, Wilcken was also a special police officer. This large gruff German had an interesting background. He came to America in 1857 and was persuaded by a persistent New York recruiting officer to join the U.S. Army. He was assigned to the Fourth Artillery and marched west that fall with Colonel Albert Sidney Johnston's Utah Expedition. However, being snowed in for the winter at Fort Bridger didn't appeal to the young emigrant and he deserted, only to be captured by Mormons on October 7, turned over to Orrin Porter Rockwell, and escorted along with a herd of liberated government cattle to Great Salt Lake City.

It happened that Wilcken would find the Mormon way of life suited him just fine. He converted, was baptized that December, and became a devout Latter-day Saint, eventually serving a foreign mission. He became a confidant of church authorities George Q. Cannon and Wilford Woodruff and for a while acted as a bodyguard to Brigham Young during the bitter antipolygamy crusades of the 1870s. Now in 1883, Watermaster Wilcken was ready to help his friend Andrew Burt arrest and jail what they thought was merely a drunken transient making a public disturbance.

Burt, a fifty-three-year-old Scot, was a determined Mormon who earned the rank of captain of police in 1859, was named chief in 1862, and in February 1876 was elected city marshal. He was a lawman almost from the day he arrived in Utah in the fall of 1851. Those who knew him swore he was absolutely fearless; "a braver man never lived . . . he had the courage of a lion," was the way the *Deseret News* put it.

From city hall, the two officers strode up First South, crossed State Street, and turned down Main. Grice, meanwhile, had walked up the east side of the street until he encountered the lawmen. Sam Joe Harvey, he told them, had frightened Mrs. Grice and some luncheon customers with his revolver, then pushed his way through the kitchen and out into a back alley.

As Burt and Wilcken scanned the noon crowds along the city's busiest street, Grice recounted the events of the morning. Harvey was looking for a job, he said, and Grice had offered him work as a laborer around his farm on the outskirts of town. Grice would pay two dollars a day and provide Harvey transportation to and from the place. When he was told the farm was twelve miles from the city, Harvey "belched out in profanity" and began insulting the restaurant owner and his patrons. "I pushed him out the door and he pulled a pistol on me," Grice said, as Burt and Wilcken reached the corner of Main and Tribune Avenue (today's Second South).

The three turned left to check the stores as far as the corner of Commercial Street (today's Regent Street) before turning around. As they again approached the Main Street corner, Grice spotted Harvey just off the sidewalk—but now he was armed with a .45-caliber rifle and a .44 pistol!

It was later learned that after Harvey had fled the Grices' cafe, he went to a general store and bought a rifle he had seen earlier in the day. He paid the proprietor, Thomas Carter, twenty dollars for the repeater along with two boxes of cartridges. "He was nervous and dropped one of the cartridge boxes, spilling some of the ammunition," Carter remembered. Harvey had scooped up the bullets, put them in his pocket, and hurried away.

Minutes later, he would encounter Grice, Burt, and Wilcken coming up the street, directly for him. According to the *Deseret News*, as they neared the corner, "Grice pointed to a colored man who was standing on the edge of the sidewalk and said: 'That is the man, arrest him!'"

Burt was carrying a heavy cane which doubled as a nightstick. As he moved closer, Harvey raised his rifle and taking aim said, "Are you an officer?" In the next heartbeat, the ex-soldier fired; the marshal lurched to one side and stumbled into A. C. Smith & Company drugstore a few feet distant. He slumped to the floor just behind the prescription counter.

Outside, Wilcken, who was immediately behind and to the side of Burt when the shot was fired, sprang forward and caught hold of Harvey, wrenching the rifle free. He grabbed Harvey by the throat and the two locked in a desperate struggle, but Wilcken couldn't stop Harvey from using his revolver. Harvey fired again and the .44 slug tore through the fleshy part of the watermaster's left arm between the shoulder and elbow. The cowardice of the crowd was appalling, snarled the *Deseret News*, "they scrambled away in terror in every direction. Finally Mr. Wilcken threw Harvey in a ditch, and after he was overpowered the crowd returned to the scene to his aid."

Actually, Harvey had pressed the pistol against Wilcken's body and was squeezing the trigger for a second shot, when Elijah Able jumped into the fray, twisted the pistol away, and helped throw the desperado down. With blood pouring from the ugly wound in his arm, Wilcken held his own until finally Homer J. Stone rushed in to subdue the shooter. By this time other police reached the scene and took Harvey in custody. Wilken's arm was treated at the drugstore as the officers hustled their prisoner off to police headquarters.

Then things got nasty. A swarm of spectators followed the tight knot of constables as they made their way up the street. Back at Smith's drugstore, meanwhile, attention turned from Wilken's gunshot wound to the figure of the marshal slumped behind the counter. Burt had been able to make his way from the sidewalk to the inside of the store under his own power, but he was a dead man. Harvey's bullet had pierced his left arm, penetrated his heart and lungs, exited his body and lodged in his right arm. As he fell he was bleeding from five large wounds.

Dr. J. M. Benedict pronounced the police captain dead at the scene and called a wagon to take the body to an undertaker. When the throng saw Burt's sheet-covered form lifted into the wagon bed, a long, low moan erupted and the first cries of a lynching were muttered. "I say hang! Who goes with me?" shouted one man, and from the crowd a chorus of "I!" It was a belated threat.

Sam Joe Harvey was pushed into the marshal's office at city hall and searched. Officers found $165.80 in gold, silver, and greenbacks in his pockets as well as a large number of rifle and pistol cartridges. It was then an unidentified man stuck his head in and shouted Captain Burt had been shot dead. As one, the police turned on Harvey. "One of the officers . . . [struck] him violently between the eyes, felling him," the *Herald* reported.

From outside the building could now be heard excited shouts of "Get a rope! Hang the son of a b——!" The officers dragged the semi-conscious man to the back door, which opened to a yard in front of the city jail. The crowd on First South in front of city hall had become an ugly enraged mob of two thousand or more. Sensing that the prisoner was being moved, they ran to a State Street alley that opened on the jail yard and demanded Harvey be turned over.

An officer named William Salmon came to the jail door and was greeted by jeers when he ordered the mob to disband. There was a brief tussle and Salmon was shoved aside; then, Harvey, his face a bloody mask, pitched out the door into the frenzied gathering. He was swarmed over, stomped, and beaten while men ran about yelling for a rope. Harness straps cut from teams in front of city hall were passed forward and, when they were found too short, used to whip the wretched prisoner. Still he struggled to break free. His efforts and the momentum of the surging crowd carried them eastward in the jail yard until Harvey finally toppled, fifty or so feet from the jail door; at the same time a long rope made its way to the spot.

A crudely made noose was pulled roughly over Harvey's head as he squirmed to wrench free. Hands reached out to drag him another hundred feet to a stable shed west of the yard. The rope was tossed over a main beam. Men grabbed the rope and hoisted Harvey by the neck several feet from the ground. As his writhing body swung to view above their heads, the crowd gave out an excited roar of approval. Still the doomed man fought. From the moment he was pulled up he reached above his head for the rope as if to ease the noose that was strangling him. One of the

crowd leaped to a carriage nearby and kicked first one hand, then the other until Harvey let go. He gasped, his body jerking in a final spasm before his arms dropped limply to his side.

Twenty-five minutes had elapsed since the fatal shot at Burt was fired. In that time the outraged crowd at Smith's drugstore also was seized by mob fever and had marched to city hall, swelling the throng even larger. So hysterical was the atmosphere that it was dangerous for others. W. H. Sells, son of Colonel E. Sells, a prominent Utahn, was riding past the hall in a buggy and happened on the scene. Unaware that Harvey was already dead, Sells tried to reason with the mob, arguing that lynching was no answer: "let the courts handle it." In that moment Sells came close to joining Harvey on the stable beam. Only the quick thinking of Salmon, the police officer, saved him. Salmon pulled Sells into the jail and pushed him into a cell. Several other citizens who urged calm and justice were handled roughly and "came near being mobbed," according to the *Tribune*. The *Herald* said "Officer Salmon's discretion and prompt action saved Mr. Sells' life."

The horror still was not over, for the mass of angry citizens continued to clamor vengeance. Harvey's body was cut down and dragged out of the alley a short distance down State Street. There the crowd was confronted by a furious Mayor William Jennings, who demanded they disperse. Events moved quickly. The mob broke up, an inquest was convened that afternoon, and a coroner's jury comprising W. W. Riter, Joseph Jennings, and John Groesbeck heard the evidence and returned a verdict that the deceased "came to his death by means of hanging with a rope by an infuriated mob whose names were to the jury unknown."

Joe Sam Harvey was buried in Salt Lake City Cemetery that very night. Funeral services for Marshal Burt were conducted a few days later; much of the city turned out in his honor. Watermaster Wilcken recovered and continued to serve in various capacities until his death in 1915.

That ordinarily would have ended the story of that black August 25, 1883, in Salt Lake City, but there is an epilogue. Two months after the lynching, two workers loading sand from an area just west of the cemetery made a grisly discovery: a pine box. In it was a human skeleton. The cemetery sexton was notified and later explained that when the murderer Harvey's remains were buried, the grave diggers misunderstood their instructions and buried the body "near" the cemetery instead of in it. The remains were those of the lynched assassin, the *Herald* reported. No one, including the city's newspapers, questioned how Harvey's

body was reduced to a skeleton in just two months.

Then, in the spring of 1885, Officer Thomas F. Thomas was brought to trial on charges of assaulting the prisoner. After two days of conflicting testimony concerning use of clubs and brass knuckles, Thomas was acquitted.

WHERE THE BUFFALO ROAM

"OH, GIVE ME A HOME WHERE THE BUFFALO roam . . . ." The lyrics to that 1873 cowboy ballad invoke images of the Old West beyond mere words. The mighty American bison was lord of the prairies for centuries, when so many of the huge beasts roamed the plains that at times it seemed the ground itself was one great dark blanket of animals from horizon to horizon. But by the time Utah territory was being settled, the massive herds already were vanishing from the Great Basin; the last buffalo in Utah was seen in the 1830s.

So how did they find their way to Antelope Island in the Great Salt Lake? The Utah State Parks Department reports its herd of some seven hundred on the island is robust and healthy. There are varying stories of about how that came to be, but the most colorful is a 1925 account in the *Salt Lake Tribune* left by a correspondent who wrote under the pen name, "Old-Timer." The *Tribune* kept no records concerning his identity, but an educated guess would be that the writer was J. Cecil Alter, a weather bureau meteorologist whose leisure interest was western American history and who doubled as director of the Utah State Historical Society, which he helped organize in 1928.

According to Old-Timer, the bison were brought to the island in the 1880s, though recent research has adjusted that date. Rick Mayfield, director of the Utah Department of Business and Economic Development, has learned the original bunch of animals (four bulls, four cows, and four calves) once belonged to William Glasmann, rancher and Ogden newspaper publisher. In retracing the herd, Mayfield found they were bought through Charles J. (Buffalo) Jones, Garden

City, Kansas, one of several men credited by the Smithsonian Institution with saving America's bison herd from extinction.

Jones had rounded up buffalo calves on the plains of Kansas in the 1880s for his own ranch. Then with seventy or so animals acquired from Manitoba, the Kansan was able to claim the largest herd in America. A portion of that Manitoba stock was sold to Glasmann, who was developing the town of Garfield on the south shore of the Great Salt Lake. He planned to include a zoological garden and "Buffalo Park," but the project proved impractical and the bison were sold. John E. Dooley owned most of Antelope Island. He bought the Glasmann buffalo and in February 1893 ordered them shipped over to the island.

At this point, it would be wrong to tell more in anyone's words but Old-Timer's. Here is the way he wrote it that June 25, 1925:

M. C. Udy out Farmington way. He's the one as told me the story.

Yes, he was there. It was him and J. W. Walker handled the pikes and while maybe he don't know as much about hunting buffaloes as some others, when it comes to herding 'em—say, that guy's there.

Well, the way he tells it, he had been working over on Antelope Island for the Island improvement company back in the '80s. J. W. Walker succeeded him as foreman and then, when his outfit bought Bill Glasmann's buffalo herd, Walker got Udy to help him move the critters.

They was on a ranch over back of Lake Point, the way Udy tells it. Him and Walker takes a ride over there one day along about '89 intending to drive the herd of 17 bulls and cows up the lake shore to the company landing at Farmington where the old cattle boat used to load and unload its beef cargo to and from the island.

There was one old cow who'd lost a leg so they herded her onto a wagon for transport. Walker and Udy starts out with the rest on hoof and they no sooner gets outside the corral than here comes some of Glasmann's cowboys whooping it up to beat Billy Time. The buffalo take fright at the noise, and stampede.

Walker and Udy nigh kill their horses trying to head off the herd, but then Glasmann rides up to 'em and says, "Let 'em run."

The cowmen, seeing that buffalo can't be handled like range cattle, but must be coaxed rather than herded, take Bill's advice and, after about four miles of dead running, the buffalo forget what it was scared 'em and they slows to a walk.

Walker and Udy makes a wide circle round the herd. Careful not to rouse 'em into another run, they coaxes 'em along the lake shore, letting 'em browse along easy like, and that night they goes into camp near the Rudy ranch down by the old grist mill near the Jordan river and 14th North street.

Next morning they begins edging the critters along toward Farmington. 'Bout 10 o'clock they gets onto the State highway and that afternoon they brings them into camp near the boat landing down by the old Lake Shore resort.

Their company has a loading chute there for cattle. The scow would tie up at the water end of this run and on the shore end there was a corral. With cattle, all was needed was to get 'em into this corral and then drive 'em up the chute into the scow. The old boat used to handle 40, 50 head and its deck space was enclosed with heavy timbers so as to prevent any of 'em trying for a swim. Likewise to prevent capsizing the craft a length of telephone pole was run fore and aft down the middle of this pen so that they couldn't all crowd to either side. . . .

It had been easy to handle cows on this runway but buffalo was something else again. . . .

The cattle boat was a scow built with a flat bottom and it had a clumsy sail rigging that required a lot of handling. When winds were fair the passage from the island to the shore might take only a couple of hours. But there were times when the wind died out and then they had to heave to or else break out long poles [pikes] and push the boat along from a rail runway.

They lands the first shipment the same evening and comes back for more.

But the buffalo that had made [the] chute jump didn't show any inclination to get back into the corral. It took another three or four days of coaxing with hay bait to get 'em back . . . . Meanwhile Walker and Udy adds another foot of timber up the chute side and when late in the afternoon they get the strays up to the pen they rides them hard right into the boat.

The buffalo didn't know what was being done to 'em and lest they catch on and start something, the rangers decide to make this trip right away that night.

Well, they gets 'em over to the island and turns 'em loose. Right then they washes their hands of any more buffalo herding.

They're the meanest critters, so Udy tells us. Why at times while Walker was foreman at the island, they used to raid the home ranch for eats. They wasn't content to eat range grass, he says. Instead, they'd walk into a nice potato plantation about ready for harvest and kick up the tubers with their hooves. Couple o'hundred bushel a night would be wiped out when they was going good.

To stop this, Walker loaded up a shotgun with good, heavy buckshot and lets 'em have a few doses. That was about the only way to sting them enough to make them travel, Udy says.

They been out there ever since, some of them getting killed off once in a while for a Democrat barbecue or a movie, but otherwise having about their own way.

Yes, that's Antelope Island. Udy don't know why they calls it by that name. He never heard of no antelope out there, he says.

But the days of the old sail scow are long past. Walker is dead. Udy don't crave any more buffalo herding and leasees [sic] of the island are said to have been complaining that the old plains critters now [1925] numbering nearly 500 head forage too much of the range that otherwise might be used for feeding sheep or cattle. . . .

"There was only 17 when we took 'em out," Udy demures, "and they had been more or less tamed on the Glasmann ranch. It's going to be some job to get rid of 400, unless you kill 'em off. Who wants to do that? It's one of the finest buffalo herds in the world. We ought to preserve it as a reminder of the past. Leastwise, I feel that way after Will Walker and I had such a job getting 'em started."

THE HORSELESS CARRIAGE COMES TO UTAH

AH, WHAT MUST IT HAVE BEEN LIKE IN UTAH before the advent of the motor car? Do you realize the prospect of discovering a pearl in a bowl of oyster stew is more likely than locating someone who has never seen an automobile or can claim to having lived before its invention? Cars have been part of our lives forever, you say? It only seems so.

For instance, the first horseless carriage in Salt Lake City made its appearance under a century ago. On April 12, 1899, to be precise, George E. Airis, son of a well-known mining family, unveiled his new purchase in the downtown area. According to an account in the *Salt Lake Herald* of that memorable and historic occasion, the machine was a "Winton Motor Carriage," manufactured by the Winton Carriage Works in Cleveland. There were no car dealerships as we know them in those bucolic bygone days, so Mr. Airis found it necessary to order the contraption through the Salt Lake Hardware Company. The *Herald* account described the machine thusly:

> The body of the carriage resembles many of the family vehicles seen upon the streets, and differs from them in appearance by being without a tongue and by having heavy bicycle wheels, with the pneumatic rubber tires.
>
> The machinery that drives the automobile is entirely hidden from view by the box back of the seat, and consists of a gasoline engine for motive power, which drives a shaft placed near the center of the carriage. From this shaft a sprocket chain connects with the back axle of the carriage, causing it to revolve.
>
> The machinery is under perfect control of the operator from the seat, by the means of levers, one of which is used to go ahead and the other to reverse the engine. The speed is regulated by levers at the bottom of the carriage, which are pressed by the foot.

Our scribe neglected to venture a guess as to the speed of this horseless carriage, but since it was the first of its breed, the concerns of rules of the road and right-of-way apparently posed no immediate obstacle. He did, however, provide his readers with the bottom line: the price tag. A Winton was $1,500 prepaid in Salt Lake City. "This figure is remarkably low for a horseless carriage," he opined, "the Columbia carriage costing from $2,000 up."

How did the Winton perform? The *Herald's* observations came in the final paragraph. "After the engine was tried at the hardware warehouse, Mr. Airis and a friend ventured out upon the street, and took a spin over Main, State and West Temple, to the great delight of the small boy, who was out in numbers to follow them. "This is the first, but doubtless will not be the last," the *Herald's* man concluded.

There would be more horseless carriages in Utah, to be sure, but the next important newspaper coverage from the *Herald* would not come for more than a year. And it was an occasion. Lorenzo Snow, president of the Church of Jesus Christ of Latter-day Saints, known to have a "natural love for novelty" had been buzzing the streets in an automobile that was giving Salt Lake horses "the blind staggers." President Snow was no stranger to motor carriages, for it was reported that he had challenged Joseph F. Smith, president of the LDS Council of Twelve Apostles, to a fifteen-mile race over the prairie near Cove Creek in southern Utah some months earlier. "That race had its hair-raising features," reported the *Herald*, but President Snow won it. In this latest episode, the newspaper failed to mention the make of the vehicle, but it must have been a brute. Its owner was one Hyrum Silver, and his knowledge that the church leader was partial to "fast locomotion" led him to extend an invitation to tour the town.

Promptly at 2:30 on the afternoon of May 15, 1900, a chuff, chuff, chuff and a puff of exhaust smoke announced the machine had sputtered up to the door of the Beehive House on South Temple. President Snow appeared a

South Temple Street with the Gardo House on the right. Across the street from it to the left is the Beehive House. LDS Church Archives.

moment later, walked around the carriage once or twice on an inspection of the critter, stepped aboard, pulled his hat firmly down over his head, gripped the seat, and, gave the word, "All ready!"

Zip! The machine turned its bow toward the Brigham Young Monument, cutting a half-moon in the road, and was off. "It took the right-of-way from all street cars, because it went faster. The butcher boy forgot where he was to deliver the meat, while his horse stood paralyzed, and the general populace just stood and stared with wonder and admiration at the sight of the venerable old man flying down Main Street at 30 miles an hour, sublimely content, but a trifle worried, if the expression on his face indicated anything."

It was a half-hour before the automobile drove up at the president's office again, and a group of interested spectators gathered to be convinced that one could actually ride in the thing and come out alive, the *Herald* explained. A comment was sought, and President Snow, collecting his thoughts, brushed the road dust from his clothes and offered an endorsement: "It is glorious to ride in. We went all down Main Street and around Liberty Park and back up State and around here, and oh, I cannot begin to tell you what a ride we had. I didn't know what minute we might upset a street car, but the first fear soon passed."

He was thinking of getting a bicycle, he remarked, but he guessed the automobile is what he really wanted, after all. "It's quite different from driving an ox cart. That's the way I saw Salt Lake City first. But 50 years makes a great difference in most everything. In 1849 when we first came here I drove one of the ox teams over these same roads, but we made on an average of 100 miles a week. I believe that carriage," he said, pointing to the auto, "would have no difficulty covering about 35 miles an hour on good roads.

"The next time we go through Dixie [southern Utah] we can take the automobiles and do away with carrying oats in the bottom of the buggy."

"Buffalo Bill" Cody: Ever the Showman

On a brisk afternoon in early December 1902, townfolk along Salt Lake City's Main Street watched curiously as a six-horse stagecoach clattered to a stop in front of the Templeton Hotel on South Temple. Though it was still the horse-and-buggy era, Concord stagecoaches hadn't been a familiar sight in Utah's capital since the transcontinental railroad linked up at Promontory. If the stagecoach was a throwback to the old frontier days, so was its principal passenger and party this December day. He strode to the hotel desk and wrote boldly on the register: W. F. Cody, Buffalo Bill. In the space designated residence: The World.

Ever the showman, "Buffalo Bill" Cody did what he did with as much style and panache as possible. He had just completed a six-week hunting and sight-seeing tour of "the wild and woolly west" from his Scouts Rest ranch in Nebraska, through Colorado and New Mexico, and by railroad to Flagstaff, Arizona, the jumping-off spot. With Cody was an impressive entourage including Colonel McKinnon of the British Grenadier Guards and his fellow officer Major Mildway of the Queen's Own Lancers; Colonel Frank Baldwin, twice recipient of the Medal of Honor, detailed by General Nelson Miles himself for escort duty to the Cody party; Prentiss Ingraham, ghostwriter and author of *Buffalo Bill* dime novels; Colonel Allison Naylor, Washington, D.C.; Colonel Frank Bolan, U.S. Army; John M. "Arizona John" Burke, manager of Cody's "Wild West" show; Robert "Pony Bob" Haslam, former Pony Express rider; Horton Boal, Cody's son-in-law; and William C. Boal, manager of Scouts Rest. Never one to travel unprepared, Cody also brought along an official photographer, W. H. Broach of North Platte, Nebraska, and Louis Renaud, a chef d'cuisine of some renown.

Actually Bill Cody was no stranger to Utah. He had been humiliated as a twelve-year-old cattle herder during the so-called Utah War of 1857–58, when Mormon guerrilla leader Lot Smith burned a government wagon train and forced its civilian teamsters to walk back to Missouri. Cody and his teenage friend James B. Hickok were among those set afoot. Cody's most recent visit to southern Utah had been in 1885.

Now, in his late fifties, the flamboyant plainsman, idol of America's youngsters, hero of pulp novels, and the epitome of derring-do, was discovering that while fame may not always be fleeting, fortune certainly was. In the throes of marital problems and with his Irma Hotel in the Wyoming town that carried his name opening in mid-November of 1902 and already losing $500 a month in operating costs, Cody was riding a narrow financial trail. But he was Buffalo Bill and anything was possible.

Once in Flagstaff, the party was met by a cowboy contingent, fifty horses, three prairie schooners, as many mountain buckboards, and an ambulance wagon. Cody already had provided enough weapons and ammunition to outfit a small army—the hunting expedition was ready to move.

There was an ulterior motive to the tour, beyond that of showing off the West to visiting Brits. Cody, the one man in America whose reputation may have influenced the slaughter of its stupendous bison herds, herds that once blanketed the plains of the 1840s, now was lamenting the vanishing hunting grounds. Game no longer abounded, and bison had been hunted to the point of extinction on the continent. He earned his nickname and his reputation killing buffalo. During the months he was employed as a meat hunter for the Kansas Pacific contractors, he personally accounted for 4,280 animals, according to Cody's biographer, the late Don Russell. In his years on the plains, Cody hunted to feed army troops throughout his scouting career and guided numerous hunting parties. Yet down to 1884, when he killed his last buffalo, it seems doubtful to Russell that Cody's total approached ten thousand, a trifling number among the millions of bison roaming the plains.

The destruction of the vast herds came so quickly the Smithsonian Institution found itself without presentable specimens, and ironically, the eighteen animals in Cody's Wild West show became critical in saving the species from extinction. Imagine. In three years prior to 1875, 3,700,000 buffalo were killed for sport and hides; the southern plains herd ceased to exist. The herd that roamed the northern plains was gone by 1883. Lest Cody and the professional hunters suffer all the blame for this, William Hornady, a Smithsonian expert reporting on the loss of the herds, held the Indian tribes as much responsible for the slaughter as the white hide hunters.

In his report, Hornaday noted that Indians used such methods as driving a herd over a cliff or surrounding it and butchering numbers far in excess of what they needed or could use, and he claimed they took sadistic pleasure in the killing. "True," he wrote, "they did not hunt for sport, but I have yet to learn of an instance wherein an Indian refrained from excessive slaughter of game through motives of economy, or care for the future, or prejudice against wastefulness."

That then was the situation in 1902 when Cody invited a few important Brits to join him on a tour of the West. And that was why General Miles detailed Frank Baldwin, an old Indian campaigner like Cody, to act as an honorary escort "to the foreign military officers" with the expedition. Cody also wanted to put on a good front, for the dignitaries were crucial to his plans to finance his gigantic scheme for a western game park. Cody confided to a *Salt Lake Tribune* reporter that he represented a syndicate "which can command $6 million for the purpose, and the plan is to get control of 2,000,000 to 5,000,000 acres of land in the Rocky Mountain region."

Whether this was a pie-in-the-sky daydream or a genuine, if speculative, investment scheme was never clear. Cody had a history of poor investments: he shoveled thousands of dollars down glory holes in failed mining ventures, tried his hand at being a stage actor, and lent his name to an immense dime-novel publishing orgy which glorified him as America's hero, and he would, in 1905, face his most "inglorious appearance," in a Wyoming courtroom, in a divorce suit he brought against his wife.

Such was the state of Cody's affairs as the party moved out on the Flagstaff road for their first camp at old Fort Moroni at the foot of the San Francisco Mountains. Cody meant to show his guests the grandeur of the Grand Canyon; he also liked the idea of corralling a few million acres of the famous landscape for his game preserve. In a few days they reached the south rim of the canyon and from that point spotted Buckskin Mountain across the gorge—just seventeen miles distant, but a crossing that would take them some fourteen days and a three-hundred-mile detour. Scanning the John Hance trail, then the only descent on the south rim, they could plainly see the scouts on the north rim sent to meet them.

It was two weeks to Navajo Springs, Cedar Ridge, and Lee's Ferry, where they crossed the Colorado River, then to Jacobs Pools and Buckskin Mountain on the north and to Kanab in Utah's Kane County. Game was plentiful "and the larder always supplied with venison and all the other luxuries that the country afforded." During their time in the canyon they visited Bright Angel Point, Greenland Point, Point Sublime, and other "points of observation," as Cody put it. "We left the Grand Canyon as blizzards warned us that it would be death to remain and be snowed in, and descended to the Kanab Valley through a vast and gorgeous country," he said. In describing southern Utah country, Cody explained,

> Kanab is a Mormon settlement, where we found our first post office in three weeks. We were most hospitably received, and let me here say that the Mormons are by no means a backward people, but in touch with the age in which they live. They have schools, their villages are generally devoid of saloons and gambling dens, their young men and maidens are moral and respect their elders, while they have an energy and a push about them that surprised us all.
>
> Their homes are comfortable, well furnished and well stored with home products, so that they live well, while their religion, outside of polygamy, will stand the closest criticism. Of course, plural marriages are abolished among them now under the law, but theirs is a resigned acceptance of the situation among all with whom we talked. Our whole escort was Mormon, from the guide in chief to the horse wrangler. In fact, we had Brigham Young, a grandson of the prophet, with us.

Cody's party struck out overland to Salt Lake City:

In our wanderings by rail, wagon and in the saddle we have had an opportunity to see Nebraska, Colorado, New Mexico, Utah and Wyoming . . . .
We saw plenty of game of all kinds, but though found, was fast disappearing. We beheld scenery which no other land can equal. My foreign guests were even louder in singing its praises than our American contingent. . . . Outside of the National Park of the Yellowstone, America is wholly devoid of any place for the preservation of game, while every country in Europe has private preserves for just such purposes. If I meet with success in the carrying out of my plans for a private park for the preservation of our National game, I shall be more than content.

The English officers McKinnon and Milway were indeed well pleased with the trip thus far and especially tickled in the knowledge that once the canyon had been reached, most of the expedition members returned to Flagstaff rather than endure the hardships facing them if they continued the itinerary through to Salt Lake City. On the day after entering the city, they were guests for a tour of Salt Lake's points of interest, and they then took the train for New York and their return to London.

William F. "Buffalo Bill" Cody's grand plans for a game preserve did not materialize. He did not make enough money with his Wild West show to retire, and he made too much to quit. He died January 10, 1917, in Denver, of exhaustion and a heart condition. Twenty-five thousand mourners attended his funeral.

ROGUES GALLERY: A PAGE FROM POLICE HISTORY

A STACK OF OLD SALT LAKE CITY POLICE Department "mug" books long supposed destroyed have surfaced after nearly thirty years and now are part the department's historical archives. And while the circumstances surrounding their recovery are sketchy, the records are real and plans are underway for preservation of the documents, according to Lieutenant Steve Diamond, department historian. In a bygone era they would have been called rogues gallery books because they are made up of photographs of persons arrested or sought by law enforcement agencies.

For example, entry no. 318 is George Cassidy, alias Butch, alias W. Parker, age 27; 5 feet, 9 inches; 165 pounds; dark flaxen hair; blue eyes, small and deep set. He is erroneously identified as a native of New York, with an explanation that he was "born and raised in Circle Valley Scipio, Utah." The record shows he had two cut scars on the back of his head, a small red scar under the left eye; a red mark on the left side of his back, and a small brown mole on the calf of his left leg. A bullet scar was evident on the upper part and right side of his forehead. Cassidy was sentenced from Fremont

County, Wyoming, June 15, 1894, to two years for grand larceny. In another pencilled handwriting: "Pardoned by Gov. Richards."

Evidently Cassidy's photo, a duplicate of his Wyoming prison picture, was included in the gallery as a matter of information, probably from a Wyoming police circular, on an outlaw, not as a Salt Lake City record of arrest–he was never arrested in Utah.

On page 597 are unflattering profile and front views of Joe Hillstrom, alias Joe Hill, booked January 14, 1914, for murder. Hillstrom, a labor organizer and songwriter, was arrested and charged with the armed robbery and murder of a Salt Lake grocer and his son. The arrest record lists Hillstrom's identifying marks and scars: two scars on the right side of his face, "dim vax" (vaccination) scar visible on his right arm, a large scar on the back of his right forearm, and a large scar on the left side of his neck. Finally, the terse notation "Shot IWW," presumably meaning Hillstrom was executed. IWW is the abbreviation for Industrial Workers of the World, which took up Hill's cause and demonstrated unsuccessfully to

George LeRoy Parker, alias Butch Cassidy. Salt Lake City Police Museum

The books include several thousand police identification pictures dating from 1892 through the 1940s.

The lieutenant's collection of police-related history contains some interesting sidelights. One concerns a special officer assigned to the railroad yards: Times were really tough in 1903, and Ed Burroughs couldn't find the kind of employment in Parma, Idaho, that would earn a living for himself and his wife, Emma. He had tried gold dredging on the Snake River in Oregon, but that didn't work out. So when the Oregon Short Line Railroad Company offered a job in Utah, the couple pulled up stakes in April 1904 and took rooms at 111 North Fifth West, Salt Lake City. As a special railroad policeman, he would work, but not on the city payroll; Oregon Short Line would have to pony up his wages. The city would, however, provide a blue uniform, bright brass buttons, and a truncheon. Ed also acquired a used six-gun.

He would later recollect those days this way: "My beat was in the railroad yards where after nightfall I rambled and fanned bums off the freight cars and the blind baggage of the Butte Express. Kept good hours and always came home with fifty pounds of high grade ice, which I swiped while the watchman slept. I was always a good provider. This regime was not very adventurous, nor encouraging for a man of ambition. The bums and yeggs were seldom as hard boiled as they are painted and only upon one or two occasions did I even have to flash my gun."

Nevertheless, it was a rough way to earn a living—the Burroughses were so poor Ed half-soled his own shoes and even bottled his own beer. In a letter home to family in Illinois, he confided: "Can't say I am stuck on the job of policeman." After five months, Burroughs resigned. He and his wife left for Chicago. Perhaps a man of ambition and imagination could catch on there.

And he did. In fact, he went on to become a famous writer of fantasy adventure stories. Most folks are apt to recognize his full name: Edgar Rice Burroughs, creator of *Tarzan of the Apes*, the most celebrated hero in American fiction.

The other fourteen record books seem to cover turn-of-the-century arrests. One is "specialized," being limited to "bunco artists and con men," and another is devoted entirely to females arrested for offenses ranging from prostitution, drunkenness, and arson to larceny. The collection

have his sentence commuted. Hillstrom's trial and execution were sensations in 1914–15.

The mug books (there are fifteen in all) represent just one facet of a continuing effort by Lieutenant Diamond to chronicle the activities of the department since its inception in 1851. According to Diamond, the books were turned over by a former police officer who was to have destroyed the records in 1966 "because there was no room for that kind of outdated stuff" as a consequence of the move from the police station at 105 South State to headquarters at 244 East Fourth South and ultimately to the Metropolitan Hall of Justice. Instead of incinerating them, the officer stored the volumes and forgot about them. Recently he told Diamond of their existence, and the records were transferred to the police museum.

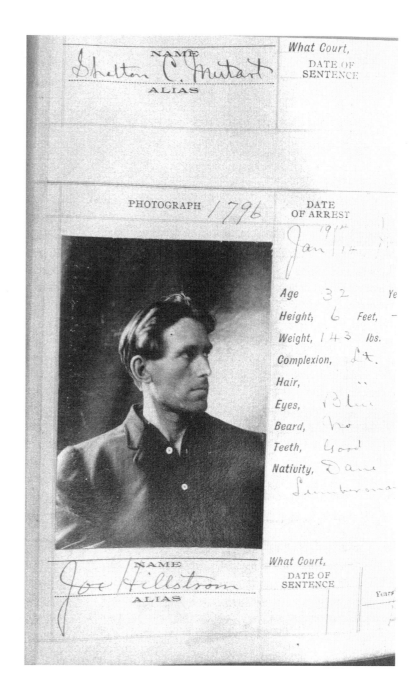

NAME ~~Shelton C. Mutart~~

ALIAS

What Court,
DATE OF SENTENCE

PHOTOGRAPH 1796

DATE OF ARREST

1914

Jan 12

Age 32   Ye

Height, 6 Feet, —

Weight, 143 lbs.

Complexion, Lt.

Hair,

Eyes, Blue

Beard, No

Teeth, Good

Nativity, Dan

Lumberma

NAME ~~Joe Hillstrom~~

ALIAS

What Court,
DATE OF SENTENCE

Years

Joe Hillstrom, alias Joe Hill. Salt Lake City Police Museum.

of criminal photos is immense: there are 702 pages of arrests in one volume alone, with three entries and photographs to a page.

Number 1 is Tom Kelly, 38, arrested 1892 for receiving counterfeit money. Suspect no. 213 is Billy McCarthey, 42; 5 foot, 8; florid complexion, red hair; and the notation: "Killed at Delta, Colo., while robbing a bank Sept. 7, 1893." Then there is the matter of James Ransom, 40, alias Jim the Pete.

(Pete is underworld slang for a safe, or safe-cracker.) Jim the Pete was arrested and sentenced March 12, 1892, to "two years in county jail at Ogden for having [blasting] powder and burglary tools." The remaining mug books document several thousand criminals.

Was it Special Officer Edgar Rice Burroughs who later said of life: It's a jungle out there?

THE OLDEST PROFESSION'S SORDID PAST IN UTAH

IN EVERY POPULATED AREA SINCE THE BEGINNING of recorded history—and Salt Lake City, high-toned protestations to the contrary, is no different—there have always been "ladies of the night." Like Manhattan's Tenderloin district, Baltimore's War Zone, and San Francisco's Barbary Coast, Ogden struggled with its notorious Twenty-fifth Street while Salt Lake City blushed over its own red light district on Commercial Street and later at the Stockade.

If, in fact, the only difference between amateur and professional standing in matters of the flesh is money, then Utah's problems in this regard did not exist until a decade after Brigham Young pronounced Salt Lake Valley "the place." The first brothels appeared near Camp Floyd (forty miles southwest of Salt Lake City) in Utah County in 1858, where elements of the U.S. Army were based after the Utah Expedition had ended that year.

But W. W. Drummond, associate justice of the Supreme Court of Utah, earns the dishonor of having imported the first known prostitute to Zion. This red-headed scoundrel managed to finagle a federal appointment out of President Franklin Pierce. Drummond then abandoned his wife and children in Oquawka, Illinois, and took up with a Washington, D.C., harlot. He traveled with her to Salt Lake City and introduced her not as Ada Carroll from the fleshpots of Washington, but as "Mrs. Justice Drummond."

She shared a seat on the court bench with Drummond, occasionally nudging him on the knee, it was said, to indicate the number of years he ought to mete out to miscreants before the bar of justice. At the same time, Drummond would unburden himself of tirades against "the deplorable Mormon practice of plural wifery." The Mormons finally caught on and Drummond fled the territory in disgrace.

After the arrival of U.S. troops under the command of Colonel Albert Sidney Johnston in 1857, the whole tone of life along what we know as the Wasatch Front changed dramatically. Brigham Young's grip on the community was broken and the outside influences he feared made the most of the fracture. Saloons operated in Salt Lake City (Ogden wasn't a problem as yet), and the stretch of road below Second South on Main Street became known as Whiskey Street. Brothels and gambling dens flourished in Frogtown, east across the creek from Camp Floyd, and did a brisk business among the several thousand troops stationed there. (Frogtown later became Fairfield.)

In the ensuing years—especially after the completion of the transcontinental railroad at Promontory in 1869—ladies of the evening came in droves (perhaps gracing Ogden's streets for the first time in numbers). During the Civil War, camp followers of General Joe Hooker did their part to help the war effort so vigorously they earned a new nickname. "Hookers" found their way to border towns, frontier towns, cattle towns, and larger settlements out West. In Utah they chose the railroad towns. Places like Corinne in Box Elder County reared back and roared in counterpoint to Salt Lake City.

The Utah capital became headquarters for women like Lou Wallace and Kate Flint. And they earned a certain social standing in the community (although that's probably a geometric contradiction). When Brigham Young's property was seized to settle court-ordered alimony to Ann Eliza Young, his divorced plural wife, the *Salt Lake Tribune* gossiped in its "City Jottings" column on November 2, 1876, "It was rumored yesterday, that Mrs. Catherine Flint had purchased Brigham's closed carriage, and would have his coat of arms erased and her own substituted." A description of Kate's coat of arms was not included.

When a baseball game between the hometown Deserets and the visiting Cincinnati Red Stockings was arranged in September 1878, with

The east side of East Temple (Main Street) in Salt Lake City, ca. 1900. Photo by C. R. Savage; LDS Church Archives.

receipts to be divided by the players, the *Salt Lake Herald* sniffed, "The highest price given for a ticket was $25 . . . [paid by] Lou Wallace, a well known courtesan. . . . She then bought three others paying the regular price of $1 for each."

Then there was the important community leader and businessman who in March 1885 lamented in his diaries, held by the Utah State Historical Society, that his brother had been lost beyond redemption to one of the city's madams. The brother was somewhere in town on a binge, and the businessman searched frantically for him, fearing for his life. "The horrible information I obtained was that he was in Kate Flint's establishment and that his associations with that notorious prostitute are well known to several police officers. He has been drinking deeply and spending money very lavishly with fast women. Some of his suppers are said to have cost him $35." (Bear in mind that in 1885 an excellent dinner in a fine restaurant could be had for under $3.)

At the annual conference of the Church of Jesus Christ of Latter-day Saints in 1886, the crime rate in Salt Lake City came under attack at a time when the Church was being blitzed by antipolygamy laws and accused of perverting the nation's morals. "There are now in the city some six brothels, 40 tap rooms, a number of gambling houses, pool tables, and other disreputable concerns, all run by non Mormons," according to a report in the *Deseret News*.

As the century rounded the corner, Salt Lake City became more "citified," as the crossroads of the West, but progress did not come without hefty baggage. Newspaper accounts help fill in the story of the city's fight against vice and corruption, but for a firsthand look at those wicked years, one must turn to a reminiscence by one of Utah's most famous sons, John Held Jr. In 1905, Held, at the tender age of sixteen, became a sports illustrator and cartoonist for the *Salt Lake Tribune*. He and another fuzzy-cheeked youngster, Harold Wallace Ross, were destined for greatness. Ross joined the *Tribune* as a cub reporter and went on to found the *New Yorker* magazine, while Held would document America's Jazz Age, illustrating the wacky world of "shieks" and "flappers" during the Roaring Twenties.

The genius that was John Held Jr.—"the Mormon Kid" to his close friends—also left a chronicle of memories of his youth in Salt Lake City, describing that period better than any newspaper story. From the book, *The Most of John Held Jr.*, his voice reaches out over the decades to paint an anecdotal image of Commercial Street and the Stockade from—ahem—personal experience.

"In those days," he writes, "the hot spots of Salt Lake were located in a tidy manner on a street that ran between 1st and 2nd South and Main and State." Then it was known as Commercial, today it is Regent Street. "Within the street were saloons, cafes, parlor houses, and cribs [small cubicles] that were rented nightly to the itinerant Ladies of the Calling. It was against the rules to solicit, so these soiled doves would sit at the top of the stairs and coo their invitation to, 'C'mon up, kid.'"

Held was acquainted with the bawdy houses and the parlor houses, too. The latter because his uncle earned a tidy sum installing electric bells in these "abodes of pastime." John Jr. remembered the names of two particular madams clearly, for their calling cards were printed to order at his father's engraving shop. "One of the madams called herself Miss Ada Wilson. Hers was a lavish house on Commercial Street. Another gave her name as Miss Helen Blazes. Her establishment catered to the big money and in it only wine was served. In the other houses, beer was the popular refreshment—at one dollar a bottle, served to the guests in small whiskey glasses. These were mere token drinks, on which the house made a good, substantial profit."

Although Held doesn't mention it, one of the prevailing stories of the period is that patrons of that "establishment" delighted in boasting they'd gone to "Hell 'n Blazes." His introduction to these places, Held said, was purely social, as a guest of his uncle, his mentor. "I was then around 15 years old, and after a few dances and light beers, I was one sick pigeon. So my baptism in the fleshpots was a dim grey puling celebration."

About that time came a hue and cry to "clean up the city." The year was 1908 and Mayor John S. Bransford was struck with the notion that prostitution was an evil that could not be eliminated, so it might as well be controlled. His idea was to move all the "fallen women" in town to a restricted area less convenient to the downtown trade and away from the city proper. The *Tribune* speculated that Commercial Street would be cleansed because of two prevailing factors: the front windows of the new Wilson Hotel on the south side of Second South looked out upon the tenderloin district, and the management realized such a view was not conducive to the prosperity of a swell hostelry. Second, property owners had agreed to transform the street, even at a financial loss to themselves. It was well known that no class of tenant paid a higher rental than prostitutes. But, the newspaper explained, the ownership has been a serious "embarrassment" to the LDS Church in its campaign against Sunday saloons and other forms of vice.

So when Mayor Bransford sprang his announcement to the city council and others that he planned to establish a red light district on the west side of town, it surprised no one. The citizenry was somewhat nonplussed, to be sure, when he also announced he was putting a professional in charge of the relocation. His choice was Mrs. Dora B. Topham, known to the denizens of Ogden's "Two-Bit Street" as the notorious Belle London. Madam Belle London, if you please. Block 64, a piece of property bordered by First and Second South and by Fifth and Sixth West, was to be the site. And at an investment of from $200,000 to $300,000 at remarkably inflated prices, the Stockade was constructed. The girls were told they didn't have to live in the Stockade, but if they were caught doing business anywhere else in the city, "things would be made most unpleasant for them."

Councilman L. D. Martin succinctly stated the case:

> From the outside of the stockade nothing can be seen of the movements within, and the offensive sights which have greeted passers-by in the neighborhood of Commercial Street will be absent. There will be but two entrances to the stockade and there will be a policeman on duty day and night at both gates.
>
> The inmates will be under thorough control. At present the city is in a terrible condition. The women have been allowed to go from Commercial Street into the residence districts, and I know of one disorderly house right on Brigham Street [South Temple] and two others on East Third South.

Workmen finished the crib rows in brick and mortar and soon a hundred or more prostitutes of every color and nationality took up residence. On December 18, 1908, the word went out to extinguish the red lights on Commercial Street. The two gates to the new bordello village made visits potentially embarrassing for former patrons of Commercial Street cribs. John Held Jr. recalled that there were several secret openings in the walled enclosure, "known to the inmates and most of the incorrigible young males of the fair city."

According to John S. McCormick, writing in the *Utah Historical Quarterly*, Belle London rented the cribs to prostitutes for from one to four dollars a day. Each crib was ten-feet square, with a door and window in the front. Soliciting was carried on from the windows. Reported the *Deseret News*: "At the windows, only two feet above the sidewalk, sits the painted denizen of the underworld calling to passers between puffs on her cigaret." A curtain or partition divided the interior of the crib. In front might be a a chair or two and a combination bureau-washstand. At the back was a white enameled iron bed. Business more on a bedsheet than a shoestring. Prospective patrons strolled the sidewalks between rows of cribs on either side and thus made their selections from various women proclaiming their attributes. This shopping ritual was called "going down the line." The half-dozen parlor houses, according to McCormick, were larger structures renting from Belle London for $175 a month. The six or so women in each house split their earnings with their madam.

The Stockade operated for three years before Belle London called it quits. She had been convicted of "inducing Dogney Grey, aged 16 years, to enter the stockade for immoral purposes." At noon on September 28, 1911, she turned out the red lights. The Stockade was torn down to rubble. It was the end of an era and authorities no longer looked the other way.

THE COVERED WAGON KEEPS ROLLING

IN 1922 FILM MOGUL JESSE L. LASKY WAS LOOKING for someone to direct a western, Emerson Hough's *The Covered Wagon*. Lasky picked James Cruze, an Ogdenite whose Danish parents had themselves come across the plains with the Mormon pioneers to settle in Utah. And Cruze (real name Jens Cruz Bose) rode the "covered wagon" to fame and fortune as director of what is now considered the first epic motion picture western.

Motion picture historian Kevin Brownlow said Lasky thought Cruze the Dane, with his powerful build and black eyes, was part Indian. It was a lucky break for the Utahn; he was perfectly suited for the project. Covered wagons were something he knew from his childhood. And because of a promise made by Cruze, Bannock Indians on the Fort Hall Reservation in Idaho were among the first in America to see the two-hour silent film blockbuster, produced at a cost of $782,000. Box office receipts from just two theaters in New York and Hollywood ultimately paid for the picture. By 1932 the worldwide gross reached an astonishing $3.8 million, and as late as 1935 it was still listed as one of the five top grossing films of all time. Today, despite some negative loss due to nitrate-base film deterioration, *The Covered Wagon* remains a silent film classic.

In many respects, the movie, adapted from Hough's novel, was a series of paradoxes. Cruze, at thirty-eight, had directed several small westerns before the *Wagon* but was considered incapable of creating sustained suspense on the screen. In fact, many critics felt he was a plodding, uninspired director; yet after the explosive debut of *The Covered Wagon*, he found himself the highest paid director in Hollywood, and two national polls in 1926 and 1928 rated this former Utahn among the world's ten greatest directors. Cruze was paid $250 a week before *The Covered Wagon*, and $400 a week during the filming. After its premiere he received offers of $1,500 a week, but Lasky wouldn't free him from his contract.

It was considered almost a documentary, describing in accurate detail the hardships of emigrant companies traveling overland in the mid-1800s. Yet on its release, *The Covered Wagon* was lambasted by cowboys and ex-soldiers for its flawed history. Among the complaints, army veterans said ox trains never swam rivers with neck yokes on; that wagon trains did not camp for the night in box canyons (one of the film's most sensational action scenes is that of an Indian attack on wagons trapped in a box canyon); and that Jim Bridger, depicted as the wagon train scout, would not have permitted such a camp.

There was also a hullabaloo about four hundred wagons traveling across the plains in a single caravan. "That could not have been possible," said old-timers, who asked, "where would the oxen and horses find pasture?" The largest number of wagons known to travel together was sixty-five, and they divided in three columns five miles apart. All of these arguments were used by the army to deny the film's inclusion in archives of the U.S. War Department.

Lasky had purchased screen rights to *The Covered Wagon* on the basis of a synopsis, but in reading Hough's novel while on a train trip to the West Coast, Lasky was mesmerized by the sweep of the story, which depicted hardships of overland travel in canvas-covered prairie schooners eighty years earlier. First serialized in the *Saturday Evening Post*, the story was a popular success and movie-goers waited for the film version with as much anticipation as they later would have for *Gone with the Wind*. Lasky was impressed with it and decided it would not be just another western potboiler on a $100,000 budget. "No sir, this is going to be the greatest movie we've made."

To play the role of heroine Molly Wingate, Cruze signed Lois Wilson; for his leading man he chose J. Warren Kerrigan to play Will Banion; and Alan Hale Sr. was cast as the villain, Sam Woodhull. Ernest Torrence played Jackson, a tough old trader, and Tully Marshall was cast as Jim Bridger.

Cruze negotiated with Otto Meek, owner of the Baker Ranch, a 200,000-acre spread in the Snake River Valley of Nevada eighty-five miles from the nearest railroad at Milford, Utah. A huge lake on the property was banked and an outlet formed to shoot the wagon-crossing sequences over the "Platte River." With a company of 127 and a large staff of carpenters and technicians, Cruze recruited almost a thousand extras from the district, some coming as far as three hundred miles for ten dollars a day. He enlisted the help of Colonel Tim McCoy as technical advisor and liaison with the tribes to sign 750 Indians from Fort Hall. McCoy was perhaps one of the most expert sign-language talkers of his time, and the Indians trusted him implicitly. Cruze also promised the Indians would see the film when it was finished.

While others collected, rented, borrowed, or built some five hundred wagons to be used, Cruze took a second camera unit to Antelope Island in the Great Salt Lake to film buffalo sequences. Always contrary beasts, the animals took three days of tough wrangling just to get them to run past the camera.

"Winds, blizzards, floods, heat, alkali dust, we had to work through it all," Lasky recalled. When the lake dam burst and the camp flooded, a terrific snow fell and Cruze had it written into the script. The wagon train formed a caravan three miles long. "Eight trucks a day carried supplies to the two or three thousand people in camp." Indians were transported with bag and baggage. Hundreds of head of stock, all kinds of foodstuffs, lumber, and fifty carloads of equipment were hauled from the Lasky studio. Leading lady Lois Wilson suffered frostbite in the snowstorm and the crew ran out of supplies and lived on apples and baked beans until provisions could be shipped in. The company remained on location for eight weeks, during which time Cruze had a replica of the Fort Bridger trading post constructed. Expenses ran to $12,000 a day.

The scenario established a wagon train heading for Oregon. During its formation, the villain, Sam Woodhull (Hale) falls for Molly (Wilson), who is in love with Banion (Kerrigan). The rivalry ends in a fight when the wagon train is about to ford the Platte. When asked by Plains Indians to pay an honest debt for ferrying him safely across the river, Woodhull kills one and brings the wrath of the tribe down on the emigrant train. The caravan divides, part headed for Oregon, the rest to California. In the denouement, Woodhull tries to kill Banion, but is himself shot by Bridger (Tully Marshall).

In the original cut the story ends with emigrants continuing to Oregon and California, but when Lasky saw the finished movie he had the ending rewritten to show both the Oregon and California groups reaching their destinations. That meant the company, three months after returning to Hollywood, would have to resume location filming in Sonora, California. The wagon train itself had become a star with a personality of its own. The wagons had to be rebuilt since the old ones had been discarded, broken up, or sold in Nevada. The new ending cost big dollars, but it gave the picture its final hurrah.

It premiered at the Criterion in New York and Grauman's in Hollywood. But there was that promise Cruze had made to the Indian extras—that they would be among the first to see it. He arranged a special print to be shipped by railroad to Pocatello, in mid-May 1923, for the sole purpose of screening the silent epic for the Bannocks at the Fort Hall Reservation. It would be shown only to members of the tribe, then returned by express to New York.

George E. Carpenter, who wrote the story for the *Salt Lake Tribune*, described the event: "It appeared that all roads led to Fort Hall. From all points of the compass came blanketed Indians astride ponies, some in autos, ranging from a ruddy Stutz to a plebian 'Henry' [Ford]; others on foot." It was standing-room-only at the school auditorium, and it was obvious a second night's

screening would be needed; and then it was doubtful everyone could be accommodated. "Joe Rainey, 72 years of age, an old time Custer scout who was present at the historic massacre, attended both shows, renewing his youth—in fact, all the Indians who were in the picture took in the big show both evenings as guests of honor."

During the screening the audience kept up a running fire of chatter, laughing heartily at the "shooting match between the scout, Jackson, and Jim Bridger, played respectively, by Torrence and Marshall, who at times run away with the picture." The horses and livestock, too, came in for enthusiastic identification, according to reporter Carpenter, with Kerrigan's big black horse the center of attraction. "We asked one of the Bannocks who took part in the picture and that night saw himself as others saw him, for the first time, what he thought of it. Did he say, 'Humph! Heap big show!'? He did not, because this is his sentiment verbatim, delivered in fair English: 'I am glad I helped, because now all over the world, people will see the Indians and what they did.'"

William Donner, superintendent of the Fort Hall Reservation, said, "If this picture will have caused a better understanding of hardships and wrongs suffered by both races it will have performed a great mission."

BEES STAR HITS THE BIG TIME

IN *THE BASEBALL ENCYCLOPEDIA: THE COMPLETE AND Official Record of Major League Baseball* is the name Anthony Michael Lazzeri, nickname "Poosh 'Em Up," and thereby hangs a tale. Lazzeri (or Lazerre, as he spelled it) has been the subject of Utah baseball folklore for as long as most fans can remember, and those stories all seemed to start in the 1920s at the *Salt Lake Tribune* with sports editor John C. Derks, for whom the community baseball field was named (and for whom, many fans still stubbornly believe, it should continue to be named).

Young Tony strolled into the Salt Lake Bees training camp in Modesto, California, in 1922 as a

wide-eyed eighteen-year-old, "a green kid off the lots," according to Derks, who was known to readers and denizens of the sports pages simply as JCD. He was green, Derks recalled, but even experienced players could tell right off that the kid had it in him to make a ball player. He had the size, the hands, some speed, the aggressiveness, and perhaps the best arm in baseball (Lazerre was a shortstop).

So team president H. W. Lane signed him and, with an eye to the future, brought the infielder along slowly, first with the Peoria baseball team in the Three I League, for a couple of seasons, and then with Lincoln in the Western League. By then

Lazerre was thought to be ready to play with the Pacific Coast League. The year was 1925.

By the end of the season, Lazerre was the sensation of the minors. He had a nickname that would, as mentioned earlier, go down in the baseball annals with his performance statistics, and he had earned the devotion of baseball fans in the West. Lane said of him, "Tony looks better striking out, than lots of players look hitting home runs." And Derks (JCD) wrote that in the eleven years Salt Lake has been in the league, there had not been a major league prospect to compare with Lazerre.

Just what did young Tony do, to deserve this adulation? Well, he Poosh 'Em Up, is what he did.

In the Utah business community there never was a more devoted fan of Lazerre than Cesare Rinetti, co-owner with Francesco Capitolo of the Rotisserie Inn, in downtown Salt Lake City. Rinetti took a liking to the young infielder from San Francisco; his Italian progenitors probably had a lot to do with it, but Tony and his San Francisco bride were a likeable couple. According to sports editor emeritus John Mooney, Rinetti "adopted" Lazerre and fed him good Italian food to build him up. Rinetti also was an avid baseball fan.

So it came to pass on a fine spring Saturday, the Bees were facing the Seattle Indians and Rinetti was in the stands at Community Baseball Park, as was JCD. (The field would not be named in his honor until 1940.) Rinetti, always the rabid rooter, shouted out in his heavy accent: "Poosh 'em up, Tony," and the crowd picked up the chant. Lazerre then drove a terrific wallop over the center field fence. The crowd went wild. Lazerre added a double to his average that day, for three runs batted in. The final tally was Seattle 2, Salt Lake 12.

Derks, who had a penchant for getting more into a headline than into the story, ran the following eight-column banner the next morning. (By the way, for years sports writers have been quoting this headline – but no one would own up to actually having seen it or could say when it appeared. After a diligent search through two years of daily *Tribune* sports pages, the Bees' story of May 24, 1925, finally surrendered.)

'Poosh Um Up, Tone,' Yella Da Fan, an' Tone She Poosh

From that day forward Lazerre was known as "Poosh 'Em Up" to the fans and "Our Tone" to John C. Derks.

The next day was a double-header for the Bees against the Indians. Lazerre collected just one hit for five trips to the bat and a stolen base in the first game (Seattle 4, Salt Lake 5), but he cracked two triples in the second game, which Salt Lake also pulled out (Seattle 8, Bees 11).

Derks must have thought to himself, it worked once, why not again? The morning headline, eight columns:

Tone She Poosh Um Down an' Den She Poosh Um Up

The subhead below (in slightly smaller type) explained:

Lazerre's Great Work Afield and With Club Factors in Twin Win

That was the last time for several months, that Derks fell back on dialect. But in July he was able to run a separate story saying, "They're After 'Our Tone'" and report a campaign in which the New York Americans (the Yankees) planned to spend $250,000 to develop its team from selected minor league players—among them, Lazerre, Salt Lake's hard-hitting shortstop.

By August, Derks, who by the way never used his full byline, and only on rare occasions signed his stories simply JCD, noted (without byline) that the boy who had been scouted and sought by the New York Yankees, the New York Giants, and the Washington Senators had been dealt to the Yankees by owner Lane for an undisclosed sum of cash and five players! Derks said the cash was estimated all the way from $1,000 to $200,000. No doubt, he added, "when the New York lads get their figures all compiled, it will be at least $250,000. Regardless, it is a fairly substantial sum." At that August writing, Lazerre was leading the Pacific Coast League in home runs with thirty-three, only ten behind the league record of forty-three established by Paul Strand. He led also in stolen bases with twenty-six and in triples with thirteen. How Lazerre does during the remainder of the season, Derks remarked, will help him set his salary when he "goes up" to the big club.

Well, young Tony bent to the task. The Bees were in contention for the pennant, but their chances were slim. Through August and September they battled, and finally came October.

The major leagues wrapped up their season, and the *Salt Lake Tribune's* front pages were devoted to the pending seven-game confrontation between the Pittsburgh Pirates and the Washington Senators. On the inside pages, JCD would have none of it. The locals were just as important and hark! On October 3, 1925, a Derks headline roared:

Our Tone She Poosh Um Oop for da Feefty-seex

The details? Lazerre sets minor league mark; he needs three to tie Babe Ruth's record for all of professional baseball.

On October 12, another Derks special:

Our Tone, She Poosh Um Oop Two Time, Maka da Feefty-eight

Lazerre now is but one home run behind Ruth.

The World Serious (Derks' words) had come and gone (Pittsburgh in seven) while the tale of Tony continued. On October 18 the clincher:

The Bambino, He's Got Nothin' on Our Tone Now

Lazerre knocks out 59th homer and ties world record.

October 19 would be the fateful day:

Gooda da Tone, She Poosh Um Up for Beat Bambino

Lazerre hits his 60th home run for the record.

The mighty Bees, however, did not win the Pacific Coast pennant that year, San Francisco did. But Lazerre went to the Yankees, and somehow, someway, his name picked up a *z*, dropped an *r*, and turned an *e* to an *i*, to become Lazzeri. He was on the batting order with Lou Gehrig, and Babe Ruth. He stayed with the Yankees for twelve years.

Tony "Poosh 'Em Up" "Lazzeri" Lazerre died August 6, 1946. John C. Derks, dean of baseball, died April 8, 1944.

DEATH IN THE UINTAS

MASASHI GOTO WAS THIRTY-TWO AND BURSTING with pride as he eased his biplane in for a landing at the Salt Lake Municipal Airport. He was on the early legs of a flight that would carry him across the United States, then across Europe to Asia, and finally to the islands of Japan.

It was a beautiful morning–July 4, 1929–and as Goto rolled the craft to a stop and switched off the ignition, he could take satisfaction in his achievement thus far. In his flying suit pocket he carried letters to family and a small folded American flag. When this flight was over, Masashi Goto would be the most famous Japanese flier in the world. It was a dream he had savored since he and his friend in Los Angeles, Takeo Watanabe, had saved enough money to build the airplane they designed–this same little biplane which had served him so well thus far.

If Goto had any premonition otherwise, he did not show it as members of the Japanese community in Salt Lake City gathered at the airport to congratulate him and shake his hand. Before the day was done, Masashi Goto's dream would be shattered–his biplane destroyed and the intrepid aviator dead in the high Uinta Mountains.

His adventure was long forgotten with the passage of time, and for years only a small granite monument on the Wolf Creek Summit road (Utah Highway 35) at the junction for Soapstone Basin and Hanna stood as mute testimony to the tragedy. The U.S. Forest Service has upgraded access to the area and relocated the monument closer to the state highway, with an automobile turnout. The monument fared well for three-score years, considering its location in a heavily wooded, but scarcely convenient spot to be noticed. It read:

This monument erected by
the Japanese Association
of Utah to
MASASHI GOTO
1896–1929
Japanese Aviator in his
flight over
America, Europe and Asia
Airplane RYOFU-Co
Crashed 3,000 feet South
East of this spot
July 4th, 1929

Goto had flown from Los Angeles to Oakland and on July 3 took off from that point to Reno, Nevada, presumably to refuel. His custom-made biplane was powered by a five-cylinder Pratt & Whitney air-cooled radial engine. The craft was fourteen-feet long with a twenty-two-foot wingspan. Japanese language newspapers on the Pacific Coast had for some time carried stories on Goto and Watanabe and their intended "round-the-world" journey.

Once the biplane was airborne out of the Salt Lake Municipal Airport in the early afternoon, Goto turned toward the Wasatch range, probably headed for Wyoming. Although his ultimate destination (New York) was widely known, he did not file a detailed flight plan, and it was never determined whether his next stop after Salt Lake City was to have been Denver or Laramie/Cheyenne.

He banked toward Parleys Canyon and set a course east, taking him over Park City. As his plane flew over the Uinta National Forest at Woodland, he ran into trouble; a thunderstorm was crackling in the vicinity of the high Uintas, and it was later theorized by experienced airmail pilots that Goto attempted to fly under the storm and, finding it impossible, tried a pancake landing. Other pilots speculated that the small airplane and its twenty-two-foot wingspan had reached its effective ceiling—that altitude above which its engine could not provide lift and then behaved as planes do under such circumstances; that is, it had gone into a nosedive or a tailspin and had struck the ground before the pilot could bring it under control.

Whatever the reason, the green and silver biplane crashed, the fuselage telescoping over the engine, throwing Masashi Goto with such force into the instrument panel that he suffered a fractured neck. Death came instantly, investigators said. His round-the-world journey had come to a heartbreaking end a mile into Dry Canyon, 8,500-feet above sea level near the Soapstone Basin.

In Salt Lake City, members of the Japanese community were still celebrating the departure of their countryman, who, it was hoped, would bring great honor to their native homeland and their adopted country as well. It was not unusual when no word was received of his successful arrival at the next city on his route. But when he failed to make contact Saturday and Sunday as well, fears for his safety began to circulate. There were no regulations requiring cross-country fliers to report their routes in advance. Where was Masashi?

Shortly before 4 P.M. on Monday July 8, Nymphus Simmons, a sheepherder, came across the wreckage in Dry Canyon. He hurried to a telephone line camp a few miles away and told them of his discovery. They tapped a wire into the line and telephoned word to Park City and Heber authorities. Wasatch County Deputy Sheriff Charles E. Bonner made an immediate try at reaching the scene but was forced to turn back on account of darkness. At daybreak a search party including Sheriff Virgil Fraughton, Deputy Bonner, and undertaker J. W. Winterose reached Dry Canyon and were met by a group of sheepherders and two men from Salt Lake, one of whom, R. F. Crandall, was camping in the area when the plane was found. The other man probably was R. H. Warner, a Boeing pilot whose company had U.S. mail contracts and who was known to have been one of the first to arrive on the scene after the sheepherder called in the location.

Crandall told searchers that because the biplane was lying flat on the canyon floor with a damaged landing gear and propellor, it appeared Goto may have piloted the plane to earth instead of plunging in a straight nosedive. He thought the flier almost made a safe landing under power. Warner noted that the pilot was still wearing his parachute, which he would have used had the plane failed him. It was his opinion based on experience that the pilot tried to fly under the storm and, when he realized it wasn't possible, attempted a crash landing, "pancaking" it in.

The search party extricated the aviator's body from the wreckage for removal to Heber. He carried a private pilot's license and identification of Masashi Goto, 1615 West 36th Place, Los Angeles. He was born in Oita, Kyushu, Japan, in 1896. In his flying suit were found drafts for $500 and $300 in cash, a small American flag, and a letter to Takeo Watanabe's father in Japan.

In Salt Lake City, Henry Y. Kasai, director of the Japanese Association of Utah, notified Watanabe in Los Angeles; and the two arranged to meet R. H. Warner in Heber. From the dead pilot's friend and partner, Warner and Kasai learned of the dream that cost Goto his life. As superintendent of the Crawford Airplane Company in Venice, California, Watanabe, who was twenty-eight, and Goto had planned for three years to make a trip around the world, using a plane over land and crossing the ocean by boat.

When they found it would be too expensive, it was decided Goto, the eldest, should make the flight. With the combined savings of the two men during those years, they spent $4,500 building the biplane, their own design, in Watanabe's garage. Goto worked as a gardener trimming lawns for extra money. It was a dream that kept them going, working for years on a homemade airplane being built during a time of aviation madness.

Charles A. "Lucky Lindy" Lindbergh hadn't crossed the Atlantic when Watanabe and Goto began their project, but his successful flight in 1927 only fired their enthusiasm—the dream of becoming the most famous Japanese fliers in the world. When their plane was completed in the summer of 1929, aviation was the international byword. Two Polish pilots were preparing a transatlantic hop from LeBourget, France, to New York. Two "hard-boiled hombres" from California named Loren Mendell and Pete Reinhart were about to begin a pioneer endurance flight which would take them past the two-hundred-hour mark for all classes of aircraft. And another pair of Americans, Roger Q. Williams and Lewis A. Yancey, bound from Old Orchard, Maine, for Rome, were forced, with gasoline tanks almost empty, to land in Spain. They were 225 miles ahead of schedule and preparing to refuel.

Instead of joyfully celebrating Goto's safe landing—the plan was to proceed to New York, then stow the plane aboard a ship for Europe, and continue the flight east across Asia to Kyushu—Watanabe was arranging for his friend's body to be shipped to Los Angeles for burial.

And the plane? It was disassembled and trucked back to Venice. Some framework, however, remained in Utah to be used as part of a memorial monument at the crash site to the valiant Goto. But in the ensuing years and the frenzy of World War II, someone toppled the monument into a creek bed. Later, Henry Y. Kasai arranged with then Utah Governor J. Bracken Lee to move the stone marker to a new site at the Soapstone-Hanna-Francis junction.

THE GOLDEN AGE OF RADIO LISTENING

"IT'S TIME FOR JACK ARMSTRONG . . . THE All-American Boy!!!" More than two generations ago, those words were as familiar to radio listeners as the television catch phrase "The Thrill of Victory; the Agony of Defeat" is today. For it was the Golden Age of Radio in America, and folks used to spend their evenings huddled around a Philco, an Emerson, a Zenith, or, if they were really well off, a Sears Silvertone that stood three feet tall and in a position of importance in the home equal to that of the family piano. It was how America entertained itself in those tough Depression days and the years of World War II.

For youngsters who grew up in that era, whose childhood began with the stock market crash of 1929 and only began to improve with the postwar fabulous fifties, it was a time for escapism into the world of imagination and radio adventure serials. And to make that world more real and exciting, there were the premiums, those precious prizes earned by mailing a required number of cereal box tops ("or reasonable facsimiles"), along with ten cents in coin, to the most famous mailing address in America—Battle Creek, Michigan, the breakfast cereal empire where these marvelous and mysterious treasures were produced.

Adventure serials came into being in the early 1930s with programs like *The Lone Ranger*, but even before that, a nightly fifteen-minute comedy called *Amos 'n' Andy* turned the infant medium of radio upside down. Sales of radios surged, from 650,000 sets in 1928 to 842,548 the following year, as the antics of Amos, Andy, the Kingfish, the Judge, the Bailiff, Lightnin', and the Fresh-Air Taxicab Company made America tune in—and stay tuned in for twenty-five years, until its younger brother, television, muscled radio aside.

In those early days there was NBC (formed in 1926), CBS (1927) and Mutual Broadcasting (1934). In Utah, KDYL Radio was the NBC affiliate and KSL was the CBS station. Dramatic serials occupied the morning hours, say, from 9:15 A.M., with *The Romance of Helen Trent*, which set out to prove (for nearly two decades) that romance could live on for a woman at thirty-five and even beyond. Unfortunately most of Helen Trent's lovers met violent death. (How else could a program continue for twenty years?) Daytime radio gave soap operas their name and reputation. *Ma Perkins* owned the longevity title, making its debut on December 4, 1933, and continuing without a break for twenty-seven years—7,065 broadcasts with the same actress, Virginia Payne, in the title role and the same sponsor, Oxydol soap.

But back to the evening adventure serials and the premiums. Those who remember *Jack Armstrong*, his sidekick cousins Billy and Betty Fairfield, and the show's father image, Uncle Jim Fairfield, who was an explorer and pilot of his own amphibious plane, also recall the neat stuff offered for a Wheaties box top and a dime: the mysterious Dragon's Eye ring that glowed with green luminescence in the dark, Jack's Explorer's Sun Watch, and his famous Pedometer, which, fastened to belt or pocket, would count every step its owner took. As Jim Harmon, radio premium historian, wrote,

"Using it, Jack was able to follow the instructions in an old pirate map and keep Billy, Betty, Uncle Jim and himself on the correct course out of the bottomless-pit death traps laid by the Cult of the Crocodile God."

Wow!

And premiums were patriotic, too. For instance, *Junior G-Man* members were issued a *Manual of Instructions to All Operatives* (obtained with Post Toasties box tops) right from Chief Special Agent-in-Charge Melvin Purvis. Purvis described secret codes and signals, passwords, whistles, and danger code signs. He detailed instructions for solving crimes and apprehending criminals, how to "shadow" a suspect, and how to judge and compare fingerprints. Yessir, with Melvin Purvis heading up the corps, how could a red-blooded American youngster go wrong?

After being cautioned never to reveal the secrets of the Junior G-Man Corps, Purvis went on to explain how he made it a rule to eat Post Toasties for breakfast every morning and why he thought all Junior G-Men ought to follow his example—because it was good for you (and what better way to collect box tops for other Junior G-Man equipment). Purvis, for those unfamiliar with the deeds of the Federal Bureau of Investigation, was the special agent-in-charge of the Chicago FBI office and all but crowded director J. Edgar Hoover off the front page with his escapades involving Baby Face Nelson and other public enemies. Purvis planned the ambush at the Biograph Theatre in Chicago and was the agent who killed John Dillinger. Hoover made life so miserable for the publicity-minded Purvis that he finally resigned from the bureau and eventually took his own life. He promoted himself into the Junior G-Man Corps radio deal in 1936, but it was short lived. Still, it recruited a lot of Junior G-Men in its time.

If being an All-American high schooler or a Junior G-Man wasn't enough, there was Tom Mix and the TM-Bar Ranch for all the "straight-shooters" in radioland. His premiums were really nifty: there was Tom Mix's Compass Magnifying Glass, his Signal Arrowhead with a magnifying lens, a reduction lens (called a "smallifying" glass), and a spinning whistle siren all in one. In 1938 he offered the clicker-key Postal Telegraph Signal Set (two Ralston cereal box tops or one box top and ten cents). Tom encouraged listeners to "get your neighbor to send for one too, so you can hook both sets together and send messages between your house and next door." They were made of cardboard and didn't weather too well, but, golly, they were "official" Tom Mix signal sets and that was worth a lot. Over the years, Tom gave away Tiger Eye rings, Siren rings, and Tom Mix TM Bar brand rings—it was the berries. Ask anyone.

There was a definite motive behind all these so-called giveaways, from the *Little Orphan Annie* Ovaltine shaker mug to the *Lone Ranger* decoder card, aside from all the boxes of cereal that were sold. It was the sponsors' way of determining how many listeners their programs were attracting. There was no Arbitron or Nielsen service to provide demographics; all they had to go on was the million or so envelopes that poured into Battle Creek after each premium was announced.

Picture for a moment a youngster filling out a request and addressing an envelope ("be certain the return address is clearly printed"), carefully including the box top and coin, adding a stamp, and posting the letter. Rare is the boy or girl of those marvelous days who will deny waiting impatiently the next morning, and the mornings for a week after, for the mailman to deliver that wonderful gift. Six weeks later, and all but forgotten, the treasure would arrive, and its proud owner could listen to the program with renewed enthusiasm.

As for the secret code messages, they would invariably end with the same pronouncement: Don't forget to tune in tomorrow, same time, same station, for the next exciting episode of . . . . And we never forgot.

A TOKEN EFFORT

THE TREASURY IS WORRIED ABOUT THE PENNY; IT seems to be going out of style. Pennies are a nuisance; there is nothing to spend them on. They won't fit parking meters anymore. Pennies have outlived their usefulness for paying sales tax. At 6.25 percent, making sales tax change is the last stronghold of the copper coin.

Was a time in Utah, though, when shoppers had to deal not only with piles of pennies but with tax tokens too. A sales tax first went into effect in 1933 at a .75 percent rate paid in rounded amounts of one cent on a dollar sale. But the State Legislature raised the rate to 2 percent (to make it easier to pay, it said) and adopted the use of tokens to pay fractions of tax on sales under fifty cents. The Utah State Tax Commission ordered two denominations: one mill and five mill.

On June 21, 1937, Utah bought its first carload of seventy thousand aluminum tokens from Osborne Register Company, Cincinnati, Ohio, to be put in circulation July 1. The one-mill disk was a bit smaller than a dime; the five-mill token slightly larger than a nickel. As the *Salt Lake Tribune* explained it, "The mill was the precise tax

on a nickel purchase; the 5-mill on a quarter purchase. A penny was the exact amount of tax on a 50-cent sale, and the tokens were used to pay the correct tax on factional amounts." Shoppers, for instance, buying an item for $2.65 paid five cents plus three mills tax.

Obviously tokens would be a world-class pain in the pocket. Everyone would be carrying around a supply of aluminum as well as pennies because businesses were required by law to collect the tax, much to the aggravation of the public. Because Utah Governor Henry Blood signed the sales tax bill into law, tokens quickly became known as "Blood money."

The extra "small change" created a fashion oddity among Utah males—the coin purse. From 1937 to the mid-1950s (and beyond by surviving senior-senior citizens today), this curious trend ordinarily consisted of the small rosette coin wallet or the larger snaplock leather pouch. Rare was the man who was without such an accessory in which to store his daily horde of pennies, nickels, dimes, quarters, halves, and those worthless, blankety-blank aluminum tokens! (The coin purse for men generally faded from the scene when tokens finally were abolished.)

In June of 1942, the burgeoning demands of World War II brought about an acute condition on the homefront. Aluminum was a scarce war material, and Utah could not replenish its supply of tax tokens with that metal. The answer was a newfangled chemical composition called plastic. Utah ordered three denominations of plastic tokens in colors—green for one mill, gray for two mill, and orange for five mill—from Ingeversen Manufacturing Company of Denver. They were all the same size, slightly smaller than a quarter.

Throughout the existence of sales tax tokens in Utah, the metal disks came in for a variety of uses, but mostly by motorists who insisted on forcing them into parking meters. And there were those under the erroneous impression the five-mill token would work in pay telephones. Other vending machines fell victim to mill jams. But tragically, the plastic tokens proved the biggest headache. Young children were inexorably attracted by the brightly colored chips, and tried to eat them. The tokens were discontinued in May 1951 and, thereafter, became another in a long line of collectible oddities.

But as an example of the truth of the adage that "you can't please everyone," take the case of the silver dollar. The "cartwheel"—the good old silver dollar—was a standard in the western states from the day it was first minted. Back east, it was all currency, but in Utah, Wyoming, Nevada, Idaho, Arizona, New Mexico, and Colorado, the coin of the realm was the cartwheel. U.S. Mints in Carson City, Nevada; Denver; and San Francisco turned them out almost exclusively for the western states, and large coins became souvenirs for flatland tourists to take home and show the neighbors.

At least in Utah, though, dollars became much like tax tokens—a blamed nuisance. In retrospect, that attitude sounds like 100 percent idiocy in light of 1990s monetary conditions, but in the 1940s and '50s, especially (there weren't many folks who had much money in the 1930s), the notion of having three or four cartwheels clanking about in a pocket was aggravating. "Can't I have paper?" was the usual lament when a shopper was handed three or four silver dollars along with the small change. Youngsters used to complain that the dollars—when they had them—would drag their jeans down, and women disliked the added weight; so the silver dollar—outside of the casinos in Nevada—became unpopular.

Today, shoppers would riot for the opportunity to receive silver anything in face value change. But silver coins went the way of the buffalo, podnuh.

Suggested Additional Reading

Alter, J. Cecil. *Jim Bridger*. Norman: University of Oklahoma Press, 1950.

Arrington, Leonard J. *Brigham Young: American Moses*. New York: Alfred A. Knopf, 1985.

Bagley, Will, ed. *The Pioneer Camp of the Saints: The 1846 and 1847 Mormon Trail Journals of Thomas Bullock*. Spokane: Arthur H. Clark, 1997.

Bolton, Herbert E. "Pageant in the Wilderness: The Story of the Escalante Expedition to the Interior Basin, 1776," *Utah Historical Quarterly* 18 (1950).

Brooks, Juanita. *Mountain Meadows Massacre*. Norman: University of Oklahoma Press, 1962.

Bryant, Edwin. *What I Saw in California*. Palo Alto: Lewis Osborne, 1967.

Burton, Richard F. *The City of the Saints and Across the Rocky Mountains to California*. New York: Alfred A. Knopf, 1963.

DeVoto, Bernard. *The Year of Decision, 1846*. New York: Houghton-Mifflin, 1943.

Estergreen, M. Morgan. *Kit Carson; A Portrait in Courage*. Norman: University of Oklahoma Press, 1962.

Flanders, Robert B. *Nauvoo: Kingdom on the Mississippi*. Urbana: University of Illinois Press, 1965.

Furniss, Norman. *The Mormon Conflict, 1850–1859*. New Haven: Yale University Press, 1960.

Hallwas, John E., and Roger D. Launius. *Cultures in Conflict: A Documentary History of the Mormon War in Illinois*. Logan: Utah State University Press, 1995.

Kelly, Charles. *Salt Desert Trails*. Salt Lake City: Western Epics, 1996.

Korns, J. Roderic, and Dale L. Morgan. "West from Fort Bridger: The Pioneering of Immigrant Trails across Utah, 1846–1850," *Utah Historical Quarterly* 19 (1951). Reprint ed., revised and updated by Will Bagley and Harold Schindler. Logan: Utah State University Press, 1994.

Madsen, Brigham D., ed. *A Forty-niner in Utah*. Salt Lake City: University of Utah Library, 1981.

———. *Gold Rush Sojourners in Great Salt Lake City, 1849–1850*. Salt Lake City: University of Utah Press, 1983.

———. *The Shoshoni Frontier and the Bear River Massacre*. Salt Lake City: University of Utah Press, 1985.

Moorman, Donald R., with Gene A. Sessions. *Camp Floyd and the Mormons: The Utah War*. Salt Lake City: University of Utah Press, 1992.

Morgan, Dale L. *The Humboldt: Highroad of the West*. New York: Farrar & Rinehardt, 1943.

———. *Jedediah Smith and the Opening of the West*. Indianapolis: Bobbs-Merrill, 1953.

———. *The Great Salt Lake*. Salt Lake City: University of Utah Press, 1995

Nunis, Doyce B., Jr., ed. *The Bidwell-Bartleson Party 1841 Emigrant Adventure: Documents and Memoirs of the Overland Pioneers*. Santa Cruz: Western Tanager Press, 1991.

Roylance, Ward J. *Utah, A Guide to the State*. Salt Lake City: Utah, A Guide to the State Foundation, 1982.

Schindler, Harold. *Orrin Porter Rockwell: Man of God, Son of Thunder*. Salt Lake City: University of Utah Press, 1983.

———. *Crossing the Plains: New and Fascinating Accounts of the Hardships, Controversies and Courage Experienced and Chronicled by the 1847 Pioneers on the Mormon Trail*. Salt Lake City: The Salt Lake Tribune, 1997.

Utley, Robert M. *A Life Wild and Perilous: Mountain Men and the Paths to the Pacific*. New York: Henry Holt, 1997.

Van Wagoner, Richard S. *Mormon Polygamy: A History*. Salt Lake City: Signature Books, 1986.

Index

McArthur, Daniel D., handcart company captain, 66

McCormick, John S., historian, quoted, 181

McCulloch, Major Ben, peace commissioner, 76–77

medicine: frontier, 89; and medical research, artificial kidney, artificial heart, 155

Meek, Joe, mountaineer at Brown's Hole, 35

Miller, Hyrum O., fishing ability of, 41

Miller, Jacob, sheep rancher, finds lens cap on Frémont Island, 39

mining interests in Utah: magnates, 152; oil development, uranium frenzy, 154

Morgan, Dale L.: historian, 3, 5, 9, 12–13; on Miles Goodyear, 27; quoted, 43, 70–71, 90, 134; and John Baptiste, 122; and Deseret Alphabet, 125

Mormon Battalion, and Pueblo sick detachment, 24

Morley, Isaac, 44

Mormon cricket (*anabrus simplex hald*), ravage fields, 32

Morris, George, 51

Morris, Joseph: dissident Mormon, 82–83; killed, 83

Morrisite massacre, 82–83

Mountain Green, trapper camp in Weber Canyon, 10

Muñiz, Andres, interpreter, Domínguez-Escalante expedition, 5

Muñiz, Antonio Lucrecio, Domínguez-Escalante expedition, 5

Murray, Eli, governor of Utah Territory, 137

N

natural wonders in Utah, 153–54

Newell, Robert "Doc," mountaineer, at Brown's Hole, 37

O

odometer, Mormon mileage counter, 23

Ogden, Peter Skene: fur brigade leader, 8; confrontation with Americans, 9; retreats, 10

Olivares, Lorenzo, member Domínguez-Escalante expedition, 5

P

Pack, John: captain of Mormon fifty, 23; in advance pioneer party, 25; and predator hunt, 43–45

Paiutes: Indian tribe, 3; at Mountain Meadow massacre, 73–74, 124

Peck, Martin H., made coin drop hammer, 48

Phillips, Leonard, and Pike-Spencer affair, 101

Piegans, and Lewis and Clark expedition, 7

Pike, First Sergeant Ralph, clubs Howard O. Spencer, 100

Pilot Peak: first emigrant arrival at, 12; mentioned, 14

Plummer, Sheriff Henry, heads bandit gang, 116–17

"plurality of wives" (polygamy): doctrine announced, 65; one of "twin relics of barbarism," 66; and Cullom Bill, 133; wives jailed for contempt of court, 141; and Woodruff manifesto, 143–44

Poll, Richard D., historian, quoted, 148–49

Pollock, James, Mormon dissident, 42

Pony Express: 78–80; famous advertisement a myth, 78–79

Porter, Major Fitz John, and Pike-Spencer affair, 100

Powell, John Wesley, 35

Powell, Lazarus W., peace commissioner, 76–77

Pratt, Addison, fishing ability of, 41

Pratt, Orson: urges Mormons to emigrate, 18; designs odometer, 23; sees Great Salt Lake, 25; leads pioneer advance party, 25; surveys Great Salt Lake City, 27

Pratt, Parley P.: reads *Emigrants' Guide* to apostles, 20; mentioned, 21; murdered in Arkansas, 72; and Deseret Alphabet, 125–26

Pratt, Silas, wounded in accidental shooting, 57

Preuss, Charles, cartographer, at Frémont Island, 37–39

prostitutes of Utah: Ada Carroll, Lou Wallace, Kate Flint, 178; Helen Blazes, Ada Wilson, Dora B. Topham (Belle London), 180

Provost, Etienne: Taos trapper, 8; probable discoverer of Great Salt Lake, 9; attacked by Shoshoni war party, 9

Pueblos of New Mexico, revolt in 1680, 3

R

Reed, James Frazier: and wagon company, 14; mentioned, 15

Rich, Charles C., on Heber C. Kimball's prediction, 49

Richards, Franklin D.: reads Frémont report to Mormon apostles, 20; mentioned, 67

Richards, Willard, 33

Robert, Henry Martyn: and best-selling book, 103–4; in Utah, 104

Robertson, Jack, mountaineer, at Brown's Hole, 35

Robison, Lewis: and predator hunt, 44; and purchase of Thomas "Peg Leg" Smith's trading post, 47

Rockwell, Orrin Porter: in Mormon pioneer advance party, 25; and predator hunt, 44; mentioned, 74–75; at Bear River battle, 84; and valley tan, 113; and Mark Twain, 114; shoots Lot Huntington, 120; and Charles H. Wilcken, 166

Rockwood, A. P., captain of Mormon hundred, 23

Ross, Glade, discovers Fort Davy Crockett ruins, 37

Ross, Harold, founder of *New Yorker* magazine, as cub reporter on *Salt Lake Tribune*, 179